Stop Replaying It

Stop Replaying It

How to End Mental Rewinds and Move On

Aria Kostova

Mindful Pages

Published in 2026

ISBN: 9788169888417 (PB)
ISBN: 9788169888400 (eBook)

Published by

Mindful Pages
Imprint of Alpha Editions LLC
312 W. 2nd St #1834
Casper, WY 82601, USA

Content

Introduction

The mind has a remarkable instinct for protection. It notices danger before you have fully named it, scans social signals before you have consciously interpreted them, and stores painful lessons so that you do not walk blindly into the same fire twice. This instinct is not a flaw. It is part of your intelligence. It is part of how you learn, adapt, repair, mature, and stay connected to other people.

Yet the same protective system can become exhausting when it refuses to stand down.

You leave a meeting and, for a moment, you simply reflect. Did I explain that clearly? Was my tone too sharp? Should I have answered differently? These questions may begin as a reasonable review. They may even be useful. But an hour later, the meeting is still playing in your head. By evening, one sentence has become evidence in an internal trial. By the next morning, you have rewritten the scene five different ways, imagined what others must now think of you, and punished yourself for a version of events that may not even be true.

That is a mental rewind.

A mental rewind is not just a memory. It is a repeated re-running of a moment, usually charged with discomfort, uncertainty, regret, shame, or fear. It is the mind returning to a conversation, mistake, message, facial expression, delay, silence, argument, joke, decision, or awkward pause as if reviewing it one more time might finally produce certainty. It is not always dramatic. Sometimes it is tiny: a line in a text, a look across a room, a slightly clumsy answer, a moment when you think you sounded foolish. Yet the size of the event does not always match the size of the mental aftermath.

This is one reason mental rewinds feel so confusing. You may know, rationally, that the situation was not catastrophic. You may even tell yourself, "It was nothing." But your body does not feel as though it was nothing. Your chest tightens. Your face heats. Your stomach turns. Your attention keeps snapping back to the same scene. The mind becomes a private cinema, screening the past with cruel precision and adding new scenes that never happened.

The usual advice is painfully inadequate: stop thinking about it.

People say this because they mean well. You may say it to yourself with equal impatience. Stop obsessing. Move on. Let it go. But the mind rarely releases a loop because it has been ordered to do so. In fact, the command to stop can make the thought louder. Now you are not only replaying the moment; you are also judging yourself for replaying it. The loop gains a second layer. First comes the original discomfort. Then comes the frustration that you cannot make the discomfort disappear.

This book takes a different approach. It does not treat mental rewinds as stupidity, weakness, vanity, drama, or over-sensitivity. It treats them as a protective process that has become overactive. That distinction matters. When you understand the mechanism, you can interrupt it without attacking yourself. You can extract the lesson without turning your identity into the crime scene. You can repair what genuinely needs repair and release what only wants another hour of your life.

The people who struggle most with mental rewinds are often not careless people. They are often conscientious people. Socially aware people. Reflective people. People who want to do well, communicate clearly, avoid hurting others, be respected, be competent, and live according to their values. Their minds are not empty; their minds are busy trying to prevent future pain. The problem is that the prevention strategy becomes its own punishment.

You replay because you care. But caring without closure becomes captivity.

Mental rewinds tend to begin with an honest impulse: I want to understand what happened. There is nothing wrong with that. Reflection is essential. Without reflection, we repeat ourselves blindly. We miss the effect we have on others. We fail to grow. But there is a clear difference between reflection and rumination, and learning to recognise that difference is one of the central skills of this book.

Reflection is specific. Rumination is circular.

Reflection asks, "What happened, what can I learn, and what will I do differently next time?" Rumination asks, "What does this mean about me, what if they hate me, why am I like this, and how can I mentally rebuild the past until it no longer hurts?"

Reflection leads to action. Rumination leads to more rumination.

Reflection has a door. Rumination has a corridor.

The aim of this book is not to make you careless. It is not to teach emotional numbness, indifference, or denial. You will not be asked to pretend that something did not bother you. You will not be asked to replace every painful thought with cheerful slogans. That kind of forced positivity often feels false because it is false. The mind does not trust language that has no respect for reality.

Instead, this book will show you how to work with reality more cleanly. You will learn to name the replay while it is happening. You will learn to separate the event from the story you are building around it. You will learn to notice when your body is signalling discomfort rather than danger. You will learn to distinguish accountability from self-punishment. You will learn how to apologise without over-explaining, repair without grovelling, wait without inventing meanings, and let things be when no useful action remains.

The phrase "move on" is often used casually, as if it were a switch. But moving on is not a switch. It is a sequence. First you notice the loop. Then you allow the feeling without feeding it. Then you extract what is useful. Then you choose whether action is needed. Then you close the scene deliberately. This book is built around that sequence because the mind often needs process, not pressure.

You will begin by understanding what mental rewinds are and why they persist. This matters because shame thrives in vagueness. When you do not understand what is happening, you may assume something is wrong with you. You may believe that a stronger person would not replay. A calmer person would not care. A more confident person would simply shrug and move on. But the truth is more precise: your attention has become caught in a threat-checking loop. The loop is not evidence that you are broken. It is evidence that your mind is trying, with excessive effort, to protect your social safety, self-image, and future choices.

Once the mechanism is visible, it becomes less mysterious. You can see how a replay starts after ambiguous feedback, a delayed reply, a public mistake, a tense exchange, or a moment when you fear you appeared foolish, unkind, incompetent, needy, rude, boring, dramatic, or wrong. Ambiguity is especially powerful because the mind dislikes unfinished meaning. A clear criticism may sting, but at least it has shape. Ambiguity spreads. A neutral expression becomes possible disapproval. A delayed message becomes rejection. A short reply becomes evidence. Silence becomes a theatre in which the mind casts every fear it can find.

This is why digital life has intensified mental rewinds. Messages can be reread. Screenshots can be imagined. Tone can be misread. Replies can be delayed. A single sentence can sit on a screen like a specimen under glass. The mind inspects it again and again, hoping to find safety in the wording. But checking rarely satisfies for long. It gives a small hit of relief, then creates another appetite for certainty. The thread is reread. The email is reopened. The post is reviewed. The loop is fed with fresh material.

The modern mind is not merely remembering conversations; it is auditing itself.

This audit culture can become brutal. You become both defendant and prosecutor. The prosecutor voice loves absolute language. You always do this. You ruined it. They definitely noticed. You made everything awkward. You should have known better. This voice can feel like discipline, but it is usually threat in formal clothing. It does not make you wiser. It makes you more frightened. And frightened minds do not learn cleanly; they scan, distort, defend, collapse, and repeat.

Accountability sounds different. Accountability says, "That landed badly. I can clarify." It says, "I interrupted twice. Next time, I will slow down." It says, "My intention was not harmful, but the impact may still need care." It says, "I can learn without making myself unworthy."

This distinction is essential. Many people are afraid that if they stop punishing themselves, they will stop improving. They fear that self-compassion is a soft escape from responsibility. In reality, punishment often keeps people stuck in the emotional drama of the mistake, while responsibility moves them towards a useful next step. Punishment loops. Responsibility acts.

You will learn to practise a form of self-compassion that does not feel artificial. Not syrupy reassurance. Not pretending everything is fine. Not excusing poor behaviour. The tone we will aim for is steadier than that: direct, humane, specific, adult. You will learn to speak to yourself as you might speak to a respected colleague who made an honest mistake and needs clarity, not humiliation. This matters because the nervous system responds not only to what you think, but to the tone in which you think it.

Mental rewinds also have a bodily life. They are not purely intellectual. A loop may intensify because your body is tired, hungry, overstimulated, tense, or flooded with stress chemistry. At night, this becomes especially obvious. The room is quiet. The day has stopped offering distractions. Fatigue lowers perspective. The mind takes unfinished material from the day and begins sorting, testing, and replaying it. At 3am, a minor moment can seem enormous because there is no competing evidence from ordinary life. There is only darkness, tiredness, and the mind's insistence that this must be solved now.

But not every problem should be solved at 3am. Some thoughts arrive with urgency but not wisdom. You will learn how to handle night-time replays with a different strategy: not debate, not analysis, not panic, but labelling, softening, parking, and gently returning the body to safety. The goal is not to force instant sleep. The goal is to end the fight that keeps the loop alive.

Throughout this book, the focus will remain practical. Insight is useful only when it changes what happens in the next real moment. You will be given small tools because small tools are the ones people actually use under stress. A five-minute release routine is more valuable than an elaborate system you abandon when anxious. A simple closing statement, repeated consistently, can be more powerful than another hour of analysis. A clear apology can end a replay faster than twelve imaginary speeches. A single sensory anchor can return you to the room more effectively than arguing with a thought that has already argued back.

You will also learn when not to act. This is an underrated skill. Mental rewinds often demand action not because action is needed, but because anxiety wants relief. You may feel an urge to send another message, explain again, apologise for something tiny, seek reassurance, check whether someone is annoyed, or reopen a conversation that has already ended. Sometimes repair is wise. Sometimes clarification is kind. Sometimes apology is necessary. But sometimes the healthiest move is to let the moment remain imperfect and incomplete.

Letting it be is not passivity. It is disciplined restraint.

To let something be, you must tolerate uncertainty. You must accept that you cannot fully control how others interpret you. You cannot enter their minds and clean up every possible misunderstanding. You cannot guarantee that nobody will ever think poorly of you. You cannot live a free life while trying to pre-approve every memory others may have of you. The cost is too high. You shrink your speech, dull your presence, and make your attention a servant of imagined judgement.

This book will not promise that you will never replay again. That would be dishonest. Replays are part of being human. Under stress, tiredness, conflict, grief, pressure, or change, old loops may return. But the aim is not a permanently blank mind. The aim is quicker recovery. Less checking. Less self-attack. Less time spent trying to edit scenes that are already over. More ability to learn, close, and re-enter your life.

Progress may look modest at first. You catch the replay after twenty minutes instead of two hours. You reread the message once instead of ten times. You apologise clearly instead of composing a dramatic essay. You notice the prosecutor voice and shift to a steadier one. You wake at night, label the loop, and refuse to conduct a full investigation in the dark. These changes may seem small, but they are not. They are the architecture of freedom.

A life with fewer mental rewinds is not a life without conscience. It is a life with cleaner conscience. You still care about your words, your relationships, your work, your values, and your effect on others. But you stop confusing suffering with sincerity. You stop believing that the amount of time spent replaying proves the depth of your responsibility. You stop using your own mind as a punishment chamber.

The past deserves to teach you. It does not deserve to own you.

As you move through this book, you will be invited to develop a new relationship with your mind's reviewing function. You will not need to hate it. You will not need to obey it blindly. You will learn to thank it for trying to protect you, then give it better instructions. Review briefly. Learn specifically. Repair proportionately. Close deliberately. Return to the present.

That is the work.

Not to erase every mistake.

Not to become perfectly unbothered.

Not to win every imagined argument.

But to stop giving yesterday unlimited access to today.

The central promise of this book is simple: you can become someone who learns from the past without living inside it. You can take the useful lesson and leave the rest. You can stop replaying the conversation, the mistake, the silence, the look, the message, the meeting, the sentence, the version of yourself you wish had appeared instead.

You can move forward with a mind that is still thoughtful, still sensitive, still responsible, but no longer trapped in endless rewinds.

Lesson taken. Scene closed. Life resumed.

Chapter 1
What Mental Rewinds Are

You say one sentence in a meeting that does not land the way you hoped. It is not a disaster. Nobody gasps. Nobody confronts you. The conversation moves on, the meeting ends, chairs scrape back, laptops close, and you walk away carrying the ordinary residue of social life: a little uncertainty, a little discomfort, a faint wish that you had chosen cleaner words.

By the time you reach the next part of your day, the sentence has followed you. It repeats while you make tea. It returns while you answer another message. It sharpens while you try to focus on work that has nothing to do with it. The words are no longer simply remembered; they are being inspected. You hear your tone again. You imagine a colleague's private reaction. You test an alternative version, then another. The scene has become a small recording with a faulty stop button.

The oddest part is that the mind presents this as usefulness. It does not announce, "I am about to waste your evening." It says, "Look again. There may be something important here." So you look again. The review feels responsible at first, even mature. You are not dismissing the moment. You are trying to learn from it. Yet somewhere along the way, the review stops behaving like learning and starts behaving like threat detection. The original sentence becomes less important than the question underneath it: *What does this mean about me?*

That is the central tension of mental rewinds. The mind is built to learn from experience, especially from experiences that carry social risk, regret, embarrassment, or uncertainty. A quick look back can help you adjust. It can help you repair. It can keep you from repeating something careless. But the same mechanism can turn against you when it mistakes repeated inspection for safety. You begin with a reasonable wish to understand what happened, and end up trapped in a private hearing where no amount of evidence is enough.

This matters because mental rewinds do not merely steal time. They alter the way you relate to yourself. A moment that could have been treated as information becomes a judgement. A clumsy phrase becomes proof of incompetence. A delayed reply becomes evidence of rejection. A mild disagreement becomes a sign that a relationship is unstable. The mind, searching for certainty, starts filling gaps with stories, and those stories often favour danger over balance. Not because you are foolish, but because a protective mind would rather over-check than under-prepare.

The cost accumulates quietly. You may become more careful with your speech, but not in a free or skilful way. You may start editing yourself before you speak, then auditing yourself after you speak. You may avoid sending messages unless every sentence feels perfectly safe. You may apologise when no apology is needed, or stay silent when a simple repair would help. Attention that belongs to the present is pulled backwards, again and again, into scenes that cannot be changed by more looking.

There is also a deeper cost: rumination can disguise itself as conscience. Many thoughtful people are reluctant to interrupt a replay because they fear that doing so would be irresponsible. They worry that if they stop examining the mistake, they will become careless, arrogant, or emotionally blunt. This fear is understandable, but it rests on a false bargain. Pain is not the price of integrity. Endless self-interrogation is not the same as accountability. You can take a mistake seriously without turning it into a sentence against your character.

The path begins by seeing the process clearly. A replay has a beginning, even when it feels automatic. It usually starts with a remembered moment and then gathers imagined alternatives around it. It persists because it offers a brief taste of control: perhaps one more analysis will prevent future embarrassment, rejection, or regret. The practical challenge is to distinguish learning from rumination before the loop consumes the evening. A useful review becomes specific and leads somewhere; a rewind becomes vague, repetitive, and increasingly personal.

The next time a scene returns with unusual force, the most important question is not whether the thought is true, false, fair, dramatic, or justified. The sharper question is simpler and more revealing: am I remembering this moment, reflecting on it, or looping inside it?

How Replays Begin

A replay rarely begins as a problem. It usually begins as something much more respectable: a review. You walk away from a conversation, a meeting, a message, a disagreement, or a small mistake, and the mind turns back towards it. At first, this can feel sensible. You are not ignoring what happened. You are checking your words, your tone, your timing, your effect. You are doing what thoughtful people do when they care about how they move through the world.

The trouble starts when the review loses its boundary. What began as a brief look back becomes a repeated return. The mind does not simply remember the moment; it re-enters it. It replays the sentence, the silence, the facial expression, the pause before someone answered. Then it adds variations. You imagine what you should have said. You hear yourself saying it better. You hear yourself saying it worse. You imagine the other person telling someone else about it. You imagine a judgement that has never been spoken. The original event becomes surrounded by invented alternatives, possible meanings, and private verdicts.

This is the beginning of a mental rewind: a remembered moment joined to imagined correction.

That distinction matters. A memory brings something back. A reflection examines it. A replay keeps running it, as if repetition itself might change the outcome. The mind behaves as though the scene is still open, still negotiable, still capable of being repaired by thinking. But the past is not a draft. You can learn from it, apologise for it, clarify it, or make a different choice next time. You cannot climb back into the scene and perform it again.

Still, the mind tries.

Consider the kind of moment that seems almost too small to explain its aftermath. You are in a meeting. Someone asks for your view. You answer quickly, perhaps too quickly, and use a phrase that sounds more blunt than you intended. Nobody reacts dramatically. The meeting continues. You finish your notes, say goodbye, and close your laptop. For a few minutes, nothing seems wrong. Then the phrase returns. You hear it with slightly more edge than it had at the time. You wonder whether it sounded dismissive. You remember that one person looked down just after you said it. Was that related? Did they think you were rude? Should you have softened it? Should you send a message? Would sending a message make it worse?

The replay has begun.

Notice how ordinary the entry point is. The mind does not require a disaster. It only requires uncertainty plus emotional charge. There is a gap in the evidence, and the mind begins to fill it. You do not know exactly how your words landed, so your attention circles the moment looking for clues. Because the stakes are social, the search feels urgent. Human beings are not indifferent to belonging, reputation, respect, trust, or acceptance. A small possible rupture can feel larger than it looks from the outside because the nervous system treats social threat seriously.

At the start, the mind may genuinely be trying to help. It asks, "Was that all right?" This can be a useful question. It may lead to a simple adjustment: next time, pause before answering; next time, choose a warmer phrase; next time, check whether the other person has finished. That is learning. It is clear, modest, and usable. But when the mind cannot find certainty, it may keep searching. "Was that all right?" becomes "What if it was not all right?" Then "What if they now think differently of me?" Then "Why do I always sound like that?" The focus shifts from behaviour to identity.

That shift is the hinge.

A healthy review stays close to the event. It asks what happened, what mattered, and what can be done. A replay drifts away from the event into self-prosecution. It no longer asks, "Was that sentence too sharp?" It asks, "Am I the kind of person who ruins things?" It no longer asks, "Could I clarify this?" It asks, "Have I damaged the way they see me?" The mind moves from practical assessment to threat scanning. It stops looking for learning and starts looking for danger.

Threat scanning is the mind's attempt to detect risk before it becomes harm. In physical danger, this can be useful. If you hear a sudden noise behind you, attention narrows, the body prepares, and the mind looks for an explanation. But the same pattern can appear after social discomfort. The "noise" is not a crash or a shout; it is an awkward pause, a delayed reply, a flat tone, a sentence that now seems questionable. The body may respond as though something is unresolved. Attention narrows. The replay sharpens. The mind searches the past for a safer interpretation.

The body often joins before you have consciously decided anything. Heat in the face. Tightness in the chest. A drop in the stomach. Restlessness in the hands. A sudden urge to check, explain, reread, apologise, withdraw, or mentally rehearse. These sensations can make the replay feel more credible. The mind thinks, "I feel alarmed, so something must be wrong." But physical arousal is not proof of danger. It is proof that the system has been activated. The body can respond strongly to uncertainty, embarrassment, fatigue, conflict, or imagined judgement, even when there is no clear evidence of actual harm.

This is why mental rewinds can feel so persuasive. They are not only thoughts; they are thoughts with bodily emphasis. The scene seems important because it feels important. The feeling then drives more thinking, and the thinking produces more feeling. A loop forms. The more you replay the moment, the more vivid it becomes. The more vivid it becomes, the more significant it appears. The more significant it appears, the more the mind insists that you must keep reviewing it.

A replay also gains strength from the illusion of correction. The mind offers alternative scripts as if they are useful preparation. "I should have said it this way." "I should have waited." "I should have smiled." "I should have explained the context." There can be value in one alternative if it points towards a future adjustment. But the replay rarely stops at one. It generates versions. The perfect sentence. The perfect tone. The perfect timing. The perfect recovery. Each imagined improvement makes the original moment look worse by comparison.

This is a subtle cruelty of hindsight. Once the pressure is gone, the mind can design elegant replies that were not available in the actual moment. It forgets the speed, surprise, fatigue, awkwardness, incomplete information, and emotional noise of real life. Then it judges your past self by the polished script of your later self. This is not fairness. It is editing after the performance and calling the actor incompetent.

The replay may also begin because the mind dislikes unfinished meaning. Some experiences have clear edges. Someone says, "That hurt me." You apologise. A plan changes. You adjust. A mistake is visible. You correct it. But many moments are ambiguous. A person responds with "fine". Someone reads a message and does not reply. A colleague seems quieter than usual. A friend uses a full stop where they normally use warmth. Ambiguity invites interpretation, and interpretation can become a trap. The mind wants to close the gap, so it starts building explanations. Unfortunately, anxious explanations often arrive faster than balanced ones.

The replay then becomes a search for certainty in a place where certainty may not exist. You cannot know exactly what someone thought. You cannot prove how long they remembered the moment. You cannot confirm every possible meaning of their expression. Yet the mind keeps trying, as if enough analysis will produce a clean answer. This is where the rewind becomes exhausting. It is trying to solve an unsolvable problem by using more of the same method that made the problem expand.

There is a clear difference between remembering, reflecting, and looping.

Remembering is the mind bringing a past event into awareness. It may be neutral, pleasant, painful, or brief. You recall what was said. You picture the room. You recognise the sequence of events.

Remembering does not necessarily demand action. It is a mental return.

Reflecting is more deliberate. It has a purpose. You look back to understand, learn, decide, or repair. Reflection can be uncomfortable, but it usually has direction. It stays connected to reality. It asks proportionate questions. It may lead to a practical conclusion: "I need to clarify that message," or "I will prepare differently next time," or "That felt awkward, but nothing further is needed."

Looping is different. Looping repeats without resolving. It asks questions that grow wider, harsher, and less answerable. It searches for a perfect meaning, a perfect explanation, a perfect version of the past. It often attacks identity rather than examining behaviour. It narrows attention until the replay feels more real than the room you are standing in. Looping is not learning with extra effort. It is learning that has lost its shape.

One reliable sign that a replay has begun is that the same material returns with no new information. You are not discovering anything. You are re-feeling it. The mind may pretend it is still investigating, but the evidence has not changed. The sentence is the same sentence. The reply is the same reply. The facial expression is the same uncertain memory. What changes is the emotional charge. Each return adds weight, not clarity.

Another sign is that the replay starts demanding impossible standards. It wants you to have known then what you know now. It wants you to have spoken without hesitation, responded without defensiveness, shown warmth without overdoing it, been honest without being blunt, confident without seeming arrogant, careful without seeming tense. The replay imagines a flawless social performance and treats anything short of it as failure. No human being can live under that standard without becoming self-conscious and tired.

A third sign is the urge to keep checking. You may reread a message, scan an email, replay a voice note, revisit a memory, or look for tiny changes in someone's behaviour. Checking can feel like relief for a moment because it gives the mind a task. But if the task is driven by anxiety rather than usefulness, the relief fades quickly. The mind asks for another check. Then another. The loop learns that discomfort should be answered with inspection, and inspection keeps the discomfort alive.

The beginning of a replay is often easier to catch than the middle. Once you are deep inside it, the scene feels urgent and personal. But early on, there is usually a small turning point. You notice the memory return. You lean towards it. You begin to test meanings. You add imagined reactions. You move from "That was awkward" to "They must think I am difficult." That early movement is important. It is the moment when a review becomes a rewind.

Catching that movement does not require harshness. You do not need to scold yourself for replaying. Scolding simply adds another layer of threat. The more useful response is recognition: "This is the mind trying to review something uncomfortable." That recognition creates a little space. It allows you to see the replay as a process, not as a command. You can still learn from the moment, but you do not have to surrender the evening to it.

Mental rewinds begin because the mind is trying to protect your future self from repeating pain. That intention deserves respect. But protection becomes costly when it relies on endless return. The mind is not wrong to care about what happened. It is wrong to assume that more replaying will create more safety. Sometimes the safest move is not to review harder, but to recognise the exact point at which review has stopped helping.

The next time a scene starts following you from room to room, pay attention to its first shape. Is it a memory asking to be noticed? Is it a reflection asking for one clean lesson? Or has it already become a loop, gathering imagined alternatives and asking you to stand trial for a moment that has ended? The answer matters, because the way a replay begins often determines how much of your life it is allowed to take.

Why the Loop Persists

A mental replay survives because it offers something seductive: the feeling that you are doing something useful. The mind does not usually return to an uncomfortable moment with the honest announcement, "I am about to keep you trapped in repetitive distress." It arrives wearing the clothes of responsibility. It tells you that one more review may reveal the lesson, one more reconstruction may prevent the same mistake, one more imagined version may finally make the whole thing feel safe.

That is why the loop can be so difficult to interrupt. It contains a promise. The promise is not pleasure, but protection. If you think harder, you will be ready next time. If you understand the exact reason the conversation felt awkward, you will never be caught off guard again. If you can identify the precise moment someone's expression changed, you can protect your reputation. If you can work out what they really meant by their short reply, you can prepare yourself emotionally before anything worse happens.

The replay persists because, for a few seconds at a time, it seems to reduce uncertainty. It gives the mind a task. Instead of sitting with the raw discomfort of not knowing, you can investigate. You can review the evidence, replay the tone, inspect the wording, compare possibilities, rehearse explanations, and try to build a complete story. This activity can feel calmer than doing nothing. It can feel like control.

But it is a costly form of control, because it rarely completes itself.

Uncertainty is one of the strongest fuels for mental rewinds. A clear event may hurt, but at least it has edges. If someone says, "That comment upset me," the path may be uncomfortable, but it is visible. You can listen, acknowledge, apologise, clarify, or adjust. A vague event is different. A pause. A delayed reply. A half-smile. A colleague who seemed quieter after your comment. A message that says "No worries" but feels colder than usual. These moments leave space for interpretation, and the mind dislikes empty space when something important may be at stake.

So it fills the gap.

It may fill the gap with caution at first. "Perhaps I should check whether that landed badly." That may be reasonable. But if no new information arrives, the mind may begin to manufacture possibilities. "Maybe they thought I was rude." "Maybe they are telling someone else." "Maybe I damaged the relationship." "Maybe this is what I always do." The replay then becomes less about the original moment and more about the imagined consequences surrounding it.

This is where the loop begins to feed itself. The mind looks for certainty in material that cannot provide it. A memory of a facial expression cannot prove what someone thought. A short text cannot reveal every shade of intention behind it. A silence cannot be forced to confess its meaning. Yet the mind keeps returning, as though pressure will produce proof. The result is not clarity, but mental abrasion. The same scene is rubbed raw by repeated attention.

Social risk makes this especially powerful. Most people can tolerate a practical mistake more easily than a social one. Sending the wrong attachment, missing a turn, or misplacing a set of keys may be frustrating, but these errors often have direct remedies. Social moments feel more delicate because they touch identity and belonging. Did I seem foolish? Did I sound unkind? Did I come across as needy? Did I disappoint them? Did I reveal something unattractive about myself? These questions are not merely about behaviour. They are about how the self is seen.

The mind treats reputation, connection, trust, and acceptance as serious matters. This is not vanity. Human beings are relational. Much of life depends on being understood well enough, trusted enough, welcomed enough, and respected enough to move through work, family, friendship, and community without constant threat. When a moment appears to put that standing at risk, even slightly, the mind may respond with urgency. It tries to prevent exclusion, criticism, conflict, embarrassment, or rejection by studying the scene for warning signs.

The problem is that the mind often cannot tell the difference between preparation and punishment once social fear is activated. It may begin with the practical question, "What can I learn?" But under pressure, that question mutates. It becomes, "What is wrong with me?" This is one reason mental rewinds persist for so long: they stop examining an event and start examining the self.

A person who thinks, "That sentence was unclear," has a manageable problem. A person who thinks, "I am terrible at speaking," has an identity threat. The second thought has more emotional force, so the mind treats it as more important. It returns to the scene not to improve one sentence, but to defend the entire self against a feared verdict. This is why a small moment can feel enormous. The replay is no longer about a sentence. It is about worth, competence, likability, maturity, intelligence, kindness, or control.

Self-image is sticky material. The mind wants a stable picture of who you are, and it becomes unsettled when an event appears to contradict that picture. If you see yourself as considerate, a moment where you may have sounded dismissive can be hard to release. If you see yourself as competent, a public mistake can replay with unusual force. If you value being calm, a moment of defensiveness may feel especially threatening. The more strongly you care about a value, the more painful it can be when a moment seems to place that value in doubt.

This is not a sign that your values are wrong. It is a sign that your mind is treating a single incident as though it has the authority to define you.

That is one of rumination's central distortions. It takes a moment and turns it into evidence. Not ordinary evidence, but character evidence. One awkward reply becomes "I am socially hopeless." One poor decision becomes "I cannot trust myself." One tense conversation becomes "I ruin relationships." The loop persists because the mind believes there is a larger case to solve. It is no longer satisfied with "What happened?" It wants a final judgement: What does this prove?

The search for that final judgement is exhausting because it is built on the wrong premise. Most human moments do not prove one clean thing. A clumsy sentence may prove that you were tired, rushed, nervous, unclear, distracted, or simply human. It may prove that a repair is useful. It may prove that next time you should slow down. It does not prove your whole character. But rumination is not careful with proportion. It widens the meaning until the event feels heavier than it deserves to be.

The loop also persists because it offers tiny rewards. This is uncomfortable to admit, but important. Replaying can briefly soothe anxiety. When you reread the message and find no obvious offence, you feel a small drop in tension. When you imagine a better response, you feel momentarily more prepared. When you decide that the other person probably was not upset, you feel relief. These brief reductions in discomfort teach the mind that replaying works.

Yet the relief does not last because nothing has truly been resolved. The mind soon asks for another check. The message is reread again. The memory is replayed again. The alternative explanation is tested again. The loop becomes self-reinforcing: anxiety triggers review, review gives temporary relief, temporary relief teaches the brain to review again. What looks like thinking is often reassurance-seeking in private form.

This is why telling yourself to stop can fail so badly. The loop is not sustained by logic alone; it is sustained by relief. If replaying has become the method your mind uses to reduce discomfort, then removing the replay can feel like removing safety. The mind may protest. It may say, "But we have not finished. We have not solved it. We have not made sure." That protest does not mean the replay is useful. It means the mind has confused certainty with survival.

Another reason the loop persists is that the replay creates the illusion of moral seriousness. Many people believe that if they stop reviewing a mistake, they are letting themselves off too easily. They worry that releasing the scene means denying responsibility. This belief is understandable, especially for people who are conscientious, sensitive to others, or determined not to repeat harmful patterns. But there is a sharp difference between accountability and endless internal punishment.

Accountability asks for truth and action. Rumination asks for repeated suffering.

Accountability says, "I interrupted. I will apologise and slow down next time." Rumination says, "Why am I like this? How many times have I done this? What if everyone sees me this way?" Accountability keeps the event at the right size. Rumination expands it until the self is on trial. Accountability can be uncomfortable, but it moves. Rumination circles.

The loop persists when suffering is mistaken for sincerity. You may feel that the amount of pain you experience proves that you care. It may feel wrong to put the moment down too quickly. Yet pain is not always evidence of growth. Sometimes pain is simply the nervous system staying activated after the useful lesson has already been taken. You can care deeply, make amends where needed, and still refuse to keep replaying the scene as payment.

There is also the lure of the perfect meaning. The mind wants to know exactly what the moment meant. Did they notice? Were they offended? Was it awkward or only slightly uncomfortable? Was your tone firm or harsh? Were you honest or insensitive? Were you misunderstood or did you communicate badly? These distinctions may matter, but the demand for exactness can become a trap. Some moments do not offer perfect meaning. They offer partial information and a need for proportion.

The replay persists by pretending that the perfect interpretation is just one more thought away. But the more you think, the more interpretations appear. You discover not certainty, but additional angles. Each angle feels relevant. Each possibility asks to be considered. The mind begins to behave like a room full of mirrors, where every view generates another view and none of them lets you leave.

This is why reflection becomes compulsion quietly. It does not cross a bright line. There is no bell that rings when useful review has ended and rumination has begun. Instead, the shift is felt in the quality of the thinking. Reflection is usually bounded. It may be uncomfortable, but it remains connected to reality and to choice. Compulsion feels urgent, repetitive, and strangely unsatisfying. It keeps asking questions that do not lead to action. It often becomes harsher over time. It narrows the world until the replay is the only thing that seems to matter.

One of the clearest signs of compulsion is the absence of new information. If you are returning to the same moment with the same evidence and the same questions, you are probably not learning anymore. You are trying to reduce discomfort by repeating the mental act of checking. The mind may call this analysis, but analysis requires fresh data, a clearer distinction, or a practical decision. Without those, the process becomes circular.

Another sign is that the replay begins to demand emotional certainty before you move on. It wants you to feel completely calm, completely forgiven, completely understood, completely safe. This is a standard that ordinary life cannot meet. You may need to act before you feel settled. You may need to let a conversation remain slightly imperfect. You may need to accept that someone's opinion is not fully knowable. You may need to carry a small amount of discomfort without turning it into an investigation.

A third sign is that the replay moves away from the present. Instead of asking, "What is the next useful step?" it asks, "How can I make the past feel different?" This is impossible. You can repair in the present. You can learn in the present. You can change future behaviour in the present. But you cannot think your way into a different yesterday. The loop persists because it keeps trying to negotiate with a closed scene.

This does not mean every replay should be dismissed. Some replays contain useful signals. A repeated discomfort may point to a needed apology, a boundary crossed, an unspoken truth, a pattern worth addressing, or a conversation that requires repair. The aim is not to treat every return of memory as meaningless noise. The aim is to recognise when the memory has delivered its message and the mind is now rereading the envelope.

There is a gentler way to understand persistence: the mind keeps returning because it does not yet feel safe enough to stop. It wants assurance that you will not repeat the mistake, lose the relationship, damage your reputation, or be caught unprepared. But the mind often asks for a form of assurance life cannot give. It wants certainty about other people's thoughts. It wants guarantees about future outcomes. It wants a version of you who never missteps. That demand is not protection. It is perfectionism under pressure.

Recognising the mechanism removes some of the shame. You are not replaying because you are weak. You are not stuck because you lack intelligence. In fact, intelligent people can build very elaborate loops. The issue is not the amount of thought available, but the function the thought is serving. Is it helping you understand and act, or is it trying to create certainty where only courage, proportion, or repair can help?

The loop persists until the mind learns that safety does not come from endless review. It comes from a different sequence: seeing the event clearly, naming what is uncertain, separating behaviour from identity, taking proportionate action if needed, and allowing the remaining discomfort to pass without feeding it. That sequence cannot begin while the replay is still being treated as an emergency.

The crucial moment is the instant you notice that thinking has become checking. The tone changes. The questions repeat. The body tightens. The imagined audience grows. The possible meanings multiply. What began as reflection now has the flavour of compulsion. At that point, the task is not to solve the past more perfectly. The task is to recognise what the mind is trying to do: it is trying to feel safe by keeping the scene alive.

And that recognition changes everything. The replay may still pull. The old promise may still sound persuasive. One more review. One more angle. One more reconstruction. But now you can hear the promise more clearly. You can see that the loop is not persisting because it has found the truth. It is persisting because it has confused repetition with protection.

The scene may contain a lesson. It may even contain a repair. But it does not require endless access to your attention. Once the useful part has been found, the loop has no further authority. It is only an old alarm ringing after the danger has passed, asking you to keep listening because silence feels uncertain.

Learning vs Rumination

Learning and rumination can look almost identical at the beginning. Both turn attention towards the past. Both ask questions. Both may arise after discomfort, embarrassment, conflict, uncertainty, or regret. Both can feel serious and necessary. This is why mental rewinds are so persuasive: they often enter through the same doorway as wisdom.

After a difficult conversation, a healthy mind naturally reviews. It asks whether the words were clear, whether the tone matched the intention, whether something requires repair, whether a future choice could be better. This is not overthinking. This is social and emotional intelligence at work. A person who never reviews their behaviour is not free; they are merely unexamined. Reflection is part of maturity. It helps you grow beyond instinct, defensiveness, and repetition.

Rumination is different. Rumination takes the raw material of reflection and removes its usefulness. It repeats rather than clarifies. It expands rather than focuses. It attacks rather than teaches. It circles the same moment while promising that another round will deliver certainty, peace, or protection. It is mental effort without forward movement.

The difference is not always found in the subject of the thinking. You may think about the same conversation in two completely different ways. One version helps you learn. The other keeps you trapped. The event itself is not the issue. The function of the thinking is the issue.

Productive learning is specific. It keeps close to what actually happened. It is interested in behaviour, context, choice, and consequence. It does not need to turn a single moment into a verdict on your entire personality. It may say, "I interrupted before they had finished. Next time I will pause." It may say, "My message was too abrupt. I can clarify." It may say, "I was tired, and I became defensive. I need to recognise that pattern sooner."

Rumination is vague. It drifts away from the event and into identity. It says, "I always ruin things." "I am terrible with people." "They must think I am impossible." "Why can I never get it right?" These thoughts may sound emotionally convincing, but they are rarely precise enough to help. They do not tell you what to do. They do not show you what to repair. They do not produce a cleaner next step. They simply make the self feel contaminated by the moment.

This is one of the clearest distinctions: learning gives you something usable; rumination gives you more of itself.

Learning is also time-bounded. It does not need unlimited access to your attention. A useful review may be uncomfortable, but it has a natural end point. You look at the moment, identify the lesson, decide whether action is needed, and return to the present. You may still feel uneasy afterwards, but the thinking has done its job.

Rumination has no natural end point because its aim is not really learning. Its hidden aim is emotional certainty. It wants you to feel completely sure that you were not wrong, not disliked, not foolish, not misunderstood, not judged, not at risk. Since life rarely provides that kind of certainty, the rumination keeps going. It keeps searching for a level of reassurance that the past cannot offer.

A useful way to separate the two is to ask: "Is this thought becoming more specific or more global?"

Specific thinking narrows towards a workable lesson. It sounds like, "The timing was poor," "I need to ask before assuming," "I should not respond when I am already tense," or "This deserves a short apology." Global thinking spreads into broad judgement. It sounds like, "I am a failure," "I cannot trust myself," "Everyone must be tired of me," or "I never handle anything properly."

Specific thinking can be acted upon. Global thinking usually cannot. You can practise pausing. You can rewrite a message. You can repair a comment. You can set a boundary. You can prepare differently. But what exactly are you supposed to do with "I am hopeless"? That kind of statement has emotional force, but no practical handle. It keeps you in pain while offering no route out.

The second useful question is: "Is this leading to an action, or only to another round of thinking?"

This question cuts through the respectability of rumination. The mind may insist that it is working hard, but effort is not the same as progress. If the thought leads to a proportionate action, it may be learning. The action might be external, such as apologising, clarifying, preparing, resting, or changing a habit. It might be internal, such as accepting uncertainty or deciding not to reopen something that does not need reopening. But there is movement.

If the thought leads only to another thought, another replay, another imagined conversation, another inspection of the same evidence, another attempt to perfect the meaning, then the process has probably slipped into rumination. The mind is no longer using the past as a teacher. It is using the past as a room to pace in.

This distinction matters because many people stay trapped by mistaking rumination for depth. They assume that the longer they think about something, the more responsible they are being. They believe that suffering proves seriousness. They may even feel guilty when they try to stop, as if releasing the replay means excusing the mistake. This is one of rumination's most convincing disguises.

But seriousness is not measured by duration. It is measured by honesty and response. You can take a mistake seriously in a few clear minutes if you are willing to see it plainly and choose your next step. You can also spend hours in mental noise and learn nothing. Time spent thinking is not proof of wisdom. Pain endured is not proof of accountability.

There is a particularly common trap here: trying to find the perfect meaning.

The mind wants to know exactly what the moment meant. Was the comment rude or merely direct? Was the silence disapproval or distraction? Was the delayed reply a sign of irritation or ordinary busyness? Did you make things awkward, or did you simply notice awkwardness because you were already anxious? These questions can seem important, and sometimes they are worth a brief look. But they become dangerous when the mind demands a final interpretation that no evidence can support.

Many human interactions do not have one perfect meaning. They are mixed, partial, layered, and shaped by more than one person's mood, history, assumptions, fatigue, and attention. A conversation can be slightly awkward without being damaging. A reply can be brief without being hostile. A person can seem distant for reasons that have nothing to do with you. A mistake can matter without defining you. The mind dislikes this messiness, so it tries to force the moment into a clean verdict.

Rumination thrives on verdicts. Learning thrives on proportion.

A verdict says, "This proves something final." Proportion says, "This may show me something useful, but it does not show me everything." Proportion allows a moment to matter at its proper size. It does not minimise genuine harm, but it does not inflate discomfort into disaster. It leaves room for complexity. It accepts that you may have been clumsy without being cruel, uncertain without being weak, wrong without being worthless.

This is where many mental rewinds lose their authority. They rely on exaggeration. They need the moment to feel bigger, sharper, more permanent, and more revealing than it is. Once you restore proportion, the replay has less to feed on. The sentence was awkward, not catastrophic. The meeting was tense, not ruined. The apology may be needed, but humiliation is not. The delayed reply is unpleasant, but not evidence. The mistake is real, but it is not the whole story.

Learning also respects context. Rumination strips context away.

If you spoke sharply after a long, draining day, context does not excuse the sharpness, but it helps explain it. If you stumbled through a presentation while nervous, context matters. If you sent a message quickly between other pressures, context matters. If a conversation went badly because both people were defensive, context matters. Learning includes these details because it wants accuracy. Rumination often rejects them because it wants a case.

The prosecutor voice has no interest in context unless context can be used against you. It will say you should have known better, should have been calmer, should have anticipated every reaction, should have controlled every word, should have performed with perfect emotional balance under imperfect conditions. It treats being human as negligence.

Learning does not do this. Learning is firm, but fair. It does not flatter you, and it does not destroy you. It asks what happened with enough honesty to be useful and enough kindness to be sustainable. That balance is not softness. It is precision. Harshness may feel powerful, but it often makes thinking less accurate. When you feel attacked, even by yourself, the mind narrows. It becomes defensive, panicked, or submissive. None of these states are ideal for clear learning.

A useful review has a clean structure, even if you do not write it down. It separates fact from interpretation. It distinguishes intention from impact. It identifies what was inside your control and what was not. It asks whether repair is needed. It takes one lesson forward. Then it stops.

Rumination refuses to stop because it keeps changing the question. Once one concern is answered, it introduces another. Perhaps the words were not that bad, but what about the tone? Perhaps the tone was acceptable, but what about the timing? Perhaps the timing was understandable, but what about the expression on their face? Perhaps their expression meant nothing, but what if they mention it later? The mind behaves as though every possibility must be neutralised before you are allowed to rest.

That is not learning. That is an anxiety system trying to achieve total social control.

And total social control is impossible. You cannot control every interpretation others make. You cannot guarantee that you will never be misunderstood. You cannot speak so perfectly that no one ever reacts from their own insecurity, distraction, or mood. You cannot revise every past moment until it becomes immune to judgement. The attempt will not make you safer. It will make you smaller.

The alternative is not carelessness. It is disciplined completion.

Disciplined completion means you give the moment a fair hearing, not an endless trial. You ask what happened. You ask what can be learned. You ask whether anything needs to be done. Then you deliberately close the review, even if some emotional residue remains. This is important: closure often comes before complete emotional comfort. Many people wait to feel fully calm before they stop thinking. But rumination can keep the body activated, which means calm never arrives. Sometimes you stop the review while discomfort is still present, and the body settles later because you have stopped feeding the loop.

This can feel unnatural at first. The mind may protest, "But we are not done." A better question is, "Are we unfinished, or are we uncomfortable?" These are not the same. Unfinished means there is a genuine next step: a message to send, a boundary to set, a preparation to make, an apology to offer, a decision to clarify. Uncomfortable means the feeling has not fully faded. Rumination often treats discomfort as evidence that more thinking is required. In reality, discomfort may simply be the echo of activation.

Learning can end with discomfort still in the room.

That sentence is worth taking seriously. A review does not have to produce perfect peace to be complete. It only has to produce enough clarity to guide the next step or confirm that no step is needed. Waiting for flawless certainty is how the loop keeps ownership of your evening.

There is a useful firmness in saying, "I have taken the lesson available." Not the ultimate lesson. Not the perfect lesson. Not the lesson that makes everyone understand you and every possible future safe. The available lesson. The one that can be drawn from the evidence you actually have. That is all a human being can responsibly take.

The available lesson might be small. "Pause before replying." "Do not send serious messages when tired." "Ask directly instead of guessing." "Clarify sooner." "Let silence remain silence." "Stop rereading once the message has been sent." Small lessons are often more powerful than dramatic self-judgements because they can be practised. They turn experience into behaviour.

Rumination prefers grand conclusions because grand conclusions feel emotionally complete. "I am bad at relationships" sounds significant. "I need to ask one more question before assuming" sounds modest. But the modest sentence is the one that can change a life. The grand conclusion simply gives the mind a heavier chain.

To learn from a replay, you must keep the lesson close to the ground. Do not ask the past to tell you who you are. Ask it what it can teach you to do with more care next time. That shift removes the false drama without removing responsibility. It allows you to grow without becoming a permanent defendant in your own mind.

The task is not to stop reflecting. The task is to protect reflection from becoming rumination. Reflection is a tool. Rumination is a treadmill wearing the mask of a tool. One helps you move through life with more skill. The other keeps you sweating in place, convinced that exhaustion means progress.

When the mind returns to a scene, the question is not, "May I think about this?" Of course you may. Some moments deserve thought. The better question is, "What kind of thinking is this becoming?" Is it specific, bounded, and linked to action? Or is it vague, repetitive, and attacking the self?

The answer tells you what to do next.

If there is a lesson, take it.

If there is a repair, make it.

If there is only another loop asking for another hour, recognise it for what it is: not wisdom, not conscience, not preparation, but rumination trying to purchase certainty with your attention.

The scene may have something to teach you. It does not have the right to keep teaching the same lesson forever.

Chapter 2
Triggers That Start Replays

Why does one passing comment slide away while another follows you for hours? Why can one delayed reply mean nothing on a steady day and everything on a tired one? Why does the mind sometimes treat a small social uncertainty as if it were urgent evidence that must be examined at once?

The answer is rarely found in the size of the event alone. A replay is not always triggered by what objectively happened. It is often triggered by what the moment appears to threaten: your competence, your kindness, your place in a group, your ability to read a room, your sense of being acceptable to people who matter. A brief pause after you speak may be harmless. A message left unanswered may be ordinary. A joke that lands flat may be forgotten by everyone else before the kettle has boiled. Yet if the moment touches a tender internal point, the mind marks it for review.

That marking can happen quickly. You may not think, "This has threatened my self-image." You may simply feel a tightening, a flush, a drop in the stomach, a sudden mental reach back towards the scene. The trigger announces itself through attention before it becomes a clear thought. Something in you says, "Go back. Check that." Once the mind obeys, the replay begins to gather detail, interpretation, and imagined consequence.

The central tension is that triggers are not always warnings of real danger. Sometimes they are signals of uncertainty. Sometimes they are echoes of old embarrassment. Sometimes they are bodily alarms looking for a story to attach themselves to. If every trigger is treated as proof that something has gone wrong, the mind becomes a nervous investigator, forever reopening ordinary human moments as possible evidence. But if triggers are dismissed too quickly, useful information can be lost. The skill lies in learning to recognise what has been activated without handing the trigger full authority over the meaning of the event.

This matters because unnamed triggers make replays feel random. When you do not know what sets the loop in motion, the mind seems unreliable, as though it can seize any moment without pattern or permission. That helplessness adds another layer of distress. You are not only replaying the conversation; you are also wondering why you are like this, why you cannot simply move on, why something so small has taken hold with such force. Naming the trigger changes the relationship. It turns a mysterious attack into a recognisable sequence.

Some triggers are built around ambiguity. The mind dislikes the open space between what happened and what it might mean. A delayed response, a vague piece of feedback, a quiet tone, an unread message, a look that could mean disapproval or distraction: these moments do not give the mind enough certainty to rest. Ambiguity is sticky because it invites completion. The mind starts supplying possibilities, and because it is trying to protect you, it often supplies the threatening ones first. A blank space becomes a screen for fear.

Other triggers are tied to shame and social rank in the broadest human sense: not hierarchy alone, but the felt question of where you stand. Did you seem foolish? Did you come across as difficult? Did you expose ignorance? Did you appear unkind when you meant to be playful? These questions can be painfully powerful because they move faster than reason. Shame does not merely say, "That was clumsy." It says, "You are exposed." It takes a behaviour and tries to turn it into an identity. That is why a badly received joke, a stumbled sentence, or a misunderstood comment can replay with such intensity. The event may be small, but the threat feels global.

The body can trigger the loop as much as the event can. A rush of heat, a tight chest, a restless pulse, a sense of agitation at night: these sensations can arrive before there is any clear interpretation. The mind then tries to explain them. It looks backwards and finds a scene that could justify the feeling. "This must be because of what I said earlier." "Something must be wrong." "I would not feel this way unless there were a real problem." In that moment, physical arousal is mistaken for evidence. The body becomes a witness the mind does not know how to cross-examine.

A clearer path begins with noticing the common doorways into replay. Ambiguous feedback and delayed replies pull the mind towards interpretation. Public speaking and visible mistakes place the self under imagined scrutiny. Interpersonal tension activates the fear of rupture. Shame turns a specific incident into a judgement about acceptability. Bodily signals add urgency, making the mind believe the past must be searched immediately. These doorways do not need to be forced open by dramatic events. They often swing on small hinges.

The work ahead is to make those hinges visible. A trigger category is not a label of weakness; it is a map of sensitivity. When you know what tends to start your replays, you are less likely to believe the loop has arrived from nowhere. You can begin to see the difference between a moment that requires action and a moment that has merely touched an old alarm. You can also recognise that feeling bad after an event does not automatically mean the event was bad in the way your mind now claims.

So the useful question is not only, "What am I replaying?" It is sharper than that: "What, exactly, did this moment touch?"

Common Replay Triggers

Mental replays often feel as though they arrive from nowhere. One moment you are moving through the day, and the next your attention has been pulled backwards into something you said, failed to say, sent, missed, misunderstood, or possibly mishandled. The mind returns to the scene with urgency, as if it has found unfinished business. Yet replays are rarely random. They have doorways. Certain kinds of moments are more likely to open them, especially when those moments contain uncertainty, visibility, emotional charge, or the possibility of social judgement.

A trigger is not always a dramatic event. This is one of the reasons people underestimate the pattern. A major argument may be obvious enough to explain a replay, but many loops begin with something smaller: a short reply, a vague piece of feedback, a pause after you speak, a facial expression you cannot interpret, a presentation that felt slightly uneven, a message left unanswered, or a conversation that ended without the warmth you expected. The event may look minor from the outside, but internally it may touch a question the mind takes seriously: *Am I safe here? Am I respected? Am I understood? Did I do damage?*

Ambiguity is one of the most common and powerful replay triggers because the mind dislikes unfinished meaning. A clear statement, even an unpleasant one, has edges. If someone says, "I was hurt by what you said," the discomfort is direct. You may need to listen, apologise, clarify, or change your behaviour, but at least the situation has shape. Ambiguity is different. It leaves the mind holding fragments. A look. A delay. A change in tone. A sentence that could mean several things. The mind begins to complete the picture, and under stress it often completes it in the most threatening direction.

This is why ambiguous feedback can be so sticky. "Interesting point." "We can revisit this later." "Let's think about it." "Fine." "No worries." These phrases may be neutral, polite, rushed, distracted, or genuinely approving. But when you are already sensitive to how you are being perceived, they can become material for interpretation. The mind does not simply accept that the meaning is unclear. It presses for a verdict. Was that approval or dismissal? Was that kindness or irritation? Was that calm or coldness? The less certain the evidence, the more the mind may try to extract certainty from it.

Delayed replies work in a similar way. A message sent into silence creates a gap, and the replay moves into that gap. At first, you may tell yourself the person is busy. Then attention returns. You reread what you sent. You notice a phrase that now seems too much, too little, too blunt, too eager, too formal, too casual. You imagine the recipient reading it with a different tone from the one you intended. The silence becomes a screen. Onto it, the mind projects rejection, annoyance, disapproval, or indifference.

The danger is not the delay itself. People reply late for countless ordinary reasons. The danger is the meaning the mind begins to build around the delay when uncertainty is intolerable. A delayed reply can become, in the space of a few minutes, an imagined social verdict.

"They are upset." "I sounded foolish." "I should not have sent that." "I have made things awkward." The replay then invites checking: open the thread again, inspect the wording, look for hidden errors, compare this reply pattern with previous ones. The mind acts as though certainty is available if only it reads closely enough.

Public speaking is another frequent doorway into replay because it combines visibility with limited control. Whether you speak in a formal presentation, a meeting, a class, a group conversation, or a casual discussion where attention briefly turns towards you, the self can feel unusually exposed. Words leave the mouth faster than the mind can polish them. You cannot control every expression in the room. You cannot know how every person interpreted your tone. Once the moment is over, the mind may begin its audit.

The replay after public speaking often has a particular rhythm. It selects one imperfect sentence, one stumble, one rushed answer, one visible hesitation, one joke that did not quite land, one moment when someone looked away. Then it edits out the rest. The mind may ignore the parts that went adequately or even well because threat has a stronger pull than balance. Attention narrows around the possible flaw. The whole experience is then judged through that narrow frame.

This is not because the mind is committed to cruelty. It is because visible mistakes feel socially risky. When other people witness you in real time, there is no private draft. You cannot quietly revise before being seen. If you value competence, clarity, intelligence, warmth, or authority, any moment that seems to compromise those qualities may be marked for later inspection. The replay asks, "What did they see?" Beneath that question is another: "Has their view of me changed?"

Interpersonal tension is also a major trigger because it threatens connection. A strained exchange with a friend, partner, colleague, parent, sibling, or acquaintance can activate the replay even when nothing openly explosive occurs. Tension does not need to be loud. It may appear as a slight withdrawal, a clipped answer, a change in rhythm, a disagreement that ends too quickly, or an unresolved feeling in the room. The mind detects possible rupture and begins to review.

The replay after tension often searches for fault. Did I push too hard? Did I sound defensive? Did I misunderstand? Did they? Should I have softened my tone? Should I have stood firmer? Did I apologise too much? Did I not apologise enough? Because relationships matter, the mind treats relational uncertainty as unfinished business. It wants to know whether the bond is intact. When no immediate reassurance arrives, it may attempt to create reassurance through analysis.

There is a painful irony here. The more important a relationship is, the more replay-prone small moments within it can become. A passing comment from a stranger may fade quickly because it has little bearing on your life. A passing comment from someone whose opinion matters may replay for hours because the emotional stakes are higher. The mind is not only reviewing the comment; it is reviewing the security of the connection.

Mistakes in performance or responsibility can trigger replays in a slightly different way. You forget something, miss a detail, make an error in front of others, send the wrong version, misunderstand an instruction, or fail to respond as well as you intended. The replay begins by examining the practical mistake, but may quickly become moral or personal. "How did I miss that?" becomes "I am unreliable." "That answer was unclear" becomes "I am not capable." The event is no longer treated as a correctable error. It becomes evidence.

This leap from incident to identity is one of the reasons replay triggers are so potent. The mind rarely says, "A small mistake occurred under ordinary human conditions." It says, "This may reveal something serious about me." Once identity enters the picture, the loop gains force. You are not simply trying to fix what happened; you are trying to defend yourself against a feared conclusion.

Another common trigger is being misunderstood. Few things provoke a replay faster than the sense that your intention and your impact have separated. You meant to be helpful, but sounded controlling. You meant to be funny, but sounded dismissive. You meant to be brief, but sounded cold. You meant to be honest, but sounded harsh. When intention is invisible and impact is uncertain, the mind can become desperate to correct the record.

Misunderstanding is difficult because it touches fairness. You know what you meant, but you cannot guarantee that others received it that way. The replay tries to bridge that gap. It rewrites the sentence, adds context, imagines explanations, drafts possible clarifications, and rehearses how you would defend the intention if challenged. Sometimes clarification is appropriate. But often the replay begins before you have any evidence that serious misunderstanding occurred. The mere possibility is enough.

A related trigger is the fear of having appeared unkind. For conscientious people, this can be especially powerful. A moment of impatience, a blunt phrase, a missed cue, a distracted response, or a joke with the wrong edge may replay because it threatens the belief that you are considerate. The mind treats possible unkindness as urgent because kindness is not a minor preference; it may be central to how you understand yourself.

This kind of replay often carries a moral tone. It does not merely ask, "Could I have handled that better?" It asks, "Was I bad?" That escalation is what makes it heavy. A practical adjustment becomes tangled with shame. Instead of taking the available lesson, the mind begins searching for proof of innocence or guilt. Neither proof usually arrives. So the loop continues.

Comparison can also trigger replays. You notice someone else speaking more smoothly, responding more warmly, managing conflict more gracefully, or appearing more confident. Suddenly, your own behaviour is reviewed under harsher lighting. A moment that might have felt acceptable on its own begins to look inadequate beside an imagined standard. You replay not only what happened, but how far it seemed to fall from the version of yourself you think you should have been.

This is especially common when the mind creates an ideal observer: a fantasy audience that notices every flaw, remembers every awkwardness, and evaluates you with a precision real people rarely sustain. The replay then becomes less about the actual room and more about the imagined court. You are no longer responding to what happened. You are responding to what you fear a perfect critic would say about what happened.

Transitions can trigger replays as well. The mind often returns to uncomfortable moments when there is a pause in activity: after a meeting ends, during a commute, while washing dishes, before sleep, after sending a message, or when moving from one task to another. These quiet spaces give the replay room to rise. During activity, attention may be held by what is in front of you. In the gap afterwards, unfinished emotional material can surface.

This does not mean quiet is dangerous. It means the mind often uses available space to process. The problem begins when processing becomes repetitive and unbounded. A brief reflection during a walk home may be useful. An hour of mentally restaging the same conversation is not. The trigger, in this case, may be less about the event and more about the absence of a clear closing ritual. The mind has not been told, "The useful review is complete."

Fatigue lowers the threshold for replay triggers. When you are tired, ordinary uncertainty can feel more threatening. A message that would not bother you in the morning may unsettle you at night. A small awkwardness may seem enormous when you are depleted. The mind has less capacity for proportion, and the body has less tolerance for discomfort. A replay that might have been easy to interrupt earlier in the day can become sticky when your system is already strained.

This is why it is unhelpful to judge the size of a replay only by the size of the event. State matters. Hunger, tiredness, overstimulation, pressure, loneliness, conflict, and emotional residue can all make the mind more vulnerable to looping. The same event can land differently depending on the condition of the person receiving it. A trigger is not only what happens outside you; it is also what the event meets inside you.

Certain personal histories can create familiar trigger categories. Someone who has often been criticised for being "too much" may replay moments where they spoke with enthusiasm. Someone who was punished for mistakes may replay small errors with disproportionate dread. Someone who has been misunderstood repeatedly may become highly alert to tone and wording. The point is not to excavate every past wound before you can change. The point is to notice that triggers often have themes.

Your themes matter more than isolated incidents. One person may be most triggered by delayed replies. Another by public mistakes. Another by signs of tension. Another by feeling morally misread. Another by situations where authority figures are present. Another by moments where they fear they sounded foolish. Once you recognise your common categories, the replay becomes less mysterious. You can say, "This is my ambiguity trigger," or "This is my being-misunderstood trigger," or "This is my visible-mistake trigger." The name does not solve the loop, but it weakens its disguise.

Naming a trigger is powerful because it moves you from content to pattern. Without naming, each replay feels like a unique emergency. With naming, you begin to see repetition. The mind may present this delayed reply as a new crisis, but you recognise the old shape. The mind may insist that this awkward sentence proves something terrible, but you recognise the familiar public-speaking aftermath. The mind may dramatise a slight tension, but you recognise the relational uncertainty trigger. Pattern recognition restores some authority to the present self.

This is not the same as dismissing the event. A trigger can point towards something real. Ambiguous feedback may deserve a clarifying question. A delayed reply may matter in a particular context. A tense exchange may need repair. A public mistake may hold a useful lesson. Naming the trigger does not mean saying, "This is all in my head." It means saying, "My system has been activated; now I need to separate activation from evidence."

That separation is essential. Activation is the feeling of urgency. Evidence is what is actually known. A replay often fuses them. "I feel anxious" becomes "Something must be wrong." "I feel ashamed" becomes "I must have done something unacceptable." "I feel unsettled" becomes "The relationship must be damaged." When you know your triggers, you are less likely to treat every bodily alarm as a factual report.

A practical way to begin mapping your own triggers is to look for repetition in the moments that follow you. Do not start with the most painful replay of your life. Start with the ordinary ones. The message you reread. The comment you rephrased in your head. The meeting you mentally revisited while making dinner. The pause that stayed with you. Ask what category the moment belongs to. Was it ambiguity? Visibility? possible rejection? perceived incompetence? fear of unkindness? relational tension? uncertainty after sending something? The category is often more useful than the detail.

The aim is to identify your top replay doorways, not to create a new reason to monitor yourself obsessively. This is important. Trigger mapping should not become another mental audit. It should be light, plain, and practical. You are looking for patterns that help you intervene earlier. You are not building a case against yourself. The purpose is not, "Here are all the ways I am sensitive." The purpose is, "Here are the situations where my mind tends to over-protect me."

Once you know the pattern, you can prepare for the vulnerable moment. If delayed replies trigger you, the vulnerable moment is not only when the reply arrives; it is the waiting period. If public speaking triggers you, the vulnerable moment may be the hour after the meeting, when the mind starts selecting flaws. If interpersonal tension triggers you, the vulnerable moment may be the silence after the conversation ends. If ambiguous feedback triggers you, the vulnerable moment may be the space before you ask for clarification or decide that no clarification is needed.

This awareness changes the timing of intervention. Many people try to stop a replay only after it has gathered force. By then, the story is vivid, the body is activated, and the imagined consequences feel persuasive. Trigger recognition allows you to catch the first movement: the instant attention turns back with urgency. That early moment is quieter. It gives you more choice.

The mind may still replay. Recognition is not magic. But the replay no longer arrives as an unexplained command. You can see the doorway it used. You can understand why this particular moment caught. You can treat the activation as information rather than instruction. That alone reduces the sense of helplessness.

Common replay triggers are not signs that you are fragile. They are signs that your mind has learned to watch certain areas closely. Some of that watchfulness may be useful. Too much of it becomes surveillance. The goal is not to remove every trigger from life; that would be impossible. Ambiguity, delay, visibility, tension, and misunderstanding are part of being human among other humans. The goal is to stop mistaking every trigger for a truth.

When a replay begins, the most useful question is not "Why am I making such a big deal of this?" That question carries judgement, and judgement tightens the loop. A better question is, "What category of trigger has been touched?" The answer may be simple, but it gives the mind something it badly needs: a map.

Shame and Status Cues

Some replays begin not because the moment was large, but because it made you feel suddenly visible. You said something and the room went quiet. You made a joke and it landed with a thud. You tried to explain yourself and heard, too late, that your tone sounded defensive. You walked away with the sense that something had shifted, even if no one said so directly. The mind marked the moment because it seemed to threaten something deeper than comfort. It threatened how you were seen.

Shame is one of the strongest accelerants of mental rewind. It does not merely say, "That was awkward." It says, "You have been exposed." It does not simply notice a mistake. It turns the mistake into a statement about your acceptability. Under shame, a clumsy sentence becomes proof that you are socially inept. A misunderstood comment becomes proof that you are careless. A joke that fails becomes proof that you are foolish. The mind stops asking what happened and starts asking what the moment reveals about you.

This is why shame-based replays have such a sharp emotional flavour. Ordinary regret may be uncomfortable, but it still leaves you with a sense of yourself as intact. You may think, "I wish I had handled that differently." Shame is more invasive. It collapses the distance between action and identity. Instead of "I did something clumsy," it whispers, "I am clumsy." Instead of "That comment did not land well," it says, "I am the kind of person people judge." Instead of "I may need to clarify," it says, "I have become unacceptable."

That shift is subtle, but it changes everything. When the mind treats a moment as a behaviour, the problem remains workable. Behaviour can be reviewed, repaired, practised, softened, strengthened, or changed. Identity feels harder. If the issue is who you are, not what you did, the replay gains weight. The mind returns again and again because it is not trying to adjust one action; it is trying to defend the whole self from a verdict.

Status cues make this process even more powerful. Status here does not mean arrogance, wealth, title, or superiority. It means your felt place among others: whether you are respected, included, trusted, valued, taken seriously, liked, or understood. Human beings are exquisitely sensitive to these signals. A small change in tone, a lack of laughter, a raised eyebrow, a dismissive response, a correction in public, or a pause after you speak can all register as possible evidence that your standing has slipped.

The mind may not use the word status, but it understands the feeling. It is the heat that rises when you think you have looked foolish. It is the drop in your stomach when someone misunderstands you in front of others. It is the sudden inner scramble when you realise your comment may have sounded unkind. It is the urge to explain, recover, soften, apologise, joke again, withdraw, or mentally edit the scene until your position feels restored.

A status cue becomes a replay trigger when the mind believes your social image has been damaged. Perhaps you wanted to sound informed, but stumbled. Perhaps you wanted to appear warm, but came across as blunt. Perhaps you wanted to contribute intelligently, but someone corrected you. Perhaps you wanted to be funny, but the humour missed. The event may be brief, yet the mind treats it as if an invisible social balance has been disturbed. It begins searching for the exact point where the damage happened.

This search can become relentless because social damage is often hard to measure. If you spill a drink, the evidence is visible. You clean it up. If you send the wrong file, you can send the right one. But if you fear that you looked foolish, the evidence is uncertain. Did they notice? Did they care? Did they remember? Did their opinion change? Did your recovery make it better or worse? The lack of certainty keeps the replay alive.

A joke that lands badly is a perfect example because it contains several replay triggers at once. There is visibility: you said something in front of others. There is ambiguity: the response was not what you expected. There is possible harm: someone may have felt dismissed, mocked, or uncomfortable. There is status threat: you may have looked foolish or socially unaware. There is identity threat: if you value being kind, perceptive, or witty, the failed joke seems to challenge how you see yourself.

The mind then begins its post-event investigation. It replays the wording. It studies the faces. It remembers who laughed and who did not. It wonders whether the silence was brief or significant. It imagines one person thinking, "That was inappropriate," and another repeating it later. It drafts possible repairs, then rejects them as excessive. It considers saying nothing, then worries silence will look careless. What began as a single social misfire becomes an all-evening tribunal.

The important point is not whether the joke genuinely required repair. Sometimes it might. If a comment hurt someone, clarification or apology may be wise. But shame distorts proportion. It can take a small awkwardness and expand it into a character crisis. Instead of asking, "Did this affect anyone, and is there a clean next step?" the mind asks, "What kind of person says something like that?" The question sounds morally serious, but it often leads away from responsibility rather than towards it.

Responsibility is specific. Shame is global.

Responsibility says, "That may have come across badly. I can check, clarify, or learn." Shame says, "I am embarrassing." Responsibility keeps contact with the facts. Shame fills gaps with accusation. Responsibility can act. Shame tends to hide, explain excessively, punish, or replay. This distinction matters because many people believe shame makes them better. They assume that if they feel bad enough, they will become more careful, kinder, smarter, or safer next time. In reality, shame often makes the mind more self-focused and less skilful.

When shame is running the replay, attention narrows around self-protection. You are not simply considering the other person's experience; you are trying to escape the feeling of being defective. That can lead to over-apologising, over-explaining, withdrawing, or seeking reassurance in ways that create more discomfort. You may send a long message when a short one would do. You may avoid someone who has not actually judged you. You may replay the moment so intensely that you miss the ordinary opportunities to reconnect naturally.

Status-based replays also create a false urgency to restore image. The mind wants to repair not only what happened, but how you are perceived. That desire is understandable. Nobody enjoys feeling diminished in the eyes of others. But image repair can become a trap when it is driven by panic. You may attempt to control an impression that is not fully knowable, or correct a misunderstanding that may not exist. The more urgently you try to manage perception, the less grounded your response becomes.

This is especially difficult for people who pride themselves on being considerate. If you care deeply about being fair, kind, and emotionally aware, a moment of possible unkindness can feel intolerable. Your replay may sound noble: "I just want to make sure I did not hurt anyone." Sometimes that is true. But the question can quietly become, "How do I make sure no one sees me as hurtful?" The difference is crucial. One is concerned with impact. The other is concerned with identity protection.

There is nothing wrong with caring about your impact. In fact, it is necessary. The danger comes when every possible impact becomes a threat to your worth. You cannot move through human relationships without occasionally being awkward, unclear, tired, distracted, too quick, too quiet, too much, or not enough for someone's preference. This does not make you unacceptable. It makes you human in contact with other humans, who are also interpreting imperfectly from inside their own moods, histories, and assumptions.

A useful way to recognise shame in a replay is to listen for its language. Shame uses final words. It says "always," "never," "everyone," "ruined," "awful," "pathetic," "unbearable." It exaggerates audience size. It imagines people remembering longer than they probably do. It treats awkwardness as contamination. It often carries a physical punch: heat, contraction, heaviness, the urge to disappear. It is less interested in what can be done than in proving that the self has been exposed.

By contrast, healthy concern sounds plainer. "That might not have landed well." "I may need to clarify." "I spoke too sharply." "I will slow down next time." "I do not know what they thought." Notice the difference in scale. Healthy concern does not deny discomfort, but it does not inflate it. It leaves room for uncertainty. It keeps the person separate from the behaviour. It allows action without self-erasure.

This separation is one of the most important skills in ending shame-based replays. "I did something clumsy" is a very different sentence from "I am unacceptable." The first sentence may sting, but it keeps you in reality. It gives you somewhere to go. The second sentence is a trapdoor. Once you fall through it, the mind starts searching the past for supporting evidence: other awkward moments, other misunderstandings, other times you felt judged. The replay then links one event to an entire identity file.

The mind is especially tempted to do this when the status cue is public. Public embarrassment has a way of making time stretch. A small stumble can feel as if it has been placed under bright light. Yet most social groups are not watching with the relentless precision of your own replay. People are usually occupied with themselves, their tasks, their worries, their next sentence, their own private discomforts. This does not mean no one notices anything. It means the replay often gives others far more attention, memory, and judgemental energy than they actually possess.

Still, the feeling of exposure can be real even when the danger is exaggerated. That is why dismissing shame rarely works. Telling yourself "Nobody cares" may be partly true, but it can feel invalidating when your body is already flooded. A better approach begins by acknowledging the signal without accepting the verdict. "This touched shame." "This felt like a status threat." "My mind is treating this as evidence about who I am." Such recognition does not solve the moment, but it prevents the replay from operating invisibly.

Once shame is named, the event can be reduced to its proper size. What actually happened? What did I do or say? What do I know, not merely imagine? Was there a clear impact? Is a repair needed, or is this discomfort without evidence? What value did this touch? Kindness? competence? belonging? respect? intelligence? calm? When you identify the value underneath the shame, the replay becomes more understandable. The mind is not randomly torturing you. It is protecting something you care about, but doing so in a crude and excessive way.

This also explains why the same event triggers different people differently. A correction in public may replay intensely for someone who values competence and fears looking uninformed. A joke landing badly may replay for someone who values warmth and fears being hurtful. A moment of being ignored may replay for someone who is sensitive to exclusion. The trigger has force because it touches a valued identity. The task is not to abandon the value. The task is to stop using shame as its guardian.

Shame is a poor guardian because it confuses improvement with humiliation. It believes that if it makes the mistake painful enough, you will not repeat it. But pain alone does not teach well. Clarity teaches. Proportion teaches. Repair teaches. Practise teaches. Shame may create a memorable emotional burn, but it often leaves the lesson vague: "Do not be like that." That is not a useful instruction. Like what? In what situation? What should change? What is the alternative behaviour? Shame rarely answers. It prefers condemnation to guidance.

Status cues become less dangerous when you learn to translate them. A failed joke may translate into, "I want to be playful without being careless." A public stumble may translate into, "I care about being competent, and I felt exposed." A misunderstood comment may translate into, "My intention and impact may have separated." A cold response may translate into, "I do not know where I stand, and uncertainty is uncomfortable." Translation turns shame into information. It replaces the global verdict with a specific concern.

This does not mean every concern requires action. Sometimes the appropriate response is a simple repair. Sometimes it is a private adjustment. Sometimes it is allowing the discomfort to fade without making it someone else's responsibility. Sometimes it is accepting that a moment was awkward and still survivable. Status can feel fragile in the immediate aftermath, but a single imperfect moment rarely has the power the replay gives it.

The more you practise separating behaviour from identity, the less authority shame has over your attention. You may still feel the sting. You may still wish you had spoken differently. You may still notice the mind trying to replay. But the sentence changes. It is no longer "I am unacceptable." It becomes, "Something in that moment touched my fear of being seen badly." That is a more accurate sentence, and accuracy is the beginning of freedom.

Mental rewinds thrive when shame is allowed to act as judge, witness, and evidence all at once. They weaken when shame is treated as a signal: intense, uncomfortable, worth noticing, but not automatically truthful. A status cue may tell you that you felt exposed. It does not get to decide what the exposure means. It may point towards a lesson. It does not get to define your character.

The next time a replay flares after you looked foolish, felt misunderstood, or feared you came across badly, listen carefully for the hidden verdict. Is the mind saying, "That was a clumsy moment," or has it already leapt to, "I am unacceptable"? The difference between those two sentences may decide whether you learn from the scene or spend the evening trying to erase yourself from it.

Body Signals as Triggers

Sometimes the replay does not begin with a thought. It begins with a sensation.

A rush of heat moves through your face. Your chest tightens. Your stomach drops. Your shoulders rise before you notice them. Your breathing becomes shallow. You wake in the dark with a sudden pulse of unease, and within seconds the mind begins searching for a reason. It reaches backwards through the day, finds the awkward message, the strange pause, the unfinished exchange, the comment that might have sounded wrong, and says, "There. That must be it."

This is one of the most overlooked ways mental rewinds begin. The event may not trigger the body as strongly as the body triggers the replay. You feel unsettled first, then the mind hunts for a scene to explain the feeling. Because the feeling is real, the explanation can seem real too. The body produces urgency; the mind supplies a story.

That sequence matters. Many people assume that if they feel anxious, ashamed, exposed, tense, or restless after an interaction, then the interaction must have contained serious danger. The body becomes treated as a witness: "I would not feel this way unless something was wrong." Yet bodily activation is not the same as proof. It is information, but it is not a verdict. It tells you that your system has been stirred. It does not automatically tell you why, how serious the situation is, or what action is required.

The body is built to respond quickly. It does not wait for a careful report. It reacts to tone, uncertainty, fatigue, conflict, memory, pressure, social exposure, lack of sleep, hunger, overstimulation, and old emotional associations. It can sound an alarm before the thinking mind has fully understood what happened. This speed can be useful in genuine danger, but it can be misleading when the threat is ambiguous or social. A tight chest after a conversation may mean there is something to clarify. It may also mean you were already tired, the room felt tense, the topic was difficult, or your body is carrying more stress than the event itself deserves.

Mental rewinds exploit this confusion. A sensation appears, and the mind assumes it must be explained. It does not like a feeling without a narrative. So it searches. The search often lands on the most emotionally available scene, not necessarily the most accurate one. The message you sent earlier. The moment your voice shook. The half-smile from a colleague. The conversation that ended abruptly. Once the mind links the sensation to a scene, the replay gains authority. "This feels bad" becomes "That must have gone badly."

That leap is the dangerous one.

Feeling bad is not the same as something being bad. Feeling ashamed is not the same as having done something shameful. Feeling afraid is not the same as being in danger. Feeling uncertain is not the same as having made a mistake. The body can be sincere and still be imprecise. It can tell the truth about activation while being unclear about meaning.

This is especially common at night. During the day, activity gives the mind other places to land. There are tasks, conversations, movement, light, noise, decisions, and ordinary interruptions. At night, the body's signals can feel louder because there is less competing input. A small wave of stress can become enormous in the quiet. You wake, notice tension, and the mind begins searching for unfinished business. Soon the conversation from earlier is replaying with theatre-like vividness. The dark does not create the issue, but it can enlarge it.

Night-time body signals can be particularly convincing because tiredness reduces perspective. The mind becomes less able to hold a balanced view. It may treat discomfort as an emergency simply because the body is depleted. A thought that would be manageable in daylight becomes severe at 3am. A minor ambiguity becomes a threat. A delayed reply becomes rejection. A clumsy sentence becomes evidence of failure. The sensation leads, and interpretation follows.

This is why the first response to a bodily trigger should not be analysis. Analysis is tempting because the mind wants to solve the feeling. It asks, "Why do I feel this way?" Then it tries to answer by replaying scenes. But if the body is activated, replaying often increases activation. The thought makes the body tighten; the body makes the thought seem more urgent; urgency demands more thinking. The loop closes.

A better starting point is to treat the sensation as a signal from the body, not a command from reality. The body is saying, "Something has activated me." It is not necessarily saying, "Go back and investigate every word." That distinction creates space. You are allowed to notice the rush of heat, the tightness, the restlessness, the heaviness, the nausea, the pulse, without immediately assigning it a dramatic meaning.

This does not mean ignoring the body. Ignoring is another form of avoidance, and avoidance often gives the sensation more power. The aim is to listen more accurately. A body signal deserves attention, but not blind obedience. It can be acknowledged in plain language: "My body is activated." "There is tightness in my chest." "I feel a rush of shame." "My system is treating something as urgent." These sentences are simple, but they prevent the mind from jumping too quickly into a story.

The body often calms when it is named without being escalated. Not always immediately, and not perfectly, but often enough to matter. The naming works because it changes the relationship to the sensation. Instead of becoming the sensation, you observe it. Instead of treating it as proof, you treat it as data. Instead of asking, "What terrible thing happened?" you ask, "What is my body doing right now?"

That question is more powerful than it looks. It returns attention to the present. It interrupts the automatic slide from sensation to replay. It also prevents a common error: using the past to justify a feeling that may be partly physical, environmental, or cumulative. Sometimes you do not feel bad because one conversation was disastrous. You feel bad because the day was long, your nervous system is overworked, and that conversation offered the mind a convenient hook.

A simple check-in can stop the hook from setting too deeply. Begin with the body before the story. What sensation is present? Where is it located? Is it heat, pressure, tightness, heaviness, restlessness, trembling, or a sinking feeling? Then ask what else may be contributing. Am I tired? Hungry? overstimulated? rushed? lonely? under pressure? carrying tension from something unrelated? Has this feeling appeared before in similar situations? The point is not to find the perfect explanation. The point is to widen the frame before the replay narrows it.

Only after that should you ask whether the event itself contains clear evidence requiring attention. Clear evidence is different from emotional intensity. A person directly said they were hurt. A mistake clearly occurred. A message genuinely needs clarification. A promise was missed. A boundary was crossed. These are workable facts. They may still be uncomfortable, but they are not the same as a body alarm looking for a case.

When no clear evidence is available, the body signal may need soothing rather than investigation. This is where many people take the wrong road. They try to settle the body by solving the story, but the story keeps changing. The mind says, "Maybe it was the tone." Then, "Maybe it was the timing." Then, "Maybe it was the look afterwards." Then, "Maybe this is part of a bigger pattern." The body never calms because the mind keeps presenting new possible threats.

Soothing begins with lowering the sense of emergency. Relax the jaw. Let the shoulders drop. Lengthen the exhale. Feel the feet on the floor. Look around the room and name what is actually present. These are not magical techniques; they are ways of reminding the system that the past is not currently happening. The replay pulls attention into a scene. Sensory grounding returns attention to the place where choice is possible.

The aim is not to force the body into calm. Forcing calm can become another battle. The aim is to stop adding fuel. A tight chest plus catastrophic interpretation becomes a loop. A tight chest plus observation has more room to pass. A rush of heat plus "I have ruined everything" becomes shame. A rush of heat plus "This is activation" becomes manageable discomfort.

This distinction is especially important for people who are highly conscientious. They may feel a bodily alarm and immediately interpret it as moral evidence. "I feel guilty, so I must have done something wrong." But guilt-like sensations can arise from many sources: conflict, fear of disapproval, old conditioning, responsibility, perfectionism, exhaustion, or the simple discomfort of not knowing how someone received you. Genuine guilt points towards a specific action or omission. Vague bodily dread often points towards activation without a clear object.

A useful test is whether the sensation leads to a specific repair or only to self-accusation. If you can name a concrete action, such as "I interrupted and should apologise," the signal may contain useful information. If the sensation produces only global claims, such as "I am awful," "I always mess things up," or "Something is wrong with me," shame has probably taken over. The body may be activated, but the story has become unreliable.

Body signals can also be triggered by memory rather than present danger. A current moment may resemble an older emotional pattern. Being corrected may recall earlier criticism. A delayed reply may echo past rejection. A tense voice may resemble previous conflict. The body recognises the pattern before the mind has sorted the difference between then and now. This does not mean you are trapped in the past. It means the body sometimes uses old maps to navigate new rooms.

When this happens, the replay may feel disproportionate because it is carrying more than the current event. You are not only responding to the meeting, the text, or the conversation. You are responding to the old meaning your system has attached to similar cues. Again, the response is not to shame yourself for being sensitive. Sensitivity is information. The task is to ask whether the present event deserves the full weight your body has placed upon it.

There is a quiet discipline in refusing to let bodily intensity decide the entire story. The feeling may be loud. It may be uncomfortable. It may demand an explanation now. But loud is not the same as accurate. Urgent is not the same as important. Familiar is not the same as true.

When the body becomes a replay trigger, the mind wants to move backwards. It wants to revisit the scene until the sensation makes sense. But sometimes the more useful movement is inward and then outward: notice the sensation, name the activation, check the evidence, return to the present, and choose the next reasonable step. Not the next anxious step. Not the next image-management step. The reasonable one.

This is how you stop "I feel bad" becoming "something terrible happened." You insert a pause between sensation and story. You allow the body to report without letting it rule. You become curious without becoming captive. The replay may still try to gather momentum, but it no longer gets to use your pulse as proof.

A body signal is a beginning, not a conclusion. It may point towards a lesson, a repair, a need for rest, a boundary, a conversation, or simply a nervous system asking to settle. The work is to discover which, without handing the replay a blank cheque. The next time your body flares and the mind rushes to reopen the past, ask the question that changes the sequence: "What am I feeling in my body before I decide what this means?"

Chapter 3
The Rumination Loop Mechanics

Why does a thought become stronger when you try to defeat it? The mind notices a painful possibility, you argue back, and for a moment it seems as though you are taking charge. You present evidence. You correct the exaggeration. You tell yourself not to be ridiculous. Yet the thought returns with a sharper edge, as if the argument has given it more oxygen. What began as one uncomfortable replay becomes a full internal debate, and the debate keeps the scene alive.

This is the paradox at the centre of rumination. The mind appears to be working against the replay, but it is often working inside it. Every rebuttal keeps attention fixed on the same material. Every attempt to prove the thought wrong repeats the image, the sentence, the expression, the possible meaning. You may win one round of the argument and still lose the evening, because attention has remained locked on the very scene you are trying to escape.

A replay is not held together by thought alone. It has moving parts. A cue appears: a memory, a bodily sensation, a delayed reply, a phrase someone used. A thought attaches itself: "That sounded foolish," "They must be annoyed," "I should have handled that better." An emotion rises: shame, fear, regret, irritation, dread. Then attention narrows. The mind's spotlight lands on the scene and everything outside it grows dim. The more attention gathers there, the more convincing the replay feels.

The central tension is that rumination often borrows the tools of intelligence and uses them against relief. Analysis, imagination, memory, moral judgement, planning, and problem-solving are all valuable capacities. They help you learn, repair, prepare, and act. But when they are recruited by threat, they can form a closed circuit. The mind does not simply ask what happened; it keeps scanning for a safer ending. It does not simply imagine a better response; it generates endless alternatives that make the original moment feel worse. It does not simply hold you accountable; it uses criticism as glue.

This matters because the loop can feel like discipline while quietly weakening your ability to respond. A harsh inner voice may appear to be keeping standards high, but harshness usually increases threat. The more threatening the tone, the more urgently the mind searches for escape. Absolute words, imagined mind-reading, and sweeping judgements do not create clarity; they create pressure. "I always do this" gives you nowhere to stand. "They definitely think I am difficult" turns uncertainty into a verdict. "I ruined it" transforms a human moment into a catastrophe. The prosecutor voice sounds powerful, but it rarely produces wisdom.

Regret adds another layer. Once the past is closed, imagination becomes strangely fluent. You can design the perfect sentence after the conversation has ended. You can picture the ideal pause, the warmer expression, the cleaner explanation, the sharper boundary, the graceful recovery. The mind calls this preparation, but too many imagined alternatives become a burden. Each polished version becomes a measuring stick used against your real, pressured, imperfect self. Instead of learning one usable adjustment, you are surrounded by unreal performances you can never go back and deliver.

The loop becomes especially costly when thinking replaces doing. Rumination can feel busy enough to disguise avoidance. You may be replaying instead of sending the clarifying message. You may be analysing instead of resting. You may be rehearsing an apology instead of making a simple one. You may be mentally correcting a past conversation instead of entering the next conversation with more steadiness. The past receives endless attention because the present contains risk. Thinking feels safer than action because action can be seen, answered, accepted, rejected, or misunderstood. Yet only action can change the present.

The mechanics are plain once the spotlight is seen clearly. A cue pulls attention towards a scene. Thought gives the scene meaning. Emotion gives it urgency. Attention makes it vivid. Self-criticism tightens the threat. Imagined alternatives multiply the regret. Problem-solving, when it loses contact with action, becomes another way to stay inside the loop. None of these parts is mysterious on its own. Together, they create the feeling of being trapped in a room whose door keeps moving.

The crucial question is not merely, "What am I thinking?" It is more exacting than that: "What is my attention doing with this thought?" If attention is feeding the replay, arguing may not free you. If criticism is intensifying threat, harsher judgement will not make you more accountable. If imagined alternatives are breeding exhaustion, one more perfect script will not bring peace. The loop begins to loosen only when its machinery is caught in motion, before the spotlight convinces you that the replay is the whole room.

Thoughts, Feelings, Attention

A mental rewind can feel like one solid experience, as if the whole loop arrives at once: the memory, the shame, the worry, the imagined consequence, the pressure to solve it. But the loop is not one thing. It is a sequence. It has parts. When those parts are blurred together, the replay feels powerful and inevitable. When they are separated, the process becomes less mysterious, and less commanding.

The usual mistake is to begin with the thought as though the thought is the whole problem. "They think I was rude." "I sounded foolish." "I have made things awkward." "I should have said it differently." These thoughts can seem like the source of distress, so the natural response is to argue with them. You try to prove they are exaggerated. You remind yourself that nobody reacted badly. You tell yourself to stop being dramatic. You build a defence case in your own head.

Sometimes that helps briefly. Often it does not.

The reason is simple: arguing with a thought can keep attention tied to the thought. The scene is replayed again so that you can disprove it. The sentence is inspected again so that you can show it was harmless. The facial expression is reconsidered again so that you can decide whether it meant anything. You may be trying to escape the loop, but your attention is still feeding it. The mind has not left the room; it has merely changed sides in the argument.

To understand the replay, you need to see the machinery beneath it. A cue appears. The cue may be external, such as a delayed reply, a tense expression, a colleague's brief comment, or the sound of your own message notification. It may be internal, such as a memory, a bodily sensation, a wave of shame, or a sudden sense that something is unfinished. The cue is the spark. It does not yet have to mean anything dramatic. It is simply the thing that turns the mind towards the past.

Then a thought attaches itself. This often happens quickly, before you have had time to choose your response. The thought gives the cue a possible meaning. A delayed reply becomes, "They are annoyed." A quiet tone becomes, "I have upset them." A memory of stumbling over a sentence becomes, "I looked incompetent." A rush of heat in the body becomes, "Something went wrong." The thought may not appear as a full sentence. Sometimes it is more like a flash of meaning, a sudden interpretation, a private certainty that feels true because it arrived with force.

After the thought comes emotion. The body and mind respond to the meaning that has just been supplied. If the thought says, "I looked foolish," shame may rise. If the thought says, "They are angry with me," anxiety may surge. If the thought says, "I ruined the opportunity," regret may tighten around the chest. Emotion gives the thought weight. It makes the interpretation feel important. This is where many people become trapped, because the feeling seems to confirm the thought. "I feel ashamed, so I must have done something shameful." "I feel anxious, so there must be danger." "I feel guilty, so I must be guilty."

But emotion is not proof. It is a response.

That distinction is essential. Emotions are real experiences, but they are not always accurate reports of the situation. They may be responding to uncertainty, tiredness, old sensitivity, imagined judgement, social pressure, or the tone of your own inner language. A feeling can be intense and still be incomplete. It can deserve care without deserving obedience. The fact that a replay hurts does not mean the replay is telling the truth at full volume.

Then attention narrows. This is the part people often miss. Once emotion rises, attention behaves like a spotlight. It lands on the scene and brightens whatever it touches. The phrase you regret becomes vivid. The pause becomes meaningful. The look becomes suspicious. The silence becomes loaded. The rest of the day disappears. The wider context fades: the normal parts of the conversation, the possibility that others were distracted, the fact that most people are not studying you as closely as you study yourself. The spotlight makes the replay feel central because it has pushed everything else into darkness.

Attention is not passive. It does not merely observe the replay; it strengthens it. What you repeatedly attend to becomes clearer, more detailed, and more emotionally available. This is why a scene can feel worse after an hour of reviewing than it felt when it happened. The event has not changed. Your attention has polished certain parts of it until they shine with artificial importance. The memory becomes less like a record and more like a magnified image.

This magnification can be brutal. A single sentence becomes the whole conversation. One uncertain expression becomes the whole relationship. A small mistake becomes the whole performance. The mind then reacts not to the original moment, but to the enlarged version attention has created. You are no longer dealing with what happened. You are dealing with what repeated attention has made it feel like happened.

This is why "just think about it rationally" is often insufficient. Rational thinking can be useful, but only if attention is not already trapped in a threat loop. When the spotlight is locked on the replay, rational arguments may become part of the performance. You produce evidence, then counter-evidence, then more evidence. You tell yourself the thought is unlikely, then the mind replies, "But what if it is true?" You answer that, and the mind finds another angle. The debate continues because the process has not been interrupted at the level where it is being maintained.

The deeper question is not only, "Is this thought accurate?" It is also, "What is my attention doing?"

If your attention keeps returning to the same scene without new information, the loop is being reinforced. If your attention is scanning for danger rather than seeking a specific lesson, the loop is being reinforced. If your attention is narrowing around one possible meaning while excluding ordinary context, the loop is being reinforced. If your attention is being used to replay, compare, imagine, prosecute, and correct the past, the thought may be only one part of the problem. The larger issue is the process.

This is a critical shift. Many people try to end rumination by finding the perfect answer to the thought. They want to know whether the other person was truly offended, whether they definitely sounded foolish, whether the message was exactly right, whether the silence meant something, whether the mistake will matter later. But some thoughts cannot be answered perfectly. They are built from incomplete evidence. The more you try to settle them through analysis, the more material you create for the loop.

A thought can be treated in several ways. It can be believed, challenged, followed, suppressed, argued with, or noticed. In rumination, people tend to believe, challenge, and follow. They believe enough to feel threatened. They challenge enough to stay engaged. They follow enough to generate another branch of the replay. Noticing is different. Noticing says, "A thought has appeared." It does not immediately treat the thought as truth, enemy, command, or emergency. It places the thought back inside a larger process.

That larger process might sound like this: "A cue has activated a thought. The thought has triggered emotion. Emotion has narrowed attention. Narrowed attention is making the replay feel more convincing." This is not cold analysis. It is practical seeing. It helps you step back from the content of the replay and recognise its structure. Once you see the structure, you are less likely to be hypnotised by the latest interpretation.

The mind will often resist this. It prefers content because content feels urgent. "But what if they really are annoyed?" "But what if I really did sound rude?" "But what if this matters?" These questions may deserve a brief and proportionate answer later, but when the loop is hot, they are often bait. They pull you back into the replay. They ask you to keep looking at the scene from inside the same narrowed spotlight.

Process awareness changes the order. Instead of chasing every question, you ask what stage of the loop you are in. Is this the cue stage, where something has just reminded you of the moment? Is this the thought stage, where the mind is attaching meaning? Is this the emotion stage, where the body is reacting? Is this the attention stage, where the scene is becoming vivid because you keep returning to it? The answer matters because each stage calls for a different kind of response.

At the cue stage, the task is to notice the trigger before it becomes a full investigation. At the thought stage, the task is to recognise interpretation as interpretation. At the emotion stage, the task is to allow the feeling without treating it as proof. At the attention stage, the task is to shift the spotlight, not by force, but by deliberate redirection. You cannot always stop the first thought from appearing. You can learn not to build a theatre around it.

The spotlight motif is useful because it explains why replays feel so convincing. Whatever stands in the light appears important. The mind assumes that because something is vivid, it must be significant. But vividness is not the same as truth. A replay can be vivid because it is emotionally charged, recently repeated, or connected to shame. It can be vivid because you have rehearsed it many times. It can be vivid because your body is activated. None of that proves that the replay deserves the authority it is claiming.

A useful question, then, is: "What is outside the spotlight?" This does not mean inventing comfort or pretending the moment was perfect. It means restoring context. What else happened in the conversation? What evidence is missing? What ordinary explanations exist? What do you actually know? What do you only fear? What part of the day has your attention ignored because one scene has become so bright? Context does not always erase concern, but it reduces distortion.

There is also a relationship between attention and identity. The more you attend to a replay, the more personally significant it becomes. A thought that might have passed through the mind becomes a statement about you. "That was awkward" becomes "I am awkward." "That was unclear" becomes "I am not competent." "That may have sounded blunt" becomes "I am unkind." Attention gives the thought a place to settle. Repetition makes it familiar. Familiarity then masquerades as truth.

This is why rumination can feel as though it is revealing who you are, when it may only be repeating what you fear. The mind confuses frequency with accuracy. If you have thought "I ruined that" many times, the thought becomes easier to access. Because it is easier to access, it feels more plausible. Because it feels more plausible, you return to it again. The loop creates its own evidence by becoming familiar.

Breaking this pattern does not require you to replace every negative thought with a positive one. That can become another argument. It is more useful to replace fusion with observation. Instead of "I ruined that," you might notice, "My mind is producing the thought that I ruined that." The difference may seem small, but it creates distance. The original sentence makes the thought sound like a fact. The second sentence places it back where it belongs: as an event in the mind.

Distance is not denial. You can still examine whether the thought contains useful information. You can still repair what needs repair. You can still learn. But you are no longer swallowed by the first interpretation. You have moved from being inside the replay to observing the replay. That shift reduces the pressure to solve everything immediately.

The emotional part of the loop also needs this kind of careful handling. Many people try to think their way out of an emotion that first needs to be felt and named. Shame, anxiety, regret, and embarrassment often intensify when they are fought. The mind adds commentary: "I should not feel this way." "This is ridiculous." "Why am I still bothered?" Now there is the original feeling and a second layer of judgement about the feeling. The loop thickens.

A cleaner response is to name the emotion plainly. "This is shame." "This is anxiety." "This is regret." "This is embarrassment." Naming does not make the emotion vanish, and it does not need to. Its purpose is to prevent the emotion from becoming a hidden director of the replay. When shame is unnamed, it writes the story in secret. When shame is named, you can hear its influence. You can recognise that the replay may be harsher because shame is present.

The same is true of attention. When narrowed attention is unnamed, the replay seems like the whole truth. When narrowed attention is named, you can say, "My spotlight has locked onto this moment." That sentence restores choice. You may not feel free instantly, but you are no longer treating the spotlight as reality itself. You can begin to widen it.

Widening attention is not vague distraction. Vague distraction often fails because the mind remains half-attached to the replay. You scroll, but the scene continues. You watch something, but the thought keeps returning. You try to work, but your attention is split. Widening attention means deliberately reconnecting with something specific in the present: the weight of your feet, the sound in the room, the task in your hands, the next sentence you need to write, the cup you are washing, the door you are opening. Specific attention gives the mind somewhere real to land.

This matters because rumination thrives in abstraction. It loves imagined conversations, possible interpretations, invisible judgements, future consequences, and alternate versions of the past. The present interrupts that abstraction. The present says, "This is the room. This is the body. This is the next action." It does not answer every question, but it changes the ground. The replay can continue only while attention keeps funding it.

There will be times when the thought has useful content. Perhaps you did speak too sharply. Perhaps a clarification would help. Perhaps there is a lesson about timing, preparation, boundaries, or tone. Process awareness does not mean dismissing content. It means refusing to let content hijack the entire system before it has been examined properly. A useful thought can be handled once the spotlight is no longer burning a hole through the scene.

The order matters: settle attention enough to see clearly, then decide whether there is anything to learn or do. If you try to decide while attention is narrowed and emotion is high, you are more likely to over-apologise, over-explain, withdraw, accuse yourself, or create unnecessary action simply to discharge discomfort. When attention has widened, the same event may look different. Not perfect. Not irrelevant. Just proportionate.

A mental rewind is not defeated by winning an argument with every thought it produces. It weakens when the system that powers it is understood. Cue, thought, emotion, attention. Meaning, activation, spotlight, repetition. These are the mechanics. Once you can see them, the replay becomes less like fate and more like a process you can interrupt.

The next time a scene starts to pull you back, do not rush straight into the courtroom of the thought. Pause at the doorway. Ask what cued it. Notice the meaning the mind has attached. Name the emotion rising around it. Then look at the spotlight itself. Where has attention gone? What has it enlarged? What has it excluded? That is often where the loop reveals its secret: not in the thought alone, but in the attention that keeps making the thought feel true.

Why Self-Criticism Hooks You

Self-criticism often arrives with the voice of responsibility. It does not always sound wild or irrational. Sometimes it sounds disciplined, moral, even mature. It tells you that you are only being honest with yourself. It says you should not let yourself off too easily. It insists that if you feel bad enough about what happened, you will become better, safer, kinder, sharper, less likely to repeat the same mistake.

This is why self-criticism is so difficult to challenge. If it sounded obviously cruel from the beginning, you might reject it more quickly. But it presents itself as accountability. It wears the uniform of high standards. It claims to be protecting you from arrogance, carelessness, embarrassment, rejection, and future failure. In the aftermath of a replay, when your mind is already searching for certainty, self-criticism seems to offer a firm answer: *you were the problem.*

At first, that answer can feel strangely relieving. Uncertainty is uncomfortable. Not knowing how you came across, what someone thought, whether you caused harm, or whether the moment mattered can leave the mind restless. Self-criticism reduces the ambiguity by choosing a verdict. "I messed it up." "I sounded ridiculous." "I always do this." "I should have known better." The verdict hurts, but it gives the mind something solid to hold.

That solidity is deceptive. A harsh judgement can feel like clarity while actually making the loop more adhesive. Instead of helping you understand what happened, it increases the emotional threat around the scene. The more threatening the scene feels, the more urgently the mind returns to it. The more often the mind returns, the more convincing the criticism becomes. Self-criticism does not close the replay. It often fastens the mind to it.

Think of the difference between a teacher and a prosecutor. A teacher points to the mistake, names what needs to change, and gives you a workable next step. A prosecutor builds a case. It selects the worst evidence, ignores context, assumes motive, exaggerates consequence, and argues for a verdict against your character. The prosecutor voice may sound intelligent because it is detailed. It may sound principled because it is severe. But its aim is not learning. Its aim is conviction.

The prosecutor voice has familiar habits. It uses absolute words. Always. Never. Everyone. Nothing. Ruined. Hopeless. Unacceptable. It turns one moment into a pattern and one pattern into a fate. A sentence that landed awkwardly becomes "I always make things uncomfortable." A delayed response becomes "Nobody wants to deal with me." A mistake at work becomes "I cannot be trusted." These words do not describe reality carefully. They inflame it.

Self-criticism also mind-reads. It speaks as if it has access to other people's private thoughts. "They think I am incompetent." "She must be annoyed." "He definitely noticed." "They are probably talking about it." This kind of certainty feels compelling because it protects the mind from the discomfort of not knowing. But certainty manufactured by fear is not evidence. It is anxiety trying to end ambiguity by inventing a conclusion.

Another pattern is moral inflation. The replay begins with a specific behaviour and quickly expands into a judgement about worth. "I interrupted" becomes "I am selfish." "I explained badly" becomes "I am stupid." "I sounded tense" becomes "I am difficult." "I forgot to reply" becomes "I am a terrible friend." The mind moves from something you did to something you are. Once identity is involved, the loop becomes harder to release because the stakes feel much larger than the original event.

This is the hook. Self-criticism makes the mind believe the replay is no longer optional. If the moment supposedly proves something serious about you, then of course the mind must keep reviewing it. If your kindness, competence, intelligence, maturity, or likability is on trial, then one more mental hearing seems necessary. The scene becomes evidence. The replay becomes the courtroom. Attention becomes the jury that never reaches a final decision.

Harsh inner language also affects the body. You do not experience self-criticism as neutral information. The nervous system reacts to threat, including threat that comes from your own internal voice. When you tell yourself, "I ruined that," the body may tighten. When you say, "They all think I am foolish," the chest may contract, the stomach may drop, the face may heat. The body responds as though danger is present because, internally, danger has been announced.

Then the body's response becomes further proof. You feel anxious, so the thought seems more credible. You feel ashamed, so the accusation seems deserved. You feel tense, so the mind assumes the event must be serious. The loop tightens: criticism creates threat, threat creates bodily activation, bodily activation makes the criticism feel true, and the replay continues.

This is why tone matters. The same basic lesson can land very differently depending on the inner voice that delivers it. "You were awful in that conversation" does not produce the same internal state as "You were tense, and next time you need to pause before answering." One attacks the self. The other identifies a behaviour. One increases threat. The other creates room for adjustment. One keeps you trapped in the emotional meaning of the past. The other points towards a future choice.

Many people fear that softening the tone means weakening the standard. This fear is understandable, but mistaken. A calmer voice does not mean a careless voice. You can be precise without being brutal. You can be honest without being humiliating. You can admit impact without declaring yourself defective. In fact, a steadier tone often makes accountability more possible because the mind is not using all its energy defending against attack.

Self-criticism may appear to raise standards, but it often lowers the quality of learning. Under attack, the mind becomes less flexible. It narrows. It searches for escape, reassurance, or proof of innocence. It may collapse into shame or become defensive. Neither state is ideal for mature reflection. Real accountability needs enough safety for honesty. If every mistake becomes a threat to your worth, you will either avoid looking at mistakes or look at them in a distorted, punishing way.

Consider a simple social misstep. You leave a conversation and think, "I interrupted her twice. That was not good." This thought may feel uncomfortable, but it is usable. It names a behaviour. It stays close to the facts. It suggests a direction: apologise if needed, listen more carefully next time, slow down when excited. Now consider the self-critical version: "I am so rude. I always dominate conversations. No wonder people get tired of me." The second version feels more intense, but it is less useful. It turns a correctable behaviour into a global condemnation.

That intensity can be addictive in a quiet way. Harshness feels like seriousness. The mind mistakes emotional force for truth. A severe sentence can feel more honest than a balanced one simply because it hurts more. But pain is not a measure of accuracy. A thought does not become true because it wounds you. Sometimes the most accurate statement is also the least dramatic.

The prosecutor voice also loves hindsight. After the moment has passed, it speaks as though the better option was obvious all along. "You should have known not to say that." "You should have realised how it would sound." "You should have paused." "You should have handled it perfectly." Hindsight strips away the pressure, speed, emotion, fatigue, surprise, and limited information of the actual moment. It judges your past self from the comfort of later knowledge and calls the result fairness.

But real life is not performed from the editing room. You speak while tired. You answer while surprised. You respond while emotions are moving. You make choices with partial information. You do not have access to the perfect sentence until after the conversation has already ended. This does not excuse every mistake. It simply restores context. Without context, self-criticism becomes inaccurate.

Context is not an escape hatch. It is part of the truth. If you were defensive, that matters. If you were also exhausted, that matters too. If your comment landed badly, that matters. If your intention was not to harm, that also matters. If someone was hurt, the impact deserves care. If your mind is inventing injury without evidence, that deserves recognition. Accountability can hold complexity. Self-criticism usually cannot.

One of the most damaging effects of self-criticism is that it keeps the mind searching for a safer ending. After it declares that you failed, it does not let the scene close. It demands correction. It wants you to replay the conversation until you find the perfect reply. It wants you to imagine how you could have appeared calmer, kinder, sharper, warmer, more impressive, less awkward. It wants a version of the past in which the criticism has no grounds. But that version cannot be reached, because the past is closed.

So the mind keeps trying to create safety through repetition. It replays to undo shame. It imagines alternatives to undo regret. It analyses others' reactions to undo uncertainty. Yet every return to the scene also returns you to the criticism. The loop is sustained by the very voice that claims to be solving it.

A useful way to interrupt this pattern is to listen less to the content of self-criticism and more to its grammar. Does it use absolutes? Does it claim to know what everyone thinks? Does it turn one behaviour into your entire identity? Does it ignore context? Does it demand perfection after the fact? Does it leave you with a specific next step, or only with the feeling that you are wrong as a person?

The last question is especially revealing. Healthy accountability gives you a handle. Self-criticism gives you a wound. If the thought produces a clear, proportionate action, it may contain useful information. If it produces only shame, paralysis, reassurance-seeking, or another replay, it is not functioning as wisdom. It is functioning as glue.

The answer is not to replace every critical thought with empty praise. That would feel false, and false comfort rarely satisfies a serious mind. The better move is to rewrite the inner sentence so that it becomes accurate, specific, and humane. Not indulgent. Not dramatic. Clean.

"I ruined that meeting" might become "I lost my thread in one part of the meeting, and I can prepare a shorter point next time."

"They all think I am incompetent" might become "I do not know what they thought. I felt exposed because I value competence."

"I always say the wrong thing" might become "That sentence sounded blunt to me afterwards. I can clarify if there is evidence it caused a problem."

"I am awful for forgetting to reply" might become "I missed a reply. I can apologise briefly and respond now."

Notice what changes. The rewritten version does not deny the issue. It removes the attack. It replaces global judgement with behavioural clarity. It separates fact from interpretation. It leaves room for uncertainty. It gives the body less threat to react to. It also makes action easier because the problem is now the right size.

This kind of rewrite is not merely positive thinking. It is precision. A harsh statement often feels honest because it is emotionally loud, but it is frequently imprecise. "I am terrible with people" is not precise. "I interrupted because I was nervous and eager to explain" is precise. "I ruined everything" is not precise. "I may have sounded dismissive, and I can check whether clarification is needed" is precise. Precision lowers panic because the mind can work with it.

There is also dignity in speaking to yourself with restraint. Many people would never speak to a colleague, student, friend, or child the way they speak to themselves after a mistake. They would not believe cruelty was necessary for learning. They would not say, "You are hopeless," if they wanted someone to improve. They would name the issue, perhaps firmly, and then point towards the next step. The same standard should apply inwardly. You are not made more responsible by being made smaller.

When self-criticism hooks you, it often does so by pretending there are only two options: punish yourself or excuse yourself. This is a false choice. There is a third way: responsible steadiness. Responsible steadiness says, "I am willing to see what happened. I am willing to repair what needs repair. I am willing to change what needs changing. I am not willing to turn one moment into a verdict on my worth."

That stance is not weak. It is stronger than self-attack because it keeps you available for truth. It allows you to remain present rather than collapse into shame. It helps you respond rather than perform guilt. It makes learning sustainable. A person cannot grow well while constantly fearing their own inner court.

The next time the prosecutor voice appears, do not rush to obey it and do not waste the whole evening trying to defeat it. Listen for its patterns. Absolutes. Mind-reading. Identity attacks. Hindsight perfection. Missing context. Then ask what a precise, accountable, non-punishing version would sound like. The aim is not to make the moment painless. The aim is to make it workable.

Self-criticism keeps you hooked by making the replay feel morally necessary. It says the scene must remain open until you have suffered enough, understood enough, corrected enough, punished enough. But suffering is not closure. Punishment is not repair. Harshness is not truth.

A mistake may deserve attention. It may deserve apology. It may deserve a changed behaviour. It does not deserve to become a private sentence repeated until your nervous system mistakes cruelty for conscience.

Imagined Alternatives and Regret

Regret is one of the mind's most persuasive editors. It takes a finished moment and returns with a sharper line, a cleaner answer, a calmer tone, a better silence. It knows exactly what you should have said, but only after the conversation has ended. It knows when you should have paused, where you should have smiled, how you should have clarified, which word should have been removed, which sentence should have been added, and how your face should have looked while you said it.

This is why imagined alternatives feel so powerful during a mental replay. They seem useful. They appear to offer preparation, learning, even redemption. The mind says, "Next time, do it like this." That can be reasonable when it produces one clear adjustment. But replays rarely stop at one. They generate versions. Then more versions. The conversation becomes a private rehearsal room, except the performance is already over.

The first alternative may contain a genuine lesson. You remember speaking too quickly, and the mind offers a better response: slower, plainer, less defensive. That may help. It gives you something to practise. But the second, third, and fourth alternatives often do something different. They no longer teach. They compare. They place your real, pressured, imperfect response beside a polished imaginary one and make the original look worse every time.

This is the cruelty of hindsight. Your later mind has advantages your earlier self did not have. It has more time. It has distance. It has the other person's reaction, or at least your interpretation of it. It has no pressure to answer immediately. It can revise without being interrupted, questioned, surprised, tired, embarrassed, or emotionally exposed. Then it judges your past self for not performing with the elegance of a person who now has all the time in the world.

That judgement is not fair, but it feels convincing.

A real moment is lived under conditions. You speak while managing tone, facial expression, memory, uncertainty, emotion, timing, and the presence of other people. You respond with partial information. You do not know how your words will land until after they have landed. You may be tired, rushed, defensive, eager, nervous, overstimulated, or trying to be kind and clear at the same time. The imagined alternative ignores much of this. It arrives later, immaculate and unbothered, and pretends it was available all along.

This is where regret becomes distorted. Regret is not inherently harmful. At its best, regret is a moral and practical signal. It says, "Something about that did not match your values." It says, "There may be something to repair." It says, "This matters enough to learn from." A life without regret would not be a wiser life. It would be a life without sufficient feedback. The problem begins when regret is no longer allowed to point forward. Instead, it is used to punish the past.

Imagined alternatives keep regret alive by reopening the scene. Each alternate script suggests that the moment could still be perfected if only the mind works hard enough. You hear yourself answering with grace. You imagine the other person softening. You picture the room receiving you better. You construct the version in which nobody misunderstands you, nobody judges you, nobody sees your awkwardness, nobody notices your uncertainty. The fantasy offers brief relief because, for a moment, you are no longer the person who stumbled. You are the person who got it exactly right.

Then the relief turns. The imagined version makes the real version hurt more.

This is one reason alternate scripts are so addictive. They provide a short escape from regret, followed by a stronger return to it. The mind feels better while imagining the better response, then worse when it remembers that the response did not happen. That discomfort invites another alternative. Perhaps a different line would feel even more satisfying. Perhaps a more confident tone. Perhaps a warmer apology. Perhaps a sharper boundary. The mind keeps writing because it is trying to undo the emotional sting, not because it still needs instruction.

There is a difference between rehearsal and rumination. Rehearsal prepares you for a future action. Rumination restages a finished scene. Rehearsal has a target: a message to send, a conversation to have, a phrase to practise, a boundary to hold. Rumination has no real stage. It performs in the past, where nothing can be changed. It may feel like preparation because the mind is producing language, but language without a future use becomes mental noise.

A simple test is to ask whether the alternative belongs to a future situation or only to a past one. If it helps you say something more clearly next time, it may be useful. If it exists only to show how much better you could have been yesterday, it is probably feeding regret. The first creates a bridge. The second creates a wound.

Imagined alternatives also multiply because they promise control over other people's reactions. If you had used a softer word, perhaps they would not have gone quiet. If you had smiled differently, perhaps the joke would have landed. If you had explained one extra detail, perhaps they would have understood your intention. These possibilities may contain fragments of truth, but they can quickly become fantasy control. The mind begins to believe that with the perfect wording, perfect timing, and perfect expression, no one would ever misread you.

That is an impossible standard.

Human communication is not a machine in which the correct input always produces the desired output. Other people bring their own mood, history, assumptions, fatigue, sensitivities, and distractions. You are responsible for your care, honesty, timing, repair, and willingness to listen. You are not responsible for controlling every private interpretation another person might make. Imagined alternatives often forget this. They imply that if you had been perfect, uncertainty would have disappeared. But uncertainty is not always evidence of your failure. Sometimes it is simply part of being understood by another human being.

Regret becomes especially intense when the alternative script protects a valued identity. If you value kindness, your mind may replay the version in which you sounded gentler. If you value intelligence, it may replay the version in which your answer was sharper. If you value calm, it may replay the version in which you did not become defensive. If you value confidence, it may replay the version in which your voice did not shake. The alternative is not only about the words. It is about the self you wish had appeared.

That longing deserves respect. Beneath many replays is a sincere wish to live closer to your values. You wanted to be patient. You wanted to be articulate. You wanted to be fair. You wanted to be brave. You wanted to be warm without overexplaining, firm without sounding harsh, honest without causing unnecessary hurt. These are not trivial desires. But the mind turns them into suffering when it uses the ideal self as a weapon against the actual self.

The actual self is the one who has to live the moment. The actual self is the one who speaks under pressure, repairs after mistakes, learns through experience, and tries again. Growth does not come from humiliating that self with flawless imaginary performances. It comes from taking one usable instruction from the gap between what happened and what you value.

One usable instruction is enough.

This is where many people lose their way. They believe that if one alternative is helpful, many alternatives must be more helpful. But beyond a certain point, additional versions create cognitive exhaustion. The mind becomes crowded with scripts. Each one asks to be compared. Each one implies a different failure. Should you have been warmer? Briefer? More direct? Less direct? More confident? More humble? More humorous? More serious? The more alternatives you generate, the less certain you become about what was actually needed.

Too many imagined alternatives do not refine learning. They dilute it.

A useful alternative has a practical shape. It is brief. It is connected to a future behaviour. It does not require you to redesign your entire personality. It might sound like, "Next time, I will pause before answering." Or, "Next time, I will say, 'Let me think for a moment.'" Or, "Next time, I will clarify my intention sooner." Or, "Next time, I will not soften a boundary just to escape discomfort." These are small, grounded, repeatable. They can change conduct.

An unhelpful alternative is theatrical. It exists mainly to make the past feel different. It often begins with "I should have" and then expands into a scene where everyone responds perfectly. "I should have explained everything calmly and then they would have understood." "I should have made a clever point and then the room would have respected me." "I should have apologised in exactly the right way and then the awkwardness would have disappeared." These alternatives may feel satisfying, but they are built on fantasy outcomes.

The mind may resist limiting alternatives because it believes more versions mean more safety. It says, "We need to prepare." But preparation must be connected to reality. Preparing for a future conversation is useful. Preparing for a past conversation is impossible. Once the lesson has been taken, further rehearsal becomes a way of staying attached to regret.

This is where an alternative limit becomes valuable. The mind needs a boundary, not because imagination is bad, but because imagination is so productive that it can bury the lesson beneath endless revisions. An alternative limit is a deliberate decision to allow one useful rewrite and then stop. Not because the rewrite is perfect. Not because the feeling has vanished. Because the purpose of the exercise has been met.

The limit might be framed internally like this: "I get one improved version. It must teach one future behaviour." That sentence changes the task. The mind is no longer allowed to produce endless scripts for emotional relief. It must extract something usable. If the imagined alternative cannot become a future action, it is not a lesson. It is replay material.

For example, after a tense conversation, the mind may generate: "I should have said, 'I hear your point, and I need a moment before I respond.'" That is useful. It can become a future practice. But if the mind then continues with ten more versions, each designed to make you sound wiser, calmer, and more impressive, the limit has been crossed. The learning was already available. The rest is regret trying to polish the past.

Limiting alternatives can feel uncomfortable because it leaves some regret unresolved. That is normal. You may still wish the moment had gone differently. You may still feel the ache of having been imperfect in public or in relationship. The purpose of limiting is not to erase regret. It is to stop regret from taking over the entire mental field. Some discomfort can remain without requiring more analysis.

This is an important truth: you can carry regret without continuing the replay.

Regret often softens when it is allowed to become instruction. It hardens when it is turned into self-punishment. A clean instruction says, "Slow down." "Ask before assuming." "Do not joke when you are trying to hide discomfort." "Prepare your opening line." "Apologise briefly." "Let silence happen." These instructions are not glamorous, but they are liberating because they move energy forward.

Self-punishment says, "How could you?" "Why are you like this?" "You always make things worse." "You should have known." It may feel intense, but it does not tell you what to practise. It simply keeps you emotionally kneeling before the past.

There is also a hidden arrogance in some imagined alternatives, though it rarely feels like arrogance from the inside. The mind assumes that a perfect version of you could have controlled the entire scene. Perfect words, perfect tone, perfect timing, perfect face, perfect outcome. But no one has that much control. Even the most careful communication can be misunderstood. Even a sincere apology can be received awkwardly. Even a good joke can fail. Even a wise answer can land in a distracted room. Accepting this is not defeat. It is proportion.

Proportion allows you to say, "I had influence, not total control." That sentence is central. Influence means your words matter. Your tone matters. Your timing matters. Your willingness to repair matters. Total control means you believe every reaction is your responsibility. Mental rewinds thrive when influence is mistaken for total control. Imagined alternatives then become attempts to claim a power no human interaction actually grants.

The alternative limit restores the right scale. It asks, "What was within my influence?" Not "How could I have guaranteed a perfect outcome?" If the answer is that you could have paused, then take the pause forward. If the answer is that you could have been clearer, take clarity forward. If the answer is that you could have apologised sooner, take repair forward. If the answer is that you could not have known how someone would react, take humility forward.

Humility is not self-belittlement. It is an accurate understanding of your place in the exchange. You contributed to the moment. You did not author every meaning inside it. That distinction reduces regret because it stops the mind from treating the entire emotional atmosphere as your creation.

Imagined alternatives are most useful when they become small rehearsals for values. If you value patience, the alternative might show you how to pause. If you value honesty, it might show you how to speak plainly without excess force. If you value kindness, it might show you how to check impact without grovelling. If you value courage, it might show you how to stay present in discomfort instead of overexplaining. The alternative should become a bridge between regret and practice.

It should not become a museum of better selves.

A museum is for looking. Practice is for living. The mind can spend hours walking through displays of who you could have been: the calm self, the witty self, the articulate self, the perfectly compassionate self, the self who said the right thing at the right time with the right expression. But none of those displays changes the next moment unless you leave with one concrete practice.

That is the point at which regret becomes useful: when it leaves the museum and enters behaviour.

There will still be occasions when the mind returns to the alternate script. It may do so automatically. This does not mean you have failed. The mind has rehearsed that route, and familiar routes are easy to enter. The response is not to argue with every new version. The response is to recognise the category: "This is another alternative." Then ask whether it contains new usable information. If it does not, it can be declined.

Declining an alternative is not the same as suppressing a thought. Suppression says, "Do not think this." Declining says, "This version is not needed." There is a firmness in that. You are not afraid of the thought. You are simply refusing to pay it more attention than it has earned.

The mind may say, "But this version is better." Perhaps it is. That does not mean it is useful. A better imaginary line is not automatically a better use of your attention. The question is not whether the alternative is elegant. The question is whether it changes anything you can actually do.

Regret wants a time machine. Learning wants a next step.

When you understand this, imagined alternatives lose some of their spell. They may still appear, but they no longer seem like urgent assignments. You can take one instruction and leave the rest. You can honour the value beneath the regret without letting the replay continue indefinitely. You can admit that you wish the moment had gone differently and still refuse to donate another evening to redesigning it.

The past does not need a perfect script. It needs an honest lesson.

The next time your mind begins producing better lines, better pauses, better expressions, and better endings, listen for the first usable instruction. Take it seriously. Write it plainly if needed. Then stop the audition. One alternative can teach you. Ten alternatives usually punish you. The work is to know the difference before regret turns imagination into a cage.

When Problem-Solving Becomes Avoidance

Problem-solving has a clean reputation. It sounds practical, mature, responsible. When something uncomfortable happens, the mind moves towards it, examines it, tests possible explanations, considers outcomes, and searches for the best response. This can be wise. A life without problem-solving would be chaotic. You would ignore repair, repeat avoidable mistakes, and drift through situations that require attention.

But problem-solving has a shadow side. It can become a hiding place.

This happens when thinking about the problem replaces doing the thing the problem requires. You may tell yourself you are preparing, reflecting, being careful, choosing your words, waiting until you understand the situation properly. Sometimes that is true. Sometimes a pause is genuinely useful. But there is a point where preparation stops serving action and starts protecting you from it. The mind keeps working because action would involve exposure.

A follow-up email remains unsent because you are still "thinking it through". A repair conversation is delayed because you are still "finding the right moment". A difficult question is avoided because you are still "trying to understand your feelings". A new attempt is postponed because you are still reviewing the last one. On the surface, the mind appears busy and responsible. Underneath, it may be avoiding the risk of being seen, answered, misunderstood, rejected, corrected, or disappointed.

This is why avoidance can be hard to recognise in thoughtful people. It does not always look like doing nothing. Sometimes it looks like doing a great deal internally. You replay the conversation. You imagine possible replies. You draft a message in your head. You predict how the other person might respond. You rehearse your tone. You prepare for objections. You refine your explanation. You examine your motives. You revisit the scene again to make sure you have not missed anything. The activity is real, but the situation is unchanged.

Rumination often survives by pretending to be problem-solving. It borrows the language of care. "I just need to think about it a bit more." "I want to make sure I get this right." "I do not want to make things worse." "I should understand what happened before I act." These are reasonable sentences in the right context. They become dangerous when they extend indefinitely, when no new information is being gathered, and when the thinking never becomes a proportionate next step.

The crucial distinction is movement. Real problem-solving changes your relationship to the present. It leads towards a decision, a repair, a boundary, a message, a preparation, a request, a rest, or a deliberate decision to let something be. Avoidant problem-solving keeps you mentally active while the present remains untouched. It gives the mind the feeling of progress without the vulnerability of progress.

A useful question cuts through the performance: *What action am I not taking while I think?*

This question can feel uncomfortable because it removes the disguise. It does not accuse you of laziness or weakness. It simply asks whether thought has become a substitute for contact with reality. Perhaps you are not sending the message. Perhaps you are not asking for clarification. Perhaps you are not apologising. Perhaps you are not beginning the work again after a mistake. Perhaps you are not resting because resting would require admitting that no more analysis is needed. Perhaps you are not allowing a relationship to remain slightly uncertain without trying to control it.

The action you are avoiding may be small. In fact, it often is. One sentence. One question. One acknowledgement. One practical correction. One decision not to check again. One return to the task in front of you. Rumination prefers large, dramatic internal projects because they justify delay. Action is often plainer. It says, "Send the email." "Ask directly." "Apologise briefly." "Clarify the detail." "Close the laptop." "Try again." "Leave the message alone." The simplicity can feel almost insulting to a mind that has spent hours building complexity.

This does not mean action should be rushed. There are moments when immediate action would be unwise. If you are highly activated, angry, ashamed, or desperate for reassurance, a pause may prevent unnecessary damage. If the situation is genuinely complicated, time may be needed. If someone else needs space, forcing a conversation can be intrusive. The point is not to glorify impulsiveness. The point is to notice when waiting has stopped being wisdom and become fear with a thoughtful vocabulary.

Avoidance often hides inside the desire for certainty. You may be waiting until you know exactly how the other person feels, exactly what the right wording is, exactly whether the apology is necessary, exactly how the conversation will go, exactly whether the next attempt will succeed. But action rarely offers that level of certainty in advance. You send the message before you know how it will be received. You apologise before you know whether it will be accepted. You try again before you know whether you will perform better. You set a boundary before you know whether someone will understand it.

This is why rumination can feel safer than action. Thinking happens privately. Nobody can reject your imagined apology. Nobody can misread the email you never send. Nobody can judge the attempt you keep rehearsing but never make. Inside the mind, you can edit endlessly. Reality is less controllable. It answers back.

Yet reality is also where relief becomes possible. Not perfect relief. Not guaranteed comfort. But movement. A simple clarification can end hours of imagined interpretation. A brief apology can do more than an evening of self-punishment. A return to the task can rebuild confidence more effectively than replaying the earlier mistake. Even choosing not to act can be freeing when it is chosen deliberately rather than avoided anxiously. Action breaks the loop because it changes the present, while rumination keeps trying to change the past.

One sign that problem-solving has become avoidance is that the problem grows larger the longer you think about it. A short message becomes a delicate diplomatic operation. A minor clarification becomes a possible relationship rupture. A small mistake becomes a career-defining error. A simple apology becomes a statement of your entire moral character. The longer the mind rehearses, the more fragile the situation appears. This makes action feel even riskier, which leads to more thinking, which makes action feel riskier still.

Another sign is that the thinking becomes repetitive rather than constructive. You are not discovering new facts. You are not refining a decision. You are not becoming calmer. You are circling the same questions with a slightly different emotional tone each time. "Should I say something?" "What if saying something makes it worse?" "What if not saying something seems careless?" "What if they already forgot?" "What if they did not forget?" The questions multiply, but none of them leads to a chosen next step.

A third sign is that your imagined standards keep rising. At first, the task is to send a reasonable message. Then it must be warm but not needy, clear but not harsh, brief but not cold, accountable but not dramatic, casual but not careless, perfectly timed, perfectly toned, impossible to misread. The mind may call this precision. Often, it is fear of exposure. Human communication cannot be made completely risk-free. Waiting until it can be is another way of not acting.

Avoidant problem-solving also keeps you focused on how to feel safe rather than what the situation actually needs. This difference matters. The situation may need a short repair, but anxiety wants a guarantee of forgiveness. The situation may need a clear boundary, but anxiety wants everyone to approve of it. The situation may need no further action, but anxiety wants reassurance that nobody thinks badly of you. When emotional safety becomes the hidden goal, the mind may reject any practical step that does not promise complete comfort.

This is why some people over-explain. They are not only trying to communicate; they are trying to remove every possible misunderstanding in advance. They add context, then more context. They soften, justify, apologise, clarify, and qualify. The message becomes longer because the mind is trying to control the reader's reaction. But over-explaining can create the very awkwardness it was meant to prevent. It turns a manageable moment into evidence that you are anxious, uncertain, or seeking rescue from discomfort.

Other people avoid in the opposite direction. They withdraw. They decide not to send anything, not because no action is needed, but because any action feels too exposing. They tell themselves it is better to leave it, and sometimes it is. But there is a difference between calm restraint and frozen avoidance. Calm restraint feels grounded, even if slightly uncomfortable. Frozen avoidance feels tense, watchful, and unfinished. The mind keeps returning because the action has not been chosen; it has merely been feared away.

There is also the avoidance of trying again. After a mistake, the mind may replay the scene under the banner of improvement while quietly preventing the next attempt. You analyse the failed presentation instead of preparing the next one. You replay the awkward conversation instead of entering new conversations. You review the rejected idea instead of developing another. The replay protects you from fresh exposure by keeping your attention attached to old exposure. It says, "We are still learning." But sometimes the real learning is in the next attempt.

This is where compassion is necessary. Avoidance is not a character flaw to punish. It is usually a protection strategy. The mind delays because action feels risky. It analyses because uncertainty feels unsafe. It rehearses because being unprepared once hurt. It stays in thought because thought offers the illusion of control. Calling yourself cowardly will not help. Shame will only make action feel more threatening. The better response is honest kindness: "I see why I am hesitating. Now what is the smallest reasonable step?"

Smallness matters. When the mind is overwhelmed, it imagines action as a dramatic leap. But many loops break through modest movement. Open the draft. Write one clean sentence. Ask one direct question. Put the repair into two lines. Close the conversation by deciding no reply is needed. Return to the document for ten minutes. Place the phone across the room. Stand up. Wash the mug. Move the body out of the replay posture. The step does not need to solve your whole life. It only needs to return authority to the present.

The smallest reasonable step is not always external. Sometimes the avoided action is internal acceptance. You may be avoiding the action of letting uncertainty remain. You may be trying to solve what someone thinks because tolerating not knowing feels unbearable. In that case, the step is not another message or conversation. It is the decision to stop checking, stop rereading, and allow the gap to exist. That is still action. It is restraint with intention.

The body often reveals whether thinking has become avoidance. Productive planning may feel focused, even if tense. Avoidant rumination tends to feel agitated, sticky, and unfinished. The body leans towards the phone, the draft, the imagined conversation, then pulls back. There is an urge to resolve and an urge to hide. This push-pull is a sign that the mind is circling action without entering it. Noticing the body can help you identify the moment when more thinking is not giving clarity; it is postponing contact.

A clean decision often brings some discomfort, not instant peace. This is important. Many people wait for the right action to feel completely calm. But responsible action may still feel uncomfortable. Sending the clarification may still bring a pulse of anxiety. Apologising may still feel exposing. Letting the message sit unanswered may still itch. Trying again may still carry the memory of failing. Discomfort does not necessarily mean the action is wrong. It may simply mean the action matters.

This is one of the hardest lessons for replay-prone minds: peace is not always the entry requirement for action. Sometimes peace is the result of action, and sometimes it is only partial. The mind may demand certainty before it moves, but life often gives steadiness after movement. A room feels less haunted when you switch on the light; a task feels less impossible once the first plain step has been taken.

When problem-solving becomes avoidance, the mind tries to do present work with past-focused tools. It replays, rehearses, revises, and judges. But the loop cannot repair the relationship, send the message, practise the skill, set the boundary, rest the body, or complete the task. Only present action can do that. Thinking can prepare the ground. It cannot be the whole harvest.

A useful practice is to give problem-solving a boundary. Ask what decision is needed. Ask what information is missing. Ask whether that information can actually be obtained. Ask what the smallest reasonable step would be. Then notice whether the mind tries to reopen the case. If it does, the issue may no longer be problem-solving. It may be discomfort tolerance. The mind is not asking because it needs an answer. It is asking because the answer requires movement.

There are only a few honest outcomes. There is something to do now. There is something to do later at a defined time. There is information to seek. There is no useful action, and the task is to let the scene close. Anything else can become the fog in which rumination hides. "I will keep thinking" is sometimes necessary, but it should not become an indefinite residence.

The question "What action am I not taking while I think?" should be asked firmly, not cruelly. It is not a weapon. It is a lamp. It shows whether the mind is genuinely preparing or quietly postponing. It may reveal that action is needed. It may reveal that no action is needed and that the real work is release. Either way, it brings the loop back to the present, where life can actually change.

The past can teach, but it cannot act. That is the boundary rumination keeps forgetting. Once the lesson is available, continued replay often becomes avoidance dressed as diligence. The mind may still ask for another review, another draft, another imagined outcome, another hour of internal preparation. But at some point the most responsible sentence is also the simplest: "Enough thinking. What is the next honest step?"

Chapter 4
Stop the Loop Without Suppression

What if the way to stop a replay is not to force it out of your mind, but to stop treating it as the whole truth? The instinct to suppress is understandable. When a conversation starts playing again, when the old sentence returns with heat behind it, when the mind begins its familiar investigation, the first wish is simple: make it stop. Push it away. Replace it. Distract from it. Think about anything else.

But suppression often turns the replay into an opponent. The mind says, "Do not think about that message," and immediately the message becomes brighter. The more urgently you try to remove it, the more closely you monitor whether it has gone. Even the question "Am I still thinking about it?" keeps attention attached to the scene. The replay remains present, not because it is useful, but because the struggle against it has become another way of holding it.

There is a quieter alternative. Not surrender. Not indulgence. Not letting the mind roam wherever anxiety takes it. The alternative is to change your relationship to the replay while it is happening. Instead of entering the content and arguing over every detail, you step back far enough to recognise the process. Instead of saying, "This is what happened and what it means," you begin with, "This is a replay." That small change is not decorative language. It is a shift in authority.

The central tension is delicate: you cannot heal a loop by pretending you feel nothing, but you cannot end it by feeding every feeling with more story. Suppression denies the emotional charge. Rumination justifies it endlessly. The useful path sits between them. You acknowledge the feeling without handing it the steering wheel. You name the process without denying that something affected you. You return attention to the present without demanding instant calm. This is not passive. It is disciplined contact with reality.

The stakes are high because the mind learns from repetition. Each time a replay is answered with more analysis, more checking, more imagined repair, or more inner argument, the loop becomes a familiar route. The mind begins to assume that discomfort should be solved by returning to the scene. Over time, ordinary moments feel less finished. A message is not merely sent; it must be audited. A conversation is not merely over; it must be reconstructed. A feeling is not merely felt; it must be explained until it produces certainty.

That pattern can make the present feel strangely unavailable. You may be physically in the room, but mentally still inside the text thread, the meeting, the joke, the silence, the disagreement. The cup in your hand, the chair beneath you, the sound outside the window, the work waiting on the desk: all of it fades behind the replay. Life does not disappear dramatically. It becomes slightly less inhabited. That is one of rumination's quietest costs. It steals not only peace, but contact.

To stop the loop without suppression, the mind needs a different sequence. A label interrupts the trance: this is the process, not the verdict. A safe allowance of feeling prevents the secondary struggle: this emotion can be present without becoming a story that expands for another hour. A deliberate attention switch gives the mind somewhere concrete to go: not vague distraction, but a chosen anchor, then a chosen task. The movement is from content to mechanism, from emotional fight to bodily permission, from replayed scene to present action.

This approach may feel too simple to a mind that is used to complexity. Rumination likes elaborate work. It prefers full investigations, long internal speeches, careful reconstructions, and arguments with invisible audiences. But a loop is not always loosened by a more impressive thought. Often it loosens when the process is named plainly, when the feeling is allowed to exist without being inflated, and when attention is placed, deliberately and repeatedly, on something that is actually happening now.

A replay will still try to pull you back. It may insist that naming it is avoidance, that allowing the feeling is weakness, that switching attention means you are failing to take responsibility. These are familiar tactics. The loop wants to remain central because it has confused attention with safety. The question is whether you can notice the pull without obeying it immediately. When the old scene returns and asks to be treated as reality, can you pause long enough to say, "This is a replay," and let that sentence open a little space?

Naming the Process

The first move in stopping a replay is not to win the argument inside it. It is to recognise that an argument has begun.

A mental replay often feels like reality because it borrows reality's materials. It uses the words that were actually said, the message that was actually sent, the expression you actually remember, the silence that actually followed. Then it adds interpretation. It adds threat. It adds imagined consequences. Soon the mind is no longer simply recalling an event; it is living inside a meaning it has constructed around the event. The scene feels factual because it contains facts, but the loop itself is not the same as truth.

This is why naming the process matters. When you say, "This is a replay," you are not denying that something happened. You are not pretending the moment was harmless, irrelevant, or silly. You are placing the experience in the right category. You are saying, "My mind is re-running this event and adding possible meanings." That sentence creates a small but vital distance between the event and the mental machinery now surrounding it.

Without that distance, the replay becomes immersive. You do not notice that attention has narrowed. You do not notice that the same question has been asked several times without new information. You do not notice that the mind has moved from "What happened?" to "What does this prove about me?" The replay feels like a problem that must be solved immediately. Naming it reveals that the problem is partly the process itself.

Consider an awkward text. You send a message that is honest but slightly direct. A few minutes later, you remember one sentence and feel a pull to reread it. You open the thread. The wording now looks colder than it did when you sent it. You imagine the recipient reading it with offence. You picture them showing someone else. You draft a follow-up, delete it, then reread the original message again. Each return makes the message seem more dangerous, not because new evidence has appeared, but because attention has begun polishing the fear.

At that point, the mind will invite you into content. It will ask whether the phrase was too blunt, whether the timing was poor, whether the other person is annoyed, whether you should explain, whether you have damaged the connection. Some of those questions may deserve attention later. But if you enter all of them while the loop is hot, you are likely to feed the replay before you understand it. The cleaner move is to step back and name what is happening: "This is a replay after sending a message."

That wording is deliberately plain. A good process label should be short enough to use under pressure. It is not a speech. It is not a lecture. It does not require you to be calm already. It is a handle. "This is a replay." "My mind is checking." "This is the loop starting." "This is story-building." "This is post-message scanning." "This is uncertainty looking for certainty." The label does not need to be elegant. It needs to be accurate.

Accuracy is the point. Many people try to comfort themselves too quickly with phrases that their mind does not believe. "Everything is fine." "Nobody cares." "It does not matter." Sometimes these statements may be partly true, but when the nervous system is activated, they can feel thin. The mind pushes back: "But what if it is not fine? What if they do care? What if it does matter?" Now you are debating reassurance, and the replay has gained another route into your attention.

Process labelling avoids that trap because it does not overstate certainty. It does not claim to know what the other person thinks. It does not decide whether the event mattered. It simply names the mental action that is occurring. "This is a replay" is believable because it describes what you can observe directly. The scene is repeating. The mind is checking. The story is expanding. The body is reacting. That is enough to begin.

The power of the label lies in its shift from content to mechanism. Content asks, "Was that sentence wrong?" Mechanism asks, "What is my mind doing with that sentence?" Content asks, "Are they annoyed?" Mechanism asks, "Am I trying to solve uncertainty by replaying?" Content asks, "What should I have said?" Mechanism asks, "Is this becoming another imagined alternative?" This shift matters because rumination survives when you treat every new thought as a fresh emergency. Mechanism reveals repetition.

Once repetition is visible, the replay loses some of its authority. It may still feel uncomfortable. It may still pull. But it is no longer invisible. You can begin to see its familiar shape: the cue, the thought, the bodily charge, the narrowed attention, the imagined audience, the urge to check, the search for a safer ending. Naming does not end the loop instantly; it interrupts the trance that says the loop must be obeyed.

A useful label also protects you from fusing with the thought. Fusion happens when a thought is experienced as fact rather than as an event in the mind. "They think I am rude" feels like knowledge. "My mind is telling the story that they think I am rude" feels different. The second sentence does not prove the thought false. It simply stops treating it as proven. That distance is not weakness. It is mental precision.

This is where many people misunderstand the practice. Naming the process is not a trick for dismissing responsibility. It is not a way to avoid apology, repair, or learning. In fact, it often makes responsibility cleaner. When you are fused with the replay, you are more likely to overreact, over-explain, seek reassurance, withdraw, or punish yourself. When you can name the replay as a process, you are more able to ask later, with a steadier mind, whether anything actually needs to be done.

Responsibility requires proportion. Rumination destroys proportion by making the replay feel urgent, total, and morally loaded. A label restores scale. "This is a replay" means, "I do not need to solve every possible meaning right now." "This is checking" means, "Opening the message again may not give me the certainty I want." "This is story-building" means, "My mind is adding details that I do not actually know." Each label returns you to the boundary between evidence and interpretation.

The body may resist this boundary. When shame, anxiety, or regret is present, the label can feel too calm for the intensity of the feeling. The mind may say, "But this feels serious." That may be true. It does feel serious. But feeling serious and being an emergency are not the same. The label does not argue with the feeling. It makes room for the possibility that the feeling is intense because the system is activated, not because the replay deserves unlimited attention.

A practical sequence begins with one moment of recognition. You notice the replay has started. You name it in plain language. Then you add a second sentence that separates feeling from fact: "This feels urgent, but urgency is not evidence." Or, "I feel exposed, and my mind is replaying to find safety." Or, "I do not know what they thought; I know I am checking." The wording should be honest enough that your mind does not reject it. No forced brightness. No dramatic self-rescue. Just clear observation.

There is strength in such plainness. Replays often become elaborate, and elaborate thoughts can feel sophisticated. The mind produces complex interpretations, possible motives, hidden meanings, alternate versions, and imaginary conversations. A simple label cuts through that complexity without needing to answer all of it. It says, "I see the pattern." That is not a small thing. A pattern seen early is easier to interrupt than a pattern believed for an hour.

The label can be tailored to the type of replay. After a delayed reply, it might be, "This is waiting anxiety." After public speaking, "This is the post-performance audit." After interpersonal tension, "This is rupture scanning." After a mistake, "This is self-protection through replay." After a bodily rush, "This is activation looking for a story." These phrases help because they identify not only the loop, but the doorway through which it entered.

The best labels are specific without becoming another analysis project. The purpose is not to create a complex taxonomy of your mind. The purpose is to interrupt automatic belief. If the label becomes too detailed, it may turn into rumination about rumination. Keep it light. Keep it usable. You are not writing a report. You are placing a sign on the door before you walk through it again.

There is a subtle dignity in saying, "This is my mind trying to protect me." That sentence can soften the fight. The replay is not proof that you are foolish. It is not proof that you are weak. It is a protective process that has become excessive. Naming it with contempt would only add more threat. Naming it with steadiness allows you to interrupt without self-attack. "Thank you, mind, I see the warning. I am not going back into the whole scene right now."

Some people worry that if they label the replay, they will miss an important lesson. But the opposite is often true. Labelling protects the lesson from being buried under panic. A lesson is usually simple. The replay is usually noisy. Once the process is named, you can return later to the content with cleaner attention: Was there a clear impact? Is repair needed? What is the one useful adjustment? Until then, the label holds the boundary. It says, "Not every replay deserves immediate investigation."

The awkward text example shows this clearly. Without labelling, the sequence may continue for half an hour: reread, reinterpret, draft, delete, imagine, worry, reread. With labelling, the sequence changes. You notice the urge to check and say, "This is post-message replay." You feel the discomfort and say, "There is uncertainty here, not proof." You decide not to reread again unless new information arrives. The message may still feel imperfect, but the loop has been interrupted at the process level.

This is not dramatic. It is not cinematic. It is ordinary mental discipline. The replay wanted to become reality. You named it as replay. The thought wanted to become fact. You named it as thought. The feeling wanted to become evidence. You named it as activation. Each act of naming returns one piece of authority to you.

The practice becomes stronger through repetition. At first, the label may arrive late, after the replay has already taken hold. That still counts. Noticing after twenty minutes is better than noticing after two hours. Over time, the label can move closer to the beginning. You catch the first pull towards the message, the first imagined judgement, the first tightening in the chest, the first mental sentence that begins with "What if". Early naming prevents the replay from gathering unnecessary detail.

There will be days when the label does not stop the loop quickly. Fatigue, stress, conflict, and shame can make the replay more persistent. That does not mean the practice has failed. Naming is not a command that forces the mind to obey. It is a return to position. Even if the replay continues, you are practising the difference between having a thought and being ruled by it. You are building the habit of recognising process before content swallows the whole field.

The deepest value of naming is that it restores a more truthful relationship with the mind. You stop treating every mental event as a message that must be decoded. You stop treating every uncomfortable memory as a case that must be reopened. You stop assuming that repetition means importance. Sometimes repetition means only that the mind has found a familiar groove and is asking you to travel it again.

A label places a hand on the edge of that groove. It does not erase the path. It reminds you that you are not required to follow it.

The next time a scene returns and begins presenting itself as urgent reality, do not start by proving it wrong. Name it. Name the checking, the story-building, the uncertainty, the post-message scanning, the shame flare, the replay itself. Say the plain sentence before the elaborate one takes over: "This is a replay, not the whole truth." Then notice what happens in the small space that opens after the name.

Allowing Feelings Safely

A replay often survives because a feeling arrives and the mind does not know what to do with it.

The feeling may be shame, anxiety, regret, embarrassment, hurt, fear, guilt, irritation, or a vague inner agitation that refuses to name itself. It may appear as heat in the face, tightness in the chest, heaviness in the stomach, pressure behind the eyes, a clenched jaw, restless hands, or the urge to move, check, explain, apologise, withdraw, or repair everything immediately. The body speaks first, and the mind rushes in to translate.

This is where the loop gains momentum. A feeling rises, and instead of being allowed to move through the body as a feeling, it is quickly wrapped in narrative. "I feel ashamed, so I must have done something shameful." "I feel anxious, so the situation must be dangerous." "I feel guilty, so I must be guilty." "I feel exposed, so everyone must have noticed." The feeling becomes evidence. The evidence demands investigation. The investigation becomes the replay.

Many people do not actually replay because they love thinking. They replay because they are trying to make a feeling make sense. The discomfort seems too strong to be left alone. It asks for a reason. It asks for a culprit. It asks for a verdict. So the mind returns to the conversation, the message, the pause, the look, the mistake, searching for the exact cause of the emotional charge. It believes that if the story becomes clear enough, the feeling will settle.

Sometimes that works. If there is a clear repair to make, clarity can bring relief. But often the replay does not settle the feeling. It feeds it. The more you think about the moment, the more vivid it becomes. The more vivid it becomes, the more the body reacts. The more the body reacts, the more the mind believes the moment must be serious. A feeling that might have passed in waves becomes a weather system sustained by interpretation.

Allowing feelings safely means interrupting that cycle at its most human point. It does not mean liking the feeling. It does not mean agreeing with every thought that comes with it. It does not mean lying down in the middle of your day and surrendering your attention to an emotional storm. It means letting the feeling exist in the body without immediately building a case around it.

This is not indulgence. Indulgence adds drama. Allowing removes the argument.

The difference is important. Indulgence says, "Because I feel this, the story must be true, and I must keep exploring it." Suppression says, "I should not feel this, and I must force it away." Allowing says, "This feeling is here. I can notice it without turning it into a whole world." It is a steady middle path between drowning and denial.

Most replay-prone minds are skilled at narrative. They can create meanings quickly. They can detect possible implications. They can imagine how something might have landed, what it might reveal, how it might be remembered, and what it could lead to. This ability can be useful, but when emotion is high it becomes dangerous. The mind starts writing around the feeling. It does not simply say, "There is shame." It says, "There is shame because I sounded foolish, and sounding foolish means they will think less of me, and that means I have damaged my place with them." The feeling becomes the first line of a long, punishing essay.

Allowing cuts the essay short. It brings attention back to the raw experience before the mind turns it into argument. Not "Why do I feel ashamed?" Not yet. Not "What does this mean?" Not yet. Not "What should I do to make this stop?" Not yet. The first question is simpler: "Where is this feeling in my body?"

That question can seem almost too plain. But it changes the direction of attention. Rumination pulls attention outward and backward, towards the scene. Body awareness brings attention inward and present, towards direct sensation. The replay says, "Look at what happened." Allowing says, "Notice what is happening now."

A practical method can be brief. Name the feeling if you can. If the name is unclear, name the sensation. "This is anxiety." "This is shame." "This is tightness." "This is heat." "This is pressure." Then locate it. Chest. Throat. Stomach. Face. Shoulders. Hands. Jaw. Back. Give it a place rather than a story. Then stay with the sensation for a short period, gently and specifically, without trying to solve the event that triggered it.

The aim is not to stare the feeling down. It is not to force transformation. It is to stop abandoning the body for the replay. For a minute, let the sensation be known as sensation. Is it sharp or dull? Moving or still? Hot or cold? Tight or heavy? Expanding or shrinking? Does it have edges? Does it pulse? Does it change when you stop narrating it? This kind of attention is not dramatic, but it is powerful because it gives the feeling room without giving the replay fuel.

Feelings often move when they are not being constantly explained. They may rise, shift, spread, soften, or reveal themselves as something slightly different. Anxiety may have shame underneath it. Shame may have sadness underneath it. Irritation may have fear underneath it. Guilt may have a need for repair, or it may simply be the discomfort of being imperfect. You do not need to force these discoveries. The point is not emotional archaeology. The point is to let the feeling have a body before it becomes a courtroom.

There will be resistance. The mind may insist that the feeling is too important to be merely felt. It may say, "But we need to know what this means." "We need to work out whether they are upset." "We need to decide whether to send another message." "We need to review the conversation again." This urgency is familiar, but urgency is not always wisdom. Sometimes it is the nervous system asking for relief in the only way it has learned: more thinking.

A useful sentence here is: "I can feel this before I analyse it."

That sentence does not ban analysis forever. It simply restores order. Feeling first. Thinking later. If there is still a clear issue after the body has settled, you can return to it with more proportion. If repair is needed, you can repair. If a lesson is available, you can take it. If no action is required, you can let the scene close. But when analysis begins before the feeling has been allowed, the mind often analyses from inside threat. Threat is not a reliable editor.

Allowing feelings safely also means staying within your window of tolerance. If a feeling becomes overwhelming, the task is not to plunge deeper. The task is to widen support. Open your eyes if they are closed. Look around the room. Feel your feet against the floor. Touch the edge of a table, the fabric of your sleeve, the warmth of a mug. Let the body know where it is. Allowing is not a test of endurance. It is a practice of contact.

Some people fear that if they allow a feeling, it will grow without limit. This fear makes sense if your only experience of strong emotion has been either suppression or being swept away. But a feeling that is allowed without constant story often behaves less like a monster and more like a wave. It has movement. It has intensity.

It may be unpleasant. But it is not necessarily endless. What often makes it feel endless is the mind repeatedly adding fresh reasons for it to continue.

A replay says, "Here is why you should still feel ashamed." Then it supplies another detail. And another. And another. It brings back the sentence, the expression, the silence, the imagined judgement, the possible consequence. The body reacts each time as if the scene is happening again. Allowing feelings safely removes the new material. It says, "The feeling is already here. I do not need to keep proving why."

That is a radical shift for many conscientious people. They often believe feelings must be justified. If they feel guilty, they search for the offence. If they feel anxious, they search for the threat. If they feel embarrassed, they search for the evidence that others noticed. But not every feeling requires a full legal defence. Sometimes the body is simply activated. Sometimes the feeling is old. Sometimes it is intensified by tiredness, hunger, pressure, sensitivity, or the vulnerability of being seen. Sometimes it is meaningful, but not as meaningful as the replay claims.

The sentence "I feel bad" is not the same as "I did bad." This distinction may be the hinge on which many replays turn. When those two sentences are fused, the mind hunts for a confession. When they are separated, you can investigate more fairly. You can say, "I feel bad; now let me see whether there is clear evidence of harm, a need for repair, or only discomfort." That is a calmer, cleaner order.

Allowing also prevents secondary suffering. The first suffering is the feeling itself: embarrassment, regret, anxiety, shame. The second suffering is the fight against having it. "Why am I still upset?" "This is ridiculous." "I should be over this." "I am too sensitive." "Something is wrong with me." Now the replay has gained another loop. You are not only feeling the original discomfort; you are criticising yourself for feeling it. This makes the mind more threatened, not less.

A safer approach is to remove the insult. "This is uncomfortable, and it is here." "My body is having a response." "I can let this move without solving the whole story." These sentences may not feel triumphant. They are not meant to. They are meant to lower the fight. Once the fight lowers, the mind has less reason to keep returning to the scene in search of relief.

Allowing feelings safely requires boundaries. You are not giving the feeling the rest of the day. You are giving it honest attention for a contained moment. That may be a minute of noticing the body. It may be a few slow breaths while naming the sensation. It may be standing still before opening the message again. It may be placing a hand on the chest or stomach and saying, "This is activation." The practice is small because it is meant to be usable in real life.

Smallness is a strength. A method that requires perfect quiet, perfect privacy, and a perfectly calm mind will fail when you need it most. Replays often appear after ordinary moments: walking from one room to another, waiting for a reply, sitting at a desk, trying to sleep, leaving a conversation, preparing for the next task. You need a practice that can meet you there. Brief. Plain. Repeatable.

Try this sequence when a replay begins to swell. Name the process: "This is a replay." Name the feeling: "This is shame," or "This is anxiety," or "This is regret." Locate it: "It is tightness in my chest," or "It is heat in my face." Allow one minute of attention to the sensation without adding new story. Then ask, "Has the feeling changed at all?" It may not vanish. It does not need to. Even a small shift proves that the feeling is moving and that the replay is not the only way to respond.

After that minute, the mind may still want to return to the event. That is expected. The practice is not a magic door out of discomfort. It is a refusal to let discomfort automatically become rumination. You may need to repeat the label. You may need to return to the body again. You may need to choose an anchor in the room or move into a task. What matters is that the replay is no longer the only available route.

There is also a deeper kindness in allowing. It tells the body, "You do not have to shout to be heard." Many loops intensify because the system feels ignored or attacked. Suppressed feelings tend to return with more force. Over-analysed feelings tend to multiply. Allowed feelings may still hurt, but they are less likely to turn into a full internal prosecution. They are given space, not a stage.

This practice changes your relationship with emotional evidence. Instead of assuming that a strong feeling proves a serious event, you learn to treat strong feelings as signals that require wise handling. Sometimes they point to a repair. Sometimes they point to a value. Sometimes they point to tiredness. Sometimes they point to an old sensitivity. Sometimes they simply need to pass through without being recruited into a story.

The replay asks the feeling to justify itself. Allowing lets the feeling exist without justification. That is how the loop begins to lose power. You stop using the past to explain every sensation. You stop using every sensation to reopen the past. You let the body speak in its own language before the mind turns it into a narrative of blame, danger, or failure.

The next time discomfort rises after a conversation, message, mistake, or silence, pause before searching the scene for proof. Ask where the feeling is. Let it be felt as heat, tightness, pressure, heaviness, movement, or ache. Give it a minute of honest attention. Do not feed it with another imagined reaction. Do not bury it under forced reassurance. Let it move.

The feeling may be real. The story may still be incomplete. Both can be true.

Attention Switching Basics

A replay keeps its strength by holding your attention in the wrong place for too long.

The mind returns to the awkward sentence, the delayed reply, the flat expression, the mistake that now seems brighter than it did when it happened. At first, you may believe the problem is the thought itself. You try to change it, challenge it, correct it, argue with it, or drown it under another thought. But often the more decisive issue is attention. The thought may be the hook, but attention is the hand that keeps gripping it.

This is why distraction can fail. You try to watch something, scroll through something, tidy something, eat something, read something, or start another task, but the replay continues underneath. The eyes move across the page while the mind remains in the conversation. The hands fold laundry while the old sentence runs again. The body is in one place; attention is in another. That is not attention switching. That is divided attention with the replay still in charge.

A clean switch is different. It is not a desperate attempt to escape a thought. It is a deliberate movement of attention from the replay to a chosen anchor, then from the anchor to a chosen task. The anchor matters because the mind often cannot leap straight from emotional looping into focused work. It needs a bridge. A sensory anchor provides that bridge because it belongs to the present. Sound, touch, sight, breath, weight, temperature, movement: these are not imagined. They are available now.

The replay lives in mental reconstruction. It uses memory, prediction, interpretation, and imagined audience. Sensory attention interrupts that construction by returning the mind to direct contact. The sound of traffic outside the window. The pressure of your feet against the floor. The edge of the desk beneath your fingers. The colour of the wall. The warmth of a mug. These details may seem ordinary, but ordinariness is exactly the point. Rumination turns the past into theatre. A sensory anchor returns you to the room.

Many people dismiss this because it sounds too simple. They want an answer strong enough to match the intensity of the replay. But intensity is part of the trap. The mind says, "This feels huge, so the solution must be huge." Not necessarily. A loop is often maintained by repeated attention, not by the actual size of the event. If attention is the fuel, then redirecting attention is not trivial. It is the practical act of cutting the supply.

The first principle of attention switching is that you are not trying to make the replay disappear before you move. Waiting for the replay to vanish gives it too much authority. You may never feel perfectly ready. The mind may continue to offer fragments: one more sentence, one more imagined reaction, one more possible meaning. The switch begins while the replay is still present. You are not saying, "I feel calm now, so I can return to life." You are saying, "The replay is here, and I am moving attention anyway."

This is a disciplined skill, not a mood. It will not always feel natural. At first, attention may return to the replay within seconds. That does not mean you have failed. It means attention is behaving according to the path it has recently practised. You redirect it again. Not angrily. Not with a dramatic inner speech. Simply again. A replay becomes strong through repetition; a new attentional habit is also built through repetition.

The basic sequence is plain. Name the replay. Choose an anchor. Place attention on it for a brief moment. Then choose the next concrete task. The anchor is not the destination; it is the doorway. If you stay with the anchor indefinitely, the mind may drift back into analysis. The purpose is to interrupt the loop long enough to re-enter the present, then place yourself into action.

Sound is a useful anchor because it does not require much effort. You can pause and listen for the nearest sound, then a farther sound, then the quiet underneath or between sounds. The mind may still try to comment, but you do not need to follow the comment. You are training attention to receive what is happening now. A replay says, "Listen again to what you said earlier." The sound anchor says, "Listen to what is here."

Touch is another strong anchor because it gives attention a clear physical location. Feel your feet inside your shoes, your hands resting on your lap, your fingers touching a pen, your back against the chair, the fabric of your sleeve, the temperature of the air on your skin. Touch can be especially useful when the replay has created a floating, unreal quality, as though you are trapped in your head. Contact with texture and pressure reminds the body that the present is not an idea. It is a place.

Sight can widen attention when the replay has narrowed it. Look around and name simple visual facts without interpretation. Door. Window. Book. Cup. Shadow. Light. Blue folder. Wooden table. This is not about finding beauty or forcing gratitude. It is about giving the visual system a clean job. The replay has been making one mental image too bright. Sight restores the wider field.

A brief practice may look like this. You notice the replay after sending a message. You say, "This is post-message checking." You listen for one sound in the room. You feel the phone in your hand, then place it down. You look at three objects nearby. Then you choose the next task: return to the document, wash the mug, put on your shoes, open the next email, begin the meal, step outside, or sit back down to work. The switch is complete only when attention is handed to the task, not merely pulled away from the replay.

This is why vague distraction often fails. "I will do something else" is too loose. The replay can travel with you. "I will write the next three sentences of this email" is clearer. "I will rinse the plate and put it in the rack" is clearer. "I will read the next page and underline one useful line" is clearer. A chosen task gives attention a shape. Rumination thrives when attention has no assigned place to land.

The task should be modest. When the mind is looping, do not demand heroic focus. You do not need to rescue the whole afternoon in one move. You need the next clean unit of attention. One paragraph. One object put away. One glass of water. One reply written. One stretch of walking to the end of the street. One simple administrative step. The smaller the task, the less resistance the mind can build around it.

There is a reason action matters after anchoring. If you only ground yourself and then remain still with no next direction, the replay may re-enter the open space. The mind is quick. It will use any unclaimed attention. A task closes the gap. It says, "Attention belongs here now." This is not avoidance if the replay has already been recognised and no immediate repair is required. It is the refusal to keep paying attention to material that is no longer helping.

Of course, the mind may object. It may say, "But we have not solved it." "But what if this matters?" "But you cannot just move on." These objections sound responsible, but they should be examined carefully. Sometimes a practical action is needed: a clarification, an apology, a note, a decision. But if the same questions have already repeated without new information, attention switching is not negligence. It is protection from mental excess.

A useful phrase is: "Not now, not by replay." This phrase leaves room for responsibility. It does not say, "This does not matter." It says, "If this needs action, I will handle it clearly. I will not handle it by looping." That distinction is essential. Replays pretend that attention equals care. But care may require a message, a boundary, a repair, a lesson, or rest. It rarely requires another hour of mental restaging.

Attention switching also teaches the body that discomfort does not require investigation. Many replays continue because the body feels uneasy and the mind assumes unease must be solved through analysis. When you switch attention while the feeling is still present, you teach a different lesson: discomfort can be carried into the next action. You can feel a little embarrassed and still make dinner. You can feel uncertain and still finish the work. You can feel a flush of shame and still return to the room. This is how the replay loses its monopoly.

The goal is not to become perfectly detached. You are not trying to become a person who never cares, never feels, never reviews, never regrets. That would be emotional deadening, not freedom. The goal is to choose where attention goes after the useful part of reflection has ended. A thoughtful person can learn from a moment and then return attention to life. That return is not automatic for everyone. Some people must practise it deliberately.

The most difficult stage is often the first few seconds after the switch. Attention may snap back to the replay. The mind may replay the phrase again before you have fully entered the task. When this happens, do not declare the practice useless. The skill is in returning. A clean switch may need several repetitions. Each return matters because it weakens the old assumption that the replay owns your attention until it feels finished.

Finished is a dangerous word in rumination. The loop may never feel finished if the standard is perfect certainty. There may always be another possible interpretation, another alternative line, another imagined reaction. Attention switching accepts that the mind may still want certainty and moves anyway. It does not wait for the loop to bless the exit.

There is also a difference between switching and suppressing. Suppression is tense. It says, "Do not think about this." Switching is directional. It says, "Place attention here." Suppression keeps checking whether the unwanted thought is gone. Switching gives attention another assignment. Suppression is defined by the replay. Switching is defined by the chosen anchor and task.

This difference can be felt in the body. Suppression often creates tightness, resistance, and monitoring. Switching may still feel effortful, but it has more clarity. You are not wrestling with the thought. You are turning towards something else. The replay may remain in the background for a while, but it no longer sits in the centre of the room.

The practice becomes especially useful in predictable replay zones: after sending a message, after leaving a meeting, after a tense exchange, after public speaking, before sleep, or during transitions. These are moments when attention is vulnerable. Having a planned switch prevents the mind from drifting straight into review. After the meeting, touch the door handle, listen for the hallway sounds, then write one factual note and move to the next task. After the message, place the phone down, feel both feet, look at the room, then begin the planned activity. After the awkward exchange, name the replay, locate one sound, then return to the next physical action.

The plan should be ordinary enough to repeat. Do not wait until the replay is severe. Practise switching after small moments. A minor awkwardness. A slight delay. A sentence you are tempted to polish in your head. Low-stakes practice builds the attentional muscle before high-stakes discomfort demands it. When the bigger replay arrives, the route back to the present will not be completely unfamiliar.

There will still be times when reflection is necessary. Attention switching should not be used to dodge a real issue. The test is whether further thought is likely to produce a useful next step. If it is, set a bounded time to review properly. If it is not, switch. The maturity lies in knowing the difference. Not every uncomfortable thought deserves immediate engagement. Not every feeling requires a full inquiry. Not every memory is an instruction.

A simple rule can help: anchor before action, action before analysis. Anchor to return to the present. Take the next reasonable action. Analyse only if there is a clear purpose and a boundary. This prevents the mind from using analysis as the default response to every emotional flare. It also prevents attention switching from becoming mere avoidance. The sequence is balanced: present, act, review only if needed.

Over time, attention switching changes your confidence. You begin to trust that you can be pulled and still return. A replay may start, but it does not have to consume the evening. A thought may flare, but it does not automatically decide the next hour. A feeling may rise, but it does not require you to reopen the whole past. This is not the confidence of never being triggered. It is the confidence of knowing how to come back.

The room you are in matters. The task in front of you matters. The life waiting beyond the replay matters. Rumination makes the past feel like the only urgent reality, but attention is movable. It can be trained away from the old scene and towards what is present, concrete, and chosen.

The next time the replay starts, do not ask attention to leap into calm. Give it a bridge. Name the loop, choose a sound, feel a point of contact, look at what is actually around you, then place your attention into the next small task. The past may still call, but it no longer gets the whole spotlight.

Chapter 5
Extract the Lesson, Then Close

What if the mind keeps replaying not because there is more to learn, but because no one has formally ended the lesson? A conversation finishes, the room changes, the day moves on, yet internally the scene remains open. The mind returns as if the matter is still awaiting judgement. It reviews tone, intention, timing, consequence, and possible repair, but never reaches a point where it says, clearly enough to believe, "This has now been dealt with."

That unfinished quality is often mistaken for importance. The replay feels alive, so the mind assumes the issue must still be unresolved. But aliveness is not always evidence. Sometimes a scene keeps returning because the mind has not been given a clean structure for extracting what matters and leaving the rest. Without structure, meaning spreads. A small mistake becomes a character question. A practical lesson becomes a moral trial. A useful adjustment becomes a night of self-interrogation.

A replay needs an ending as much as it needs understanding. Not a false ending, where discomfort is pushed away and the lesson is ignored. Not a dramatic ending, where you punish yourself until you feel you have paid enough. A real ending has shape. It gathers the facts, separates intention from impact, identifies what can be controlled, and closes the scene with a deliberate signal. The mind often accepts closure more readily when closure is explicit, because rumination thrives in vague emotional residue.

The central tension is that you cannot close what you have refused to see, but you also cannot live well if every uncomfortable moment is granted unlimited review. The task is to take the past seriously without giving it permanent access to your attention. A lesson should be sharp enough to guide you and small enough to carry. If it becomes too large, too abstract, or too tied to identity, it stops being a lesson and becomes a weight.

This matters because replays often begin as a search for responsibility and end as a loss of agency. The mind obsesses over what cannot be controlled: whether someone understood you perfectly, whether they remembered the moment, whether their mood changed because of you, whether they judged your tone, whether they will think differently of you later. These questions feel urgent because they touch belonging and self-image, yet they rarely offer a useful handle. The more attention goes towards what cannot be controlled, the more helpless the mind feels. Helplessness then fuels more rumination.

Agency returns when the question changes. Not "How do I make sure no one thinks badly of me?" but "What part of this is mine to handle?" That shift is not cold or selfish. It is mature. Your next message may be yours. Your preparation may be yours. Your boundary may be yours. Your apology may be yours. Your choice to stop rereading may be yours. Other people's private interpretations, moods, memories, and timing are not fully yours, even when they matter to you. Confusing influence with control is one of the reasons replays become so punishing.

There is dignity in making the lesson small. Rumination prefers grand conclusions because they feel emotionally powerful: "I always ruin things," "I am not good with people," "I cannot trust myself," "I should never have spoken." But these conclusions are too broad to be useful. A real lesson sounds more grounded: "Pause before answering," "Clarify earlier," "Do not send important messages when rushed," "Ask instead of assuming," "Prepare the opening point," "Apologise briefly, then stop explaining." Such lessons may seem modest, but modest lessons change behaviour. Grand self-condemnations usually only deepen the groove.

The path from replay to closure is a movement from mental fog to usable form. The scene is turned into data: what happened, what was intended, what was learned. The field of concern is narrowed to the controllable part, so that energy is not spent trying to manage every invisible reaction. Then the mind is given a closing statement and a small physical act, because completion often needs to be felt as well as thought. A line such as "Lesson taken, scene closed" is not a slogan; it is a boundary placed at the end of a completed review.

Closure may feel uncomfortable at first because the mind often confuses unfinished emotion with unfinished business. You may still feel embarrassed after the lesson is clear. You may still feel uncertain after the apology is sent. You may still wish the moment had gone differently after the debrief is complete. None of that automatically means more thinking is required. The question is whether the replay has new information, a real next step, or only another invitation to reopen the same material. When the scene returns, can you tell whether it is asking to teach you something new, or merely asking to be kept alive?

Turning Replays into Data

A replay feels persuasive because it arrives as a story. It does not simply say, "Something happened." It says, "Something happened, and this is what it means about you, about them, about the relationship, about the future, about the kind of person you are." It gathers scraps of memory, adds emotional emphasis, fills gaps with possibility, and presents the result as if it were a reliable report. The mind does not show you raw footage. It shows you an edited version with commentary.

Turning a replay into data means removing the commentary long enough to see what is actually available. Not what you fear. Not what you imagine. Not what shame has highlighted. Not what a harsher version of you would like to submit as evidence. Data is smaller, plainer, and less dramatic. It asks for the facts of the moment before it allows the mind to build meaning around them.

This does not make the experience cold or mechanical. It makes it fair. When you are caught in a replay, the mind often treats emotional intensity as proof. If the memory burns, it must be serious. If the body tightens, something must be wrong. If you keep returning to the scene, it must contain an urgent truth. But intensity is not the same as accuracy. A replay can be loud because it touches shame, uncertainty, fatigue, fear of judgement, or an old sensitivity. Data helps you separate what happened from what the loop has made it feel like happened.

The first piece of data is the event itself. What happened, in the plainest possible terms? This question sounds simple, but it is surprisingly difficult when the replay has momentum. The mind wants to begin with interpretation: "I made the meeting awkward." "They thought I was rude." "I sounded incompetent." These are not facts. They are meanings, and some of them may be guesses. A cleaner version might be: "During the meeting, I challenged the timeline in a direct tone. One person went quiet afterwards. The meeting continued." That sentence may still be uncomfortable, but it is more usable because it has not turned uncertainty into a verdict.

The second piece of data is intention. What were you trying to do? This matters because intention is not the whole story, but it is part of the story. Impact matters. So does context. If you spoke directly because you wanted to prevent confusion, that is relevant. If you sent a brief message because you were rushing, that is relevant. If you made a joke because you wanted to ease tension, that is relevant. Intention does not erase impact, and it should not be used as a shield against responsibility. But leaving intention out gives shame too much space to invent motive. The mind may say, "I was careless," when the fuller truth is, "I was trying to be clear, but I may have sounded abrupt."

The third piece of data is the known impact. What do you actually know about how the moment landed? Not what could have happened. Not what someone might be thinking. Not what your inner prosecutor is certain everyone noticed. What do you know? Did someone say they were hurt? Did someone ask for clarification? Did the room visibly change in a way that was clear, not merely imagined? Did the conversation carry on normally? Did the person later respond warmly? This stage is essential because replays often inflate uncertain impact into confirmed harm. They take a possibility and file it as evidence.

The fourth piece of data is the lesson. What is the smallest useful adjustment available? This is where many people go wrong. They try to extract a life verdict instead of a behavioural lesson. "I need to stop being awkward" is not a lesson. It is a punishment wearing a lesson's coat. "I need to pause before replying when I feel challenged" is a lesson. "I must never be direct" is not a lesson. "I can be direct and add one sentence of warmth" is a lesson. A good lesson is specific enough to practise. It points towards a behaviour, not a personality transplant.

A replay becomes dangerous when meaning is allowed to expand without limit. One clumsy sentence becomes a statement about your intelligence. One missed cue becomes evidence of social failure. One tense email becomes proof that you cannot communicate. Turning the replay into data compresses the meaning back to a workable size. It does not minimise what happened. It prevents the mind from making the event responsible for more meaning than it can honestly carry.

A two-minute debrief is one of the most useful ways to do this. It should be brief because rumination loves open-ended review. The longer the review remains undefined, the easier it is for the mind to keep adding details, possibilities, and accusations. A bounded debrief tells the mind, "We are going to learn, not wander." The aim is not to produce the perfect interpretation. The aim is to gather enough truth to guide the next step.

The debrief can be written in plain sentences. "What happened?" "What did I intend?" "What do I know about the impact?" "What did I learn?" "Is any action needed?" These questions are simple by design. They do not invite philosophical self-examination. They do not ask, "Why am I like this?" They do not ask, "What does this prove?" They move from event to intention to evidence to lesson to action. That sequence protects you from the mind's habit of leaping straight from discomfort to identity.

Imagine a workplace moment. You are in a team discussion, and a colleague presents an idea that you believe will cause delays. You respond quickly: "That will not work unless the handover changes." The room goes a little still. Your colleague says, "Right," and continues, but the energy feels different. Later, your mind begins its replay. You hear yourself as dismissive. You imagine your colleague feeling embarrassed. You see yourself as difficult, blunt, uncooperative. The meeting becomes an internal accusation.

A data-based debrief changes the frame. What happened? You challenged an idea directly during a meeting. What did you intend? You wanted to prevent a practical problem and protect the project timeline. What do you know about the impact? The colleague gave a short response; you do not know whether they felt dismissed. What did you learn? The point may have been useful, but the delivery could have included more acknowledgement. Is action needed? Perhaps a short message would be appropriate: "I realised I came in quickly on that point. I meant to flag the handover risk, not dismiss the idea." That is learning without self-attack.

Notice what the debrief does not do. It does not declare you rude. It does not declare you innocent. It does not pretend the moment was perfect. It does not require you to know your colleague's private thoughts. It does not turn one meeting into a referendum on your character. It keeps the scene close to the ground, where action is possible.

This is the strength of data: it gives the mind something firm without feeding the drama. Rumination often feels unbearable because it operates in fog. It deals in maybes, imagined reactions, exaggerated meanings, and emotional conclusions. Data does not remove uncertainty entirely, but it reduces unnecessary uncertainty. It says, "Here is what is known. Here is what is guessed. Here is what can be learned. Here is what can be done." That is enough.

The difference between a debrief and a replay is direction. A debrief moves towards closure. A replay moves towards more replay. A debrief narrows. A replay widens. A debrief produces one or two usable sentences. A replay produces a sprawling inner monologue. A debrief asks, "What is the lesson?" A replay asks, "How many ways can this be reinterpreted until I feel safe?" The question tells you which process you are in.

There is also an ethical benefit to turning replays into data. It makes responsibility cleaner. When you are trapped in shame, you may become more focused on escaping the feeling of being wrong than on understanding the actual effect of your behaviour. You may over-apologise to soothe yourself, under-apologise to avoid exposure, or keep reviewing without ever taking a useful step. Data brings you back to the matter itself. If harm is clear, repair it. If the lesson is clear, take it. If the evidence is absent, do not invent it just to satisfy anxiety.

This is especially important when the replay involves other people's perceptions. You cannot responsibly claim full knowledge of another person's private reaction unless they have told you. You may sense tension. You may infer. You may have reason to check. But inference is not certainty. Rumination often treats guessed perception as fact because uncertainty feels intolerable. A data approach allows you to say, "I do not know." That sentence can be uncomfortable, but it is honest. It also prevents you from building an entire emotional case on imagined evidence.

Turning replays into data also protects against excessive self-blame. A replay often removes context because context complicates the prosecution. It forgets that you were tired, surprised, rushed, under pressure, missing information, or responding to a difficult situation. Context is not an excuse. It is part of accuracy. A fair debrief includes context without using it to dodge accountability. "I was tired and spoke too sharply" is more truthful than either "I had no choice because I was tired" or "I am awful for speaking sharply." Accuracy lives between excuse and attack.

A useful debrief should end with one of three outcomes. There is a repair to make. There is a lesson to carry forward. There is no further action available, and the scene can close. These outcomes are intentionally limited. Rumination thrives when the mind believes there must be a hidden fourth option: continue thinking until emotional certainty arrives. But emotional certainty is not always available. A clear enough conclusion is often the best and most honest ending.

The words "clear enough" matter. Replays often demand perfect clarity before they will release the scene. Perfect clarity about what happened, what was intended, how it landed, how it will be remembered, what it means, and whether it will matter later. This is an impossible standard. Human interactions rarely provide complete knowledge. A data-based debrief respects the limits of what can be known. It takes the available lesson, not the imaginary perfect one.

There is a quiet discipline in stopping after the available lesson. The mind may object. It may say, "But what if there is more?" There may be more. There is always more if you allow the mind to keep digging. More interpretations, more motives, more imagined futures, more possible misunderstandings. The question is not whether more thoughts can be produced. The question is whether more thought is likely to produce useful action. If not, continuing is not responsibility. It is rumination with a serious expression.

Writing the debrief is often more effective than keeping it in your head. The mind can loop endlessly in private because each return feels slightly different. On paper, repetition becomes visible. You see that the same concern has appeared again. You see where fact ends and interpretation begins. You see whether the lesson is practical or punitive. Writing also gives the mind a record, which can reduce the urge to keep remembering. The lesson has been captured. It does not need to be held open by repeated thought.

The debrief should be brief enough that it cannot become another replay. A few sentences are often sufficient. Long emotional essays may feel relieving at first, but they can deepen the groove if they repeat the same accusations and imagined consequences. The purpose is to distil, not expand. Think of it as taking a tangled thread and pulling out the one usable strand. Once you have it, stop pulling.

A strong debrief uses neutral verbs. "I said." "They replied." "I intended." "I noticed." "I learned." "I will." Neutral verbs lower the temperature. They keep the mind from sliding into exaggerated language such as "ruined," "humiliated," "destroyed," "failed," or "proved." Dramatic verbs may match the feeling, but they often distort the event. The language you use in the debrief shapes the state from which you learn.

The most important boundary is this: do not allow the debrief to become an identity trial. The moment may reveal a behaviour. It may reveal a pattern. It may reveal a need for repair, rest, preparation, courage, patience, or clearer boundaries. It does not get to define your whole self. If the debrief begins producing sentences such as "I am the kind of person who..." or "This proves I always...", return to data. What happened? What was intended? What is known? What is learned? What is next?

A replay wants to turn experience into accusation. A debrief turns experience into instruction.

That instruction may be very small. "Slow down." "Ask directly." "Do not reply while activated." "Add warmth before critique." "Prepare the opening line." "Stop after one apology." "Let silence remain unfilled." These small instructions are powerful because they can be used. They give the future self something to do. A global condemnation only gives the present self something to suffer.

There will be times when the data shows that a repair is needed. This is not failure. In fact, it is often the cleanest outcome. If you discover that your words may have caused a clear impact, the debrief can point towards a proportionate action. The action should match the size of the issue. A short clarification for a small ambiguity. A direct apology for a clear hurt. A boundary adjustment for a repeated pattern. A practical correction for a practical error. Data protects repair from becoming either avoidance or over-performance.

There will also be times when the data shows that no action is needed. This may be harder than it sounds. The mind may still want to do something to relieve discomfort. It may want to send a message, explain, apologise, check, or reopen the scene. But if the evidence is thin and the lesson has been taken, no action may be the most responsible action. Not every emotional flare deserves a social intervention. Sometimes the work is to tolerate the feeling without exporting it into the relationship.

A data-based approach gives you a way to decide. It asks whether the action is needed by the situation or demanded by anxiety. If the situation needs it, act. If anxiety demands it but the evidence does not support it, pause. This distinction becomes easier when the replay has been translated into facts. Anxiety thrives in blur. Data sharpens the edges.

The practice is not about becoming detached from your life. It is about becoming trustworthy with your own mind. When your mind learns that uncomfortable moments will be reviewed fairly, briefly, and specifically, it does not have to keep dragging them back for another hearing. It begins to understand that lessons will be captured, repairs will be considered, and scenes will not be left open indefinitely. Closure becomes more believable when learning has been done properly.

Turning replays into data is not glamorous work. It is plain, disciplined, and deeply humane. It respects the part of you that wants to learn, while protecting you from the part that wants to prosecute. It allows concern without exaggeration, responsibility without punishment, and reflection without endless return.

The next time a scene starts replaying, resist the first invitation to interpret it dramatically. Take it down to data. What happened? What did I intend? What do I actually know? What have I learned? What, if anything, is mine to do? Once those questions have been answered honestly enough, the replay has served its useful purpose. The rest is only noise asking to be mistaken for wisdom.

Finding the Controllable Part

A replay becomes exhausting when the mind tries to manage what no human being can fully manage. It wants to know what someone thought, how they interpreted your tone, whether they noticed the hesitation, whether they remembered the awkward phrase, whether their mood changed because of you, whether they will privately revise their opinion. The mind treats these invisible possibilities as if they are tasks. It leans towards them with effort, as though enough thinking could reach inside another person and tidy the whole thing up.

This is one of rumination's cruelest tricks: it points your attention towards the least controllable part of the situation, then blames you for feeling helpless. You cannot make someone understand you perfectly. You cannot guarantee that a message lands exactly as intended. You cannot choose the mood another person brings to the exchange. You cannot control whether someone forgets the moment quickly or thinks about it later. You can influence these things, sometimes powerfully, but influence is not ownership.

The distinction between influence and control is not a minor technicality. It is central to freedom from replay. Influence says, "My words, timing, tone, preparation, repair, and boundaries matter." Control says, "Every reaction, interpretation, memory, and emotional response belongs to me to manage." Influence keeps you responsible. Control makes you captive. When the mind confuses the two, a normal human exchange becomes an impossible assignment.

Replays often begin with a controllable concern and then drift into uncontrollable territory. You may start by asking, "Did I explain that clearly?" That is a useful question. It can lead to a clearer follow-up, better preparation, or a slower response next time. But the replay quickly expands: "What if they thought I was incompetent? What if they tell someone else? What if they now see me differently? What if they remember this next week?" These questions feel urgent, but they do not give you a handle. They pull you away from action and into speculation.

A controllable part has a clear edge. It is something you can do, stop doing, adjust, ask, prepare, repair, decline, practise, or leave alone on purpose. Your next message is usually within your control. Your willingness to apologise for a clear impact is within your control. Your decision to reread the thread or put the phone down is within your control. Your preparation before a meeting is within your control. Your choice to pause before answering is within your control. Your boundary around an unhelpful conversation is within your control.

Other people's private reactions are not.

This does not mean other people's reactions do not matter. Of course they matter. Relationships are built from impact, response, interpretation, repair, and trust. But something can matter deeply without being fully controllable. That is the emotional difficulty. The mind dislikes that middle ground. It wants either total responsibility or total dismissal. Mature reflection asks for something more precise: "What part belongs to me, and what part must remain outside my control?"

A simple way to find the controllable part is to draw an invisible circle around the situation. Inside the circle place only what you can genuinely influence through your own behaviour. Outside the circle place what you cannot command, guarantee, or know. The circle is not a wall of indifference. It is a boundary of responsibility. It prevents you from trying to carry the entire social atmosphere on your back.

Take a delayed reply. The replay says, "They are annoyed. I sounded too needy. I should send another message. I need to know what they think." The controllable circle asks for cleaner sorting. Inside the circle: the message you already sent, whether it was respectful, whether one clarification is genuinely needed, when you will check again, whether you will stop rereading. Outside the circle: the person's schedule, mood, attention, interpretation, and response time. Once the circle is clear, the next step usually becomes less dramatic.

Take a workplace example. You challenged an idea in a meeting and later worry that you sounded dismissive. Inside your control: whether your point was necessary, whether your tone could have been warmer, whether a brief follow-up would be useful, how you phrase critique next time, how you prepare for similar discussions. Outside your control: whether someone felt momentarily embarrassed but chose not to say so, whether they later forgot, whether another person privately agreed or disagreed, whether everyone interpreted the moment the same way. The replay wants all of it. Responsibility only asks for your part.

This sorting reduces helplessness because helplessness often comes from attempting the impossible. If your task is to make sure nobody misjudges you, you will feel anxious because the task cannot be completed. If your task is to speak with care, clarify where needed, and repair proportionately, the task becomes possible. It may still be uncomfortable, but discomfort is not the same as impossibility.

The mind resists this because uncontrollable questions can feel more emotionally important than controllable ones. "What do they think of me?" feels larger than "What is my next message?" "Will they remember this?" feels more urgent than "What did I learn?" "Did I damage my image?" feels more compelling than "Is there a specific repair?" Yet the larger question is often the less useful one. Rumination is skilled at making the unanswerable feel central.

One strong prompt is: "What is mine to do, and what is not mine to manage?" This sentence is firm without being cold. It does not excuse poor behaviour. It does not deny impact. It simply divides responsibility from fantasy control. "Mine to do" might be apologise, clarify, prepare, pause, listen, ask, stop checking, rest, or try again. "Not mine to manage" might be someone else's mood, speed, memory, hidden judgement, or willingness to respond warmly.

Another useful prompt is: "What would still be my part even if I never got perfect certainty?" This question matters because many replays are fuelled by waiting for certainty before acting. You may want to know exactly whether someone was offended before deciding whether to clarify. You may want to know whether your mistake will matter before deciding what to learn. You may want to know whether you are judged before deciding whether to let the scene go. But often you must act, or choose not to act, with incomplete information.

Incomplete information is not a failure of reflection. It is the condition under which most human decisions are made. You rarely know the full meaning of a conversation. You rarely know the precise effect of your tone. You rarely know how much of a moment another person carried away. A replay demands certainty because uncertainty feels unsafe. The controllable circle asks for responsibility despite uncertainty.

This is where proportion enters. A proportionate action matches the evidence you have, not the fear you can imagine. If there is clear harm, repair clearly. If there is possible mild awkwardness, a light clarification may be enough, or no action may be needed. If there is no evidence beyond your anxiety, the controllable part may be to stop checking and return attention to the present. The action should be fitted to the known facts, not inflated by the mind's worst-case script.

Over-controlling can create new problems. When the mind tries to manage every possible interpretation, it may push you towards excessive explanation. You send a long message to prevent a misunderstanding that may not exist. You apologise repeatedly for a moment that required one clean acknowledgement. You soften a boundary until it no longer protects you. You monitor someone's tone so closely that natural connection becomes strained. The effort to control perception can make you less grounded, not more.

Under-controlling creates another problem. You may avoid a repair because you cannot control the outcome. You may say nothing because you cannot guarantee the response. You may refuse to try again because you cannot guarantee success. This, too, is rumination's influence. The mind says, "If you cannot control all of it, do not enter any of it." But agency does not require total control. It requires willingness to take the part that is yours.

Finding the controllable part is not always emotionally satisfying. The mind may prefer a grand answer. It may want to resolve the entire relational field, secure everyone's approval, and erase the possibility of judgement. The controllable part may be much smaller: send one sentence, make one note, stop one checking behaviour, prepare one question, accept one unknown. This can feel inadequate because the anxiety is large. But large anxiety does not always need large action. It needs accurate action.

There is power in small accuracy. "I cannot know what they think, but I can clarify my intention." "I cannot control whether they reply warmly, but I can send a respectful message." "I cannot change how I sounded yesterday, but I can adjust my tone next time." "I cannot stop every possible judgement, but I can stop rereading." These sentences reduce the replay because they return you from imaginary control to actual agency.

Agency is calming because it gives the mind a place to stand. Rumination keeps you suspended between fear and fantasy. Control brings you back to ground. Not perfect ground. Human ground. The place where you can say, "This is what happened. This is what I can influence. This is what I cannot own. This is the next reasonable step."

Sometimes the controllable part is an external action. You send the email. You make the apology. You ask the question. You set the boundary. You prepare differently. Sometimes it is an internal action. You stop rereading. You let the silence remain unfilled. You decline to assign meaning to a delay. You allow the feeling without turning it into evidence. You decide that no further action is needed and stand by that decision.

That last one is often the hardest. Doing nothing deliberately can feel almost impossible to a replay-prone mind because anxiety interprets stillness as negligence. But no action is not the same as avoidance when it follows a fair review. If the facts do not support repair, if the lesson has been taken, if another message would only seek reassurance, then leaving the scene closed may be the most controlled and responsible choice available.

The controllable circle also helps with self-respect. Without it, you may become overly responsible for other people's comfort and insufficiently responsible for your own steadiness. You may treat every shift in mood as your assignment. You may try to pre-empt every possible disappointment. You may become so focused on not being misread that you lose the clarity of what you actually mean. Control, properly understood, includes your boundaries. It includes your right not to manage every reaction.

This is not selfishness. It is relational honesty. Other people are allowed their responses. You are allowed your part. The relationship between those two realities is where adult communication lives. Rumination tries to collapse that space by making you responsible for both sides. Finding the controllable part reopens the space. It lets you care without taking over.

A useful practice after a replay is to write three short sentences. "What I can control is..." "What I can influence but not guarantee is..." "What I cannot control is..." Keep the answers plain. Do not turn the practice into a legal argument. The purpose is to stop the mind from smuggling uncontrollable material into your responsibility pile. Once the sorting is done, choose one next step from the first sentence. If no step exists, the next step is closure.

For example: "What I can control is sending a brief clarification if needed." "What I can influence but not guarantee is whether my colleague understands my intention." "What I cannot control is whether they were already in a bad mood or how long they remember the meeting." From there, the next step may be obvious. Send the clarification, or decide it is unnecessary. Either way, the mind has a boundary.

The phrase "if needed" deserves care. Anxiety often declares everything needed. The need must come from the situation, not merely from discomfort. Ask whether the action would serve clarity, repair, preparation, or a genuine boundary. If it would only serve the immediate relief of checking how you are perceived, it may not be needed. Relief is pleasant, but it is not always the same as wisdom.

As you practise, you may notice that many replays lose force once the uncontrollable part is named. The mind still dislikes uncertainty, but it no longer gets to disguise uncertainty as responsibility. "I do not know what they thought" becomes a clean fact, not an emergency. "I cannot guarantee how this lands" becomes part of communication, not proof that you should keep editing. "I cannot control their memory" becomes a limit, not a failure.

Limits can feel disappointing. They can also feel merciful. You are not built to manage every private response to your existence. You are built to act with as much care, courage, honesty, preparation, and repair as you can reasonably bring. That is already demanding enough. The rest belongs to the wider human field, where other people have their own minds, moods, histories, and responsibilities.

The replay will often return to the uncontrollable part because that is where the emotional charge lives. It may ask again, "But what do they think?" You can answer without re-entering the loop: "I do not know. My part is..." Then name the controllable part again. This may need repetition. Not as a ritual of reassurance, but as a boundary of attention. The mind is being trained to stop treating the unknowable as a task.

Finding the controllable part is not about shrinking your care. It is about refining it. Care becomes more useful when it is directed towards what can actually be done. It becomes harmful when it tries to occupy other people's minds, edit the past, or guarantee the future. A replay may insist that everything is yours to solve. A clear mind answers, "No. This part is mine. That part is not."

Once that line is drawn, the next step can be simple. Not always easy, but simple. Do what is yours. Release what is not. Then close the scene before the mind tries to turn uncertainty back into labour.

Closing Statements That Work

A replay does not always end when the lesson has been found. This is one of the most frustrating parts of rumination. You may already know what happened. You may already know what you meant. You may already know what you would do differently. You may even know that no further action is needed. Yet the mind returns again, as though the scene is still open and waiting for another review.

This is because the mind often needs a signal of completion. It does not always infer closure simply because you have thought enough. Rumination thrives in unfinished mental space. If the review fades vaguely, the loop can return later with the same invitation: "Look again. Maybe there is more here." A closing statement gives the mind a boundary. It says, clearly and deliberately, "The useful part has been taken. The scene is no longer available for endless review."

A closing statement is not a magic phrase. It is not a spell, a slogan, or a way to trick yourself into indifference. It works only when it follows honest review. If you use it to bypass a needed apology, ignore a real repair, or dismiss a lesson you are avoiding, the mind will not trust it. The statement must be earned by a clean process: the facts have been named, the controllable part has been identified, and any necessary next step has been chosen. Then closure becomes credible.

This credibility matters. The mind rejects false reassurance because false reassurance leaves too many loose ends. "It is fine" may not work if part of you knows that something needs clarifying. "Forget it" may not work if the feeling has not been acknowledged. "Move on" may not work if the lesson has not been captured. A good closing statement does not deny the scene. It confirms that the scene has been processed enough.

The best closing statements are short, plain, and repeatable. They do not argue with the replay. They do not explain the whole situation again. They do not attempt to make you feel instantly calm. They mark the end of the review. "Lesson taken, scene closed." "I have done the useful thinking." "This has been reviewed; I am not reopening it now." "My part is handled." "No further action is needed." "The next step is chosen." Each phrase draws a line between reflection and rumination.

The wording should fit the situation. If there is a lesson but no repair, "Lesson taken, scene closed" may be enough. If a repair has been made, "Repair sent, scene closed" may feel more precise. If the replay is demanding certainty about another person's thoughts, "I do not know their mind; my part is complete" may be stronger. If the loop is trying to reopen a message you have already checked, "This has been read once; no more checking" may be the cleanest line. The statement works best when it names the boundary the replay is trying to cross.

Tone matters as much as wording. A closing statement should sound firm, not frantic. If it carries panic, the mind hears fear. If it carries contempt, the body hears threat. The ideal tone is steady and adult: clear enough to interrupt the loop, kind enough not to create a second fight. You are not shouting the replay down. You are closing the meeting.

This is a useful way to think about it. When a meeting has served its purpose, someone has to end it. If no one does, people drift, repeat points, reopen settled matters, or create work that does not need to exist. A mental replay behaves similarly. Without closure, it keeps adding agenda items. The same sentence is discussed again. The same possible reaction is raised again. The same imagined alternative is proposed again. A closing statement acts as the chairperson's final line: the decision is made; the meeting is over.

For closure to become more than a thought, pair the statement with a small action. The body often understands completion through movement. Stand up. Close the notebook. Put the phone face down. Wash a mug. Send the email. Step outside. Turn off the lamp. Open the next document. Move from the chair where you have been replaying into a different physical position. The action does not need to be symbolic in an ornate way. It simply gives the mind and body evidence that attention is leaving the scene.

This pairing is especially useful because rumination is not only mental. It has posture, rhythm, and physical habit. You may replay while hunched over the phone, lying awake, staring at a screen, standing at the sink, sitting in the same chair after a call. If you say a closing line but keep the same posture, same object, same thread, and same mental environment, the loop may continue. A small action changes the setting. It tells the nervous system, "We are moving now."

The action should match the closure. If the next step is a repair, the action may be sending the message and then putting the phone down. If the next step is no action, the action may be closing the app and starting the task in front of you. If the lesson has been captured in writing, the action may be closing the notebook. If the replay is happening at night, the action may be turning your body to a comfortable position after naming that the review is closed. The statement marks the boundary; the action crosses it.

Many people make the mistake of waiting until they feel completely finished before they close the scene. This gives rumination too much power. Emotional residue can remain after the useful thinking is complete. You may still feel a little embarrassed. You may still wish you had said it differently. You may still dislike the uncertainty. Closure does not require perfect comfort. It requires enough clarity to stop feeding the loop.

This is uncomfortable but liberating. The mind often says, "I cannot close this until I feel calm." But the replay itself may be the reason calm has not arrived. Continued review keeps the nervous system activated. At some point, closure has to come before calm, not after it. You close because the review is complete, and the body may settle later because the review has stopped.

A closing statement should therefore be based on completion of process, not completion of feeling. "I have identified the lesson." "I have chosen the action." "I have made the repair." "I have decided no action is needed." These are process completions. They are clearer than "I feel fine now," because you may not feel fine immediately. The statement tells the truth: the work is complete even if the emotion is still moving through.

There is a difference between a closing statement and suppression. Suppression says, "Do not think about this." Closure says, "This has been reviewed enough." Suppression is afraid of the replay. Closure recognises its limit. Suppression pushes the thought away without learning. Closure takes the lesson and ends the review. Suppression often creates pressure. Closure creates structure.

There is also a difference between closure and avoidance. Avoidance refuses to look. Closure looks, learns, acts if needed, and then stops looking. Avoidance leaves the scene emotionally unfinished. Closure makes an honest decision about what remains to be done. The replay may accuse closure of avoidance because it wants more access to your attention. Do not let that accusation decide the matter. Ask instead: "Has the useful work been done?"

If the useful work has not been done, do it briefly. If it has been done, close.

A practical closing statement has three qualities. It is specific to the situation. It is believable to the mind. It points attention away from further replay. "Everything is perfect" is rarely believable. "I have taken the lesson I can take" is more credible. "Nobody cares" may be too sweeping. "I do not have evidence that more action is needed" is steadier. "I must never think about this again" is too forceful. "I am not reopening this tonight" is more workable.

The phrase "not now" can be useful when the mind is activated but a decision truly needs to wait. For example: "This is not for 11pm. I will review it after breakfast." This is closure with a time boundary, not indefinite postponement. It prevents the mind from pretending that the only options are solve it immediately or ignore it forever. Some issues genuinely deserve a calmer review later. The key is to name the time and then stop the night-time hearing.

For ordinary replays, however, setting another review can become a loophole. The mind may use scheduled review as permission to keep the scene alive. Be honest. If the issue is small and the lesson is already clear, do not create a future appointment for rumination. Use a clean closing line: "There is no more useful thinking here." That sentence may feel severe to the loop, but it is merciful to your attention.

Closing statements are especially effective when they are consistent. If you create a new phrase every time, the mind may treat each one as another thought to evaluate. A familiar phrase becomes a cue. It teaches the system that a certain point has been reached. "Lesson taken, scene closed" can become recognisable through repetition. The words begin to carry the memory of previous exits. They tell the mind, "This is the doorway out."

Do not expect the replay to vanish the first time you use a closing statement. The loop may return a minute later. When it does, repeat the statement without restarting the review. This is crucial. If every return of the replay receives a fresh investigation, the statement loses authority. The mind learns that it only has to knock again. Instead, respond with the same boundary: "Already reviewed. Scene closed." Then return to the chosen action.

This repetition should be calm, not combative. The aim is not to wrestle the mind into obedience. The aim is to withhold further fuel. A replay feeds on engagement. Even arguing with it can be engagement. A closing statement is a refusal to negotiate after the decision has been made. The mind may bring another angle. You do not have to attend the meeting again.

There will be times when the replay returns with a new piece of genuine information. Someone replies. You remember a fact that changes the situation. You realise a repair is actually needed. In that case, closure can be reopened responsibly. But this is different from reopening because the same old fear feels loud again. New information deserves attention. Recycled anxiety does not automatically deserve another review.

Learning this distinction builds trust. You are not banning thought. You are creating standards for when thought earns attention. That is a mature mental boundary. The mind begins to understand that it will be listened to when it brings useful information, but not when it brings the same accusation dressed in slightly different clothing.

Closing statements also help protect relationships. Without closure, replays often leak into behaviour. You may seek reassurance repeatedly, send unnecessary follow-ups, over-apologise, withdraw, or act tense around someone who has moved on. A clear internal ending reduces the pressure to use other people as proof that you are safe. It lets you engage from steadiness rather than from the urge to settle your nervous system through their response.

They protect work as well. A replay after a meeting can consume the focus needed for the next task. A replay after a message can interrupt an entire afternoon. A closing statement, paired with action, returns attention to what is next. This does not mean becoming emotionally robotic. It means refusing to let one scene colonise the rest of the day.

The strongest closing statements often include responsibility and release in the same breath. "I have taken responsibility for my part; I am releasing what is not mine." "I have made the repair; I am not managing their response." "I have learned the lesson; I am closing the scene." These statements are effective because they do not split the world into denial or obsession. They hold the middle: accountable, but not captive.

That middle is the heart of moving on. Moving on is not an act of forgetting. It is an act of completion. You complete the review. You complete the action if one is needed. You complete the boundary around what is outside your control. Then you return to life before the mind can turn review into residence.

A closing routine can be very small. Write the lesson in one sentence. Say the closing statement. Do the paired action. Return attention to the next task. That is enough. If the replay returns, repeat the closing statement, not the whole analysis. This is how closure becomes repeatable. Not dramatic. Not perfect. Repeatable.

The phrase you choose should feel like something you can respect. It should not be overly sweet if sweetness irritates you. It should not be harsh if harshness activates shame. It should not be clever if cleverness pulls you back into thinking. Plain language is usually best. "Done enough." "My part is complete." "Lesson taken, scene closed." "No more review." "I am moving to the next right thing."

Over time, the statement becomes more than a sentence. It becomes a line of practice. It teaches your mind that every replay does not get infinite hearings. It teaches your body that discomfort can remain while attention moves on. It teaches your future self that mistakes, awkwardness, and uncertainty can be processed without becoming permanent mental possessions.

The next time a replay asks for another round, do not ask whether the scene feels completely settled. Ask whether the useful work has been done. If the answer is no, do the smallest honest piece. If the answer is yes, say the line and move the body. The mind may still mutter from the doorway, but the meeting is over.

Chapter 6
Self-Compassion That Does Not Feel Fake

Why does kindness towards yourself sometimes feel less believable than criticism? A harsh sentence can land with brutal authority: "You made that awkward." "You should have known better." "You always do this." It feels unpleasant, but strangely convincing. A kinder sentence, by contrast, may sound weak, artificial, almost embarrassing. "It is okay" can feel too smooth. "You are doing your best" can feel too easy. The mind rejects it, not because it wants pain, but because it does not trust comfort that seems to ignore reality.

This is the problem with much self-compassion as people first encounter it. It is often mistaken for softness, excuse-making, or a sentimental attempt to decorate a mistake with nicer language. For a conscientious person, that can feel morally wrong. If something went badly, surely the answer is not to soothe yourself too quickly. If you hurt someone, surely you should not rush to feel better. If you made a poor choice, surely discomfort has a purpose. These concerns are valid. Any useful form of self-compassion must respect them.

The kind of self-compassion that helps with mental rewinds is not a warm fog placed over the facts. It is not "I am fine" when you are not fine. It is not "Nothing happened" when something did happen. It is not "I did nothing wrong" when there may be something to learn or repair. Real self-compassion is sharper than that. It is the practice of staying on your own side while telling the truth.

The central tension is that people often confuse punishment with accountability. Punishment says, "You are bad, and you must suffer enough to prove you care." Accountability says, "Something happened, and your next responsibility is to see it clearly, repair what needs repair, and adjust what can be adjusted." Punishment keeps attention trapped in shame. Accountability moves attention towards truth and conduct. One creates a private courtroom. The other creates a path.

This matters because the tone of your inner language changes what becomes possible after a mistake. When the mind is attacked, it tends to defend, collapse, deny, exaggerate, or replay. It does not become wiser simply because it has been frightened. Harshness may feel like seriousness, but it often produces blur rather than clarity. A steady inner voice can name the issue more accurately because it is not busy trying to survive the accusation. It can say, "That was too abrupt," without adding, "Therefore I am impossible."

Self-compassion also matters because replays thrive on identity threat. A mistake that stays at the level of behaviour can usually be handled. A mistake that becomes a verdict on the self becomes sticky. "I interrupted" is workable. "I am selfish" is a wound. "My message was unclear" is workable. "I am useless at communication" is a trap. The mind keeps returning because it is trying to defend your worth from a charge that should never have been framed that way. Compassion does not remove responsibility; it returns responsibility to the right size.

The language needed here must be credible. It should sound like something a wise, direct colleague might say: honest, humane, specific. Not sugary. Not dramatic. Not cruel. A harsh script can be replaced without replacing standards. A mistake can be acknowledged without becoming an identity. An impact can be cared for without endless self-punishment. The aim is to develop a voice that can hold three truths at once: what happened matters, your values matter, and your worth is not decided by one imperfect moment.

From there, responsibility becomes cleaner. The mind can acknowledge impact without drowning in shame. It can name intention without using intention as a shield. It can choose repair without over-explaining in search of reassurance. It can learn without demanding humiliation as payment. This is the difference between growing from a mistake and being mentally dragged behind it. The former requires courage. The latter only requires repetition.

So the question is not whether you should be kind to yourself in a vague, decorative way. The question is whether your current inner voice is helping you become clearer, steadier, and more responsible, or whether it is keeping the replay alive under the banner of high standards. When the next mistake returns in your mind, listen closely: is the voice guiding you towards repair, or merely making you suffer?

Replacing Harsh Scripts

Harsh scripts are the sentences the mind reaches for when something has gone wrong. They are usually quick, familiar, and severe. They arrive before you have had time to examine the facts properly. "That was stupid." "You sounded ridiculous." "You always make things awkward." "Why are you like this?" "They must think you are impossible." The words may feel private, but they shape the entire replay. They decide whether the moment becomes a lesson or a wound.

A harsh script often feels believable because it has force. It sounds certain. It cuts through ambiguity. It offers a conclusion at the exact moment uncertainty is most uncomfortable. If you do not know whether your comment landed badly, the harsh script supplies a verdict. If you do not know whether someone is annoyed, it invents their judgement. If you do not know whether a mistake matters, it treats it as proof of failure. The mind mistakes severity for truth because severity feels firm.

But firmness is not accuracy. A sentence can be painful and still be poorly reasoned. A thought can feel honest while exaggerating, mind-reading, or ignoring context. Harsh scripts do not become reliable simply because they hurt. In fact, the more dramatic the inner language becomes, the less useful it often is. "I ruined everything" may match the emotional temperature of shame, but it rarely matches the facts. "I spoke too quickly and may need to clarify" is less dramatic, but much more workable.

Replacing harsh scripts does not mean replacing truth with comfort. This is where many people resist the idea. They fear that if they stop speaking brutally to themselves, they will lose standards. They worry that kindness will become an excuse, that softness will blur responsibility, that a gentler sentence will let them avoid what needs to be faced. This fear is understandable, especially for conscientious people. But it rests on a false choice. The choice is not between cruelty and denial. The better choice is between punishment and precision.

Precision is the standard to aim for. A precise inner script identifies the behaviour, keeps context in view, separates fact from interpretation, and points towards a next step. It does not flatter. It does not minimise. It does not collapse into self-attack. It tells the truth in a way the nervous system can actually use. A precise script might say, "That reply was sharper than I intended. I can slow down and add warmth next time." This is not indulgent. It is responsible.

Harsh scripts, by contrast, often blur the very lesson they claim to teach. "You are terrible at conversations" does not tell you what to practise. "You should never have spoken" does not help you speak better. "Everyone thinks you are difficult" gives you no reliable evidence and no useful action. The script may produce shame, but shame is not the same as guidance. A good correction should make the next right action clearer. If the sentence only makes you feel smaller, it is not correction. It is punishment.

One reason harsh scripts are so sticky is that they often come from old training. Somewhere along the way, the mind may have learned that mistakes should be met with threat. Perhaps criticism was treated as motivation. Perhaps embarrassment felt dangerous. Perhaps being wrong carried consequences that taught the body to overreact. Perhaps high standards were confused with harshness. Whatever the origin, the script becomes automatic through repetition. It may sound like your own voice now, but familiarity does not make it wise.

The first task is to hear the script clearly. Many people do not notice the exact wording of their inner criticism because they are already fused with it. The sentence feels like reality rather than language. Slow it down. What did the mind actually say? Not the general mood, not the vague feeling, but the sentence. "I am useless." "I made it weird." "They will never respect me." "I always overdo it." When the words are visible, they can be examined. A script you can hear is a script you can rewrite.

Listen for exaggeration. Harsh scripts love absolute language: always, never, everyone, nothing, ruined, impossible, hopeless. These words should make you cautious. They are rarely precise. If the mind says, "I always say the wrong thing," ask what actually happened this time. If it says, "Everyone noticed," ask what evidence exists. If it says, "I ruined the relationship," ask whether that conclusion is known, feared, or imagined. The aim is not to argue endlessly. It is to remove inflated language so the truth can be handled at its real size.

Listen also for mind-reading. "They think I am incompetent." "She is annoyed with me." "He must have lost respect." These thoughts may feel persuasive, especially when a replay is fuelled by shame, but they often pretend to know more than they know. A credible rewrite might be, "I do not know what they thought. I felt exposed because that moment touched my fear of looking incompetent." This sentence does not give false reassurance. It simply refuses to promote a fear into a fact.

Another pattern is identity attack. This is when the mind turns an action into a definition of the self. "I interrupted" becomes "I am selfish." "I sounded nervous" becomes "I am weak." "I forgot to respond" becomes "I am a bad friend." Identity attacks are dangerous because they make the replay feel morally urgent. If the whole self is on trial, the mind will keep returning to the scene. A better script keeps behaviour separate from identity: "I interrupted because I was eager and tense. I can apologise briefly and practise pausing." This gives you both truth and direction.

A useful replacement script has three parts: the fact, the humane context, and the next step. The fact keeps you honest. The humane context keeps you accurate. The next step keeps you moving. For example: "I spoke over him twice. I was nervous and trying to explain myself. Next time, I will pause before responding." Notice the balance. The sentence does not excuse the interruption. It does not pretend it was ideal. It also does not turn the interruption into a global judgement.

This structure is especially helpful after social missteps. Suppose you made a joke that landed badly. A harsh script might say, "You are so embarrassing. Why do you always ruin the mood?" A more useful script would say, "That joke did not land the way I intended. I wanted to lighten the moment, but it may have sounded off. I can let it pass unless there is clear impact, and I can be more careful with humour when tension is present." The rewrite keeps responsibility without feeding humiliation.

Or imagine you sent a message that now seems too abrupt. The harsh script says, "You sounded cold. They must think you are rude." The replacement says, "The message was brief, and I am worried it may read as cold. I do not know how it landed. If clarity is genuinely needed, I can send one warm follow-up; otherwise, I will stop rereading." This script protects both care and boundary. It prevents the mind from turning uncertainty into endless checking.

Or take a mistake at work. The harsh script says, "I cannot believe I missed that. I am incompetent." The replacement says, "I missed a detail that mattered. I need to correct it and adjust my checking process. This is a mistake to fix, not a verdict on my capability." That last sentence matters. It restores proportion. It makes the problem actionable instead of existential.

A replacement script should sound like a respected colleague: direct, calm, specific, and fair. Not syrupy. Not falsely cheerful. Not evasive. Imagine someone competent sitting beside you after the mistake. They would not say, "You are awful." They would not say, "Everything is perfect." They would say something closer to, "Here is what happened. Here is what matters. Here is what to do next." That is the tone to cultivate inwardly.

The mind may reject this at first. It may say the kinder script is too generous. It may insist that harshness is the only way to prevent repetition. But consider whether the harsh script has actually worked. Has it made you clearer, calmer, braver, more accountable? Or has it made you replay more, hide more, apologise excessively, avoid action, or fear future attempts? A method should be judged by its results, not by how severe it sounds.

Real accountability does not require self-contempt. It requires contact with truth. If your inner language is so threatening that you cannot look at the mistake without collapsing into shame, then the language is not serving accountability. It is interfering with it. A steadier script allows the mind to stay present. It makes it possible to say, "Yes, that happened," without sliding into "Therefore I am unacceptable."

There is also a bodily reason to change the script. Harsh words can activate the nervous system. The body hears danger in the inner tone, even when the danger is self-generated. A sentence such as "You ruined it" can tighten the chest, heat the face, and intensify the urge to replay. A sentence such as "That was not ideal, and I can handle the next step" gives the body less threat to fight. The content matters, but the tone matters too. You are not only thinking; you are creating an internal climate.

This does not mean every replacement script should be gentle in the same way. Some moments call for firmness. If you genuinely caused harm, the script should not be soft enough to avoid responsibility. It might say, "That affected them, and I need to apologise without defending myself." That is compassionate because it is truthful and clear. Compassion is not always soothing in the easy sense. Sometimes it is the steadiness that allows you to do the difficult thing without making the whole self a casualty.

The best scripts are believable. Do not reach for sentences your mind cannot trust. If "I did nothing wrong" feels false, do not use it. If "I am amazing" feels irrelevant, leave it. Begin closer to the ground: "This feels uncomfortable, and I can look at it fairly." "I may have handled part of that badly, but I can choose the repair." "I do not need to punish myself to learn." Believability matters because the aim is not performance. The aim is regulation and clarity.

A good script often begins by softening the absolute. "I always mess up" becomes "I did not handle that moment as well as I wanted." "They definitely hate me" becomes "I am afraid they are upset, but I do not know that." "I ruined the meeting" becomes "One part of the meeting felt awkward, and I can learn from it." "I am awful" becomes "I feel ashamed, and shame is making this global." These changes may look small on the page. Inside the mind, they are substantial. They move you from accusation to observation.

The rewrite should also include what remains unknown. This is a mature form of honesty. "I do not know what they thought." "I do not know whether they noticed." "I do not know if this mattered to them." These statements can be uncomfortable because they leave uncertainty in place. But they are cleaner than pretending to know. Harsh scripts often invent certainty because uncertainty feels unsafe. Replacing them means allowing some unknowns to remain unknown without turning them into punishment.

There is a danger of turning script replacement into another perfection project. The mind may begin asking, "Did I rewrite that correctly? Was the compassionate sentence good enough? Am I doing this right?" Do not let the practice become a new replay. The aim is not to craft a perfect inner paragraph. The aim is to interrupt the harsh pattern and return to accuracy. A plain sentence is enough.

The practice can be simple. Write the harsh script exactly as it appears. Then ask what part is fact, what part is interpretation, and what part is attack. Keep the fact. Question the interpretation. Remove the attack. Add one next step if one is needed. The result is not necessarily comforting, but it should be usable. If it is not usable, it is probably still too global or too harsh.

For example, the harsh script "I made everyone uncomfortable" can be examined. Fact: you made a comment and the room became quiet. Interpretation: everyone was uncomfortable. Attack: you made it all wrong. A usable rewrite: "After my comment, the room went quiet. I do not know exactly why. If this happens again, I can pause and ask, 'How is that landing?'" This turns a replay into a practice point.

Another example: "I am too much." Fact: perhaps you spoke with enthusiasm or sent a longer message than usual. Interpretation: your energy was excessive. Attack: your personality is a problem. A better script: "I shared more than I planned because I was excited. I can notice the other person's pace next time without making my enthusiasm wrong." That rewrite protects both self-awareness and self-respect.

Another: "I should have handled that perfectly." Fact: the moment was difficult and you wish you had responded better. Interpretation: perfection was available and required. Attack: anything less is failure. A steadier script: "That was a difficult moment, and I handled it imperfectly. I can identify one adjustment rather than demand a flawless past." This sentence closes the door on impossible standards.

Notice how replacement scripts often include one key idea: one adjustment. Harsh scripts demand total transformation. They say you must become a different person immediately. A credible script asks for one adjustment. Pause. Clarify. Listen. Ask. Prepare. Apologise. Stop checking. Rest. Try again. One adjustment is how growth becomes possible. Total self-condemnation may feel grand, but it rarely changes behaviour.

The language "I can" is useful because it restores agency. "I can clarify." "I can slow down." "I can repair." "I can practise." "I can let this be." Harsh scripts often trap you in what has already happened. "I should have." "Why did I?" "How could I?" These questions pull attention backwards. "I can" turns attention towards the next moment. It does not erase regret. It gives regret somewhere to go.

There will be times when the harsh script returns even after you rewrite it. That is normal. Familiar scripts do not disappear because you challenged them once. The mind may offer the old line again: "You ruined it." You do not need to begin the whole debate again. You can answer with the replacement: "One part went badly; I have my next step." Then move attention. Repetition builds the new path.

Consistency matters more than intensity. A single dramatic act of self-kindness will not undo years of harsh scripting. But repeated precision will change the atmosphere. Each time you remove an identity attack, you teach the mind that mistakes will be handled, not weaponised. Each time you replace mind-reading with uncertainty, you teach the mind not to invent evidence. Each time you turn a global judgement into one practical adjustment, you teach the mind that learning is possible without humiliation.

Replacing harsh scripts also changes the way you relate to other people. When you are less busy defending against inner attack, you can listen more cleanly. You can apologise without making the apology about your own shame. You can receive feedback without collapsing into a verdict. You can notice impact without drowning in self-criticism. You can repair with dignity instead of panic. Inner language is not only private; it shapes outward behaviour.

This is why the practice is not self-indulgent. It is relationally responsible. A person trapped in shame often seeks rescue, hides, over-explains, or becomes defensive. A person grounded in fair self-talk is more available for genuine repair. They can say, "I see that affected you," without needing the other person to immediately reassure them that they are not bad. That is a stronger form of accountability than self-punishment ever offers.

There is a quiet courage in refusing to speak to yourself with cruelty after a mistake. Cruelty can feel familiar, even righteous. Fairness may feel unfamiliar, even suspicious. But fairness is the ground on which real change stands. You do not need a softer fantasy. You need a truer voice.

A harsh script says, "Suffer so you will learn."

A better script says, "Look clearly, take responsibility, and choose the next right action."

The next time a replay begins, listen for the sentence driving it. Do not accept the script simply because it arrived first or hurt most. Write it down if you need to. Strip away exaggeration, mind-reading, identity attack, and impossible hindsight. Keep the fact. Keep the value. Keep the lesson. Then say the replacement in a tone you could respect.

Not fake. Not flattering. Not cruel.

Clear enough to guide you. Kind enough to keep you standing.

Accountability Without Punishment

Accountability is one of the most misused words in the inner life. It should mean the willingness to see clearly, own your part, repair what needs repair, and change what can be changed. Yet inside a mental replay, accountability often becomes something harsher and less useful. It becomes a private sentence. The mind says, "If I punish myself enough, I will prove that I care." It treats suffering as evidence of integrity.

This is a trap. Punishment can feel morally serious, but it often prevents the very clarity that responsibility requires. When the inner voice becomes threatening, the mind does not become wiser. It becomes frightened, defensive, ashamed, or paralysed. It searches for relief instead of truth. It replays the scene not to understand it, but to escape the accusation that now surrounds it. A mistake that could have been handled becomes a courtroom.

Accountability without punishment begins with a stronger premise: you can be responsible without being brutal. You can admit that your words had an impact without declaring yourself awful. You can recognise that you acted poorly without turning the action into your identity. You can apologise without collapsing. You can change without humiliating yourself first. In fact, you are more likely to change when your mind is steady enough to see the lesson accurately.

Punishment tends to blur the issue. It uses sweeping language. "I ruined everything." "I am terrible." "I always do this." "I should never speak." These sentences may feel intense, but they do not help you act. They do not show you what to repair, what to practise, what to avoid, what to say next, or what boundary to set. They create emotional heat without practical light. Accountability, by contrast, is specific. It asks, "What happened? What was my part? What was the impact? What is the next clean action?"

This distinction is crucial for people who replay conversations and mistakes. Many replay-prone minds are not trying to avoid responsibility. They are trying to perform responsibility through repeated self-punishment. They believe that if they stop attacking themselves, they will become careless. They fear that kindness will make them complacent. But punishment is not the engine of conscience. Conscience does not need cruelty to work. It needs honesty, proportion, and follow-through.

Consider the difference between two inner responses after interrupting someone in a tense discussion. Punishment says, "I am so rude. I never listen. No wonder people get frustrated with me." Accountability says, "I interrupted twice because I felt defensive. That may have made it harder for them to finish. I can apologise briefly and practise pausing before I respond." The second response is not softer in the weak sense. It is more exact. It names the behaviour, recognises the possible effect, and points towards repair.

A useful accountability structure has three movements: acknowledge impact, name intention, choose repair or adjustment. Each movement matters, and none requires self-attack.

To acknowledge impact is to look at what your behaviour may have done outside your own intention. This is where maturity begins. You may not have meant to sound dismissive, but someone may still have felt dismissed. You may not have meant to dominate the conversation, but you may still have taken up too much space. You may not have meant to be cold, but your message may still have read abruptly. Intention matters, but it does not cancel impact. It simply sits beside it.

This can be uncomfortable, especially if you see yourself as kind, thoughtful, or careful. When impact does not match identity, shame often rushes in. The mind wants to choose between innocence and guilt. Either "I did nothing wrong" or "I am awful." Accountability refuses both extremes. It says, "My intention may have been decent, and the impact may still need care." That sentence is adult. It leaves room for complexity. It allows repair without self-erasure.

Naming intention is not the same as making excuses. This is where the inner prosecutor often becomes suspicious. It says, "Do not mention intention. You are just defending yourself." But intention is part of accurate learning. If you spoke sharply because you were trying to protect a deadline, that context matters. If you went quiet because you were overwhelmed, that matters. If you made a joke because you wanted to ease tension, that matters. The point is not to use intention to avoid impact. The point is to understand the gap between what you meant and what may have landed.

That gap is where much of human growth happens. You learn that honesty may need warmth. You learn that humour may need timing. You learn that directness may need acknowledgement. You learn that silence may be read as disinterest, even when it comes from processing. You learn that good intentions still require skilful delivery. Punishment usually misses these lessons because it is too busy condemning. Accountability studies the gap carefully enough to improve the next attempt.

The third movement is repair or adjustment. Repair is needed when there is a clear or likely impact that can be addressed. It may be a brief apology, a clarification, a correction, a check-in, a changed behaviour, or a practical fix. Adjustment is needed when the lesson is mainly for future conduct. Perhaps no message is required, but you need to prepare differently next time. Perhaps no apology is needed, but you need to stop responding when tired. Perhaps the mistake was minor, but the pattern deserves attention.

The key word is proportionate. Punishment pushes towards excess. It may make you over-apologise, write a long explanation, seek reassurance, or turn a small moment into a major emotional event. Avoidance pushes in the other direction. It may make you minimise, disappear, or refuse to look. Accountability chooses the action that fits the situation. Not the action that best relieves shame. Not the action that best protects pride. The action that serves truth and repair.

A proportionate apology, for example, does not need to become a confession of your entire character. If you interrupted someone, you might say, "I realised I cut across you earlier. I am sorry. I will slow down next time." That is enough for many ordinary moments. It owns the behaviour. It acknowledges impact. It names an adjustment. It does not demand reassurance. It does not ask the other person to comfort your shame. It does not turn the apology into another replay.

When intent was good but impact was off, accountability might sound like, "I meant to be direct so we could solve the issue, but I can see it may have landed as dismissive. I am sorry for that. I will make more room for your view before jumping to the practical point." This kind of language is strong because it holds both sides. It does not hide behind intention, and it does not pretend intention is irrelevant. It repairs the bridge between what was meant and what was received.

Punishment, on the other hand, often keeps you self-focused. This may seem surprising because punishment feels like remorse, but it can actually pull attention away from the other person and towards your own distress. You become absorbed in how bad you feel, how awful you are, how frightened you are of being judged, how urgently you need to be forgiven. The original impact can get lost beneath your internal emergency. Accountability brings attention back to the relational fact: what happened, who was affected, and what clean step is needed.

This is why self-punishment can become a subtle form of avoidance. If you spend the evening replaying how terrible you are, you may never send the simple repair. If you collapse into shame, you may avoid the conversation that would actually matter. If you keep analysing your guilt, you may delay the behavioural change that would prevent repetition. The mind can look busy while the real responsibility remains untouched.

Accountability asks for movement. Punishment asks for suffering. They are not the same.

The belief that punishment prevents future mistakes is deeply tempting. The mind says, "If this hurts enough, I will remember not to do it again." Pain can make an event memorable, but memory is not the same as skill. To behave differently, you need a clear alternative. "Do not be awful" is not an alternative. "Pause before replying when I feel defensive" is. "Never mess up again" is not a plan. "Check the file before sending" is. "Stop being too much" is not guidance. "Notice the other person's pace before adding more" is.

Real change is usually behavioural, not theatrical. It happens through specific adjustments repeated in ordinary moments. Harsh punishment may create dramatic emotion, but it rarely creates a reliable practice. A person becomes more accountable by learning what to do next, not by proving that they can suffer intensely after doing wrong.

There is also the matter of trust. If your mind knows that every mistake will be met with attack, it may begin to hide from mistakes. It may minimise them, justify them, or delay looking at them. This is not because you lack values. It is because the cost of honest reflection has become too high. When accountability is non-punishing, the mind can approach mistakes more readily. It learns that truth will be handled firmly, but not violently. That makes honesty safer.

This does not mean accountability should be comfortable. It often is not. Admitting impact can sting. Apologising can feel exposed. Changing behaviour can require humility. Sitting with someone else's disappointment without rushing to defend yourself can be difficult. But discomfort is different from punishment. Discomfort can be clean. Punishment is contaminated by contempt.

Clean discomfort says, "This matters, and I need to respond well." Punishment says, "This proves something shameful about me." Clean discomfort may lead to repair. Punishment often leads to spiralling. Clean discomfort respects the situation. Punishment makes the self the centre of the drama. The goal is not to avoid discomfort; it is to remove contempt so that discomfort can do its proper work.

A practical accountability review can be brief. Ask what happened in observable terms. Ask who, if anyone, may have been affected. Ask what you intended, without using that intention as a shield. Ask what part was within your control. Ask whether repair is needed now or adjustment is enough for next time. Then act, close, and stop paying punishment as if it were a moral debt.

The closing matters. Without closure, accountability easily slips back into rumination. After you apologise, the mind may still ask, "Was that enough? Did they believe me? Do they still think badly of me?" Some of these questions may arise naturally, but they are not always yours to solve. Once you have made a proportionate repair, the other person's response belongs to them. You can stay open to further conversation, but you do not need to keep punishing yourself while you wait.

This is where accountability without punishment becomes an act of respect for both people. You respect the other person by acknowledging impact and changing what needs changing. You respect yourself by refusing to turn responsibility into self-destruction. You respect the relationship by keeping the repair clean, not burdening it with excessive shame. You respect the future by converting the mistake into practice.

A replay may still try to reopen the case. It may say, "You have not suffered enough." Answer carefully: suffering is not the measure of responsibility. The measure is whether you have seen clearly, owned your part, repaired where needed, and adjusted your conduct. If those have been done, punishment has no further role. It is only noise wearing a judge's robe.

The most accountable sentence is often simple: "I did that, it had this impact, and this is what I will do now." No drama. No self-erasure. No denial. No performance of guilt. Just truth with a direction.

That is the standard. Not innocence. Not perfection. Not endless internal sentencing. Accountability without punishment means becoming the kind of person who can face a mistake directly, respond proportionately, and keep their dignity intact. The mistake gets your attention. The lesson gets your commitment. The punishment does not get your life.

Chapter 7
Repair, Apologise, or Let It Be

You send the message, then see the sentence differently the moment it leaves your hands. It looks sharper now. Less warm. Too brief. Too much. You read it once, then again, and the mind begins arranging possible consequences. Perhaps they will understand. Perhaps they will not. Perhaps a quick follow-up would help. Perhaps a follow-up would make you look anxious. Perhaps saying nothing is rude. Perhaps saying something is worse.

The phone becomes heavier than it should be. You place it down, pick it up, check the thread, notice there is no reply, and feel the old machinery begin. The replay does not simply ask whether repair is needed. It asks whether you are safe, whether the connection is intact, whether your intention survived the wording, whether silence means judgement. A simple question becomes tangled: should I act, apologise, clarify, wait, or leave it alone?

This is where many mental rewinds become socially expensive. The mind overestimates the damage and underestimates the power of a proportionate response. It imagines that a repair must be perfect, emotionally complete, and impossible to misunderstand. It forgets that many human moments need only a small bridge: a clean clarification, a brief apology, a steady check-in, or no further action at all. The replay wants certainty before it moves. Relationships often require something humbler: care without control.

The central tension is that not every uncomfortable moment requires repair, but some do. Ignore a real impact and the lesson remains unfinished. Chase every possible impact and life becomes a series of unnecessary explanations. The skill is not to apologise more, explain more, or withdraw more. The skill is to choose the right-sized response. Repair is not a performance of guilt. Apology is not a plea to be reassured. Letting something be is not neglect when the useful work has already been done.

This matters because the aftermath of a moment can shape the relationship as much as the moment itself. A clumsy sentence handled plainly may pass with little damage. The same sentence followed by panic, over-explanation, repeated checking, or cold avoidance can make the situation larger than it needed to be. The aim is not to manage every impression, but to complete the social loop where completion is genuinely needed. Clear impact, an ongoing relationship, and a feasible next step give repair its proper place. Without those, anxiety may try to manufacture a task.

Apology needs the same discipline. A good apology is often shorter than the replay wants it to be. It names the behaviour, recognises the impact, and points towards a better next action. It does not require a long defence of intention, a dramatic confession, or a hidden request for the other person to make your shame disappear. When intention was good but impact was off, the task is not to prove innocence. It is to acknowledge the gap. That kind of language is quiet, adult, and surprisingly relieving because it stops the mind from rehearsing elaborate speeches it will never send.

There is also a form of courage in choosing no action. Some moments do not need repair. They need a lesson, a breath, and release. The mind dislikes this because no action leaves uncertainty in place. Someone may have noticed. Someone may have misunderstood. Someone may have forgotten. You may never know. Letting it be asks you to tolerate that open space without filling it with another message, another apology, another check, another attempt to secure your image. This is not passivity. It is restraint with purpose.

The path here moves through judgement, language, restraint, and waiting. Repair begins with criteria rather than panic. Apology becomes simple enough to use without spiralling. No action becomes an active decision rather than a frightened freeze. Slow or ambiguous replies are handled with a waiting plan, so silence does not become a blank screen onto which the mind projects rejection, irritation, or disaster.

The difficult question is not, "How can I make this feeling go away?" That question often leads to reassurance-seeking. The sharper question is, "What does this situation genuinely require from me?" Sometimes the answer will be repair. Sometimes it will be apology.

Sometimes it will be patience. Sometimes it will be the disciplined discomfort of leaving the phone alone while the mind insists that one more check will finally settle everything.

Choosing Repair Actions

A mental replay often asks the wrong question first. It asks, "How do I make this discomfort stop?" That question feels urgent, especially after a sentence lands badly, a message reads colder than intended, or a conversation ends with a strange quietness. The body wants relief. The mind wants certainty. The quickest imagined route is usually some form of repair: send another message, apologise, clarify, soften, explain, check, reopen, make sure.

But repair is not meant to be a sedative for anxiety. Repair is meant to serve reality.

This distinction matters because replay-prone minds often overestimate damage. They take a possible awkwardness and treat it as confirmed harm. They take a delayed reply and treat it as emotional evidence. They take a brief silence and treat it as a broken connection. Once the mind imagines damage, it begins planning repair as if repair must be immediate, perfect, and complete. Yet many moments are not damaged in the way the replay claims. Some are merely uncomfortable. Some are ambiguous. Some need a light touch. Some need nothing at all.

A good repair action begins with proportion. It asks what the situation actually requires, not what shame is demanding. The aim is not to erase every possible misunderstanding or guarantee that nobody thinks badly of you. That kind of repair becomes image management. The aim is to address a clear or likely impact in a way that is simple, respectful, and fitting. Repair should reduce unnecessary confusion, acknowledge genuine effect, or reopen contact where something has been strained. It should not turn a small moment into a large performance.

There are three useful criteria for deciding whether repair is needed: clear impact, ongoing relationship, and a feasible next step. These criteria bring the mind back from panic to judgement. They do not remove all uncertainty, but they prevent anxiety from declaring every social discomfort an emergency.

Clear impact means there is some evidence that your words or actions affected someone. This evidence may be direct: someone tells you they felt hurt, confused, dismissed, pressured, or excluded. It may be behavioural: the exchange changed sharply after a specific moment, a practical mistake caused inconvenience, or a misunderstanding is now shaping what happens next. Clear impact does not mean you know every private thought inside the other person. It means there is enough reality to respond to, rather than only a fear your mind has generated.

This is where many replays need slowing down. "They might have been upset" is not the same as "They were upset." "That could have sounded rude" is not the same as "I was rude." "They have not replied yet" is not the same as "I damaged the relationship." Possible impact deserves awareness, but awareness is not always a command to act. The more anxious the mind becomes, the more it treats possibility as proof. Repair chosen from proof is usually steadier than repair chosen from panic.

The second criterion is the ongoing relationship. Repair matters most where there is a continuing connection, shared work, trust to maintain, or future contact that would benefit from clarity. A comment that may have confused a colleague you work with regularly deserves different consideration from an awkward sentence spoken to someone you are unlikely to meet again. This does not mean strangers do not matter. It means repair should be fitted to the living context. Where there is ongoing relationship, small unresolved moments can sometimes create avoidable distance. A brief check-in can protect the connection without making the moment dramatic.

The third criterion is a feasible next step. Repair should be something you can actually do in a clean, bounded way. A brief apology. A clarifying sentence. A corrected document. A follow-up question. A changed behaviour. If the imagined repair requires controlling someone's opinion, rewriting the whole interaction, explaining every hidden motive, or making your discomfort disappear, it is not a feasible repair. It is rumination wearing social clothing.

Feasible repair is usually smaller than the replay wants it to be. The replay imagines a speech. Repair may need a sentence. The replay imagines a full emotional debrief. Repair may need a short acknowledgement. The replay imagines you must prove your character. Repair may only require you to clarify your meaning. The mind under shame tends to overbuild. Good repair is often modest because it is aimed at the actual gap, not the entire fear.

Imagine you made a comment during a discussion and later realised it could have been misunderstood. Perhaps you said, "That approach is risky," intending to refer to the plan, but afterwards you worried that it sounded like a criticism of the person who suggested it. The replay begins: "They probably think I dismissed them. I should have said it differently. I need to explain myself properly." A proportionate repair would not require a long defence. It might simply be: "I realised my comment about the approach being risky may have sounded abrupt. I meant the timeline risk, not your idea as a whole." That is clear. It names the possible misunderstanding. It does not beg for reassurance. It completes the social loop.

This kind of repair works because it is specific. It does not say, "I am so sorry if I was awful earlier." That places emotional weight on the other person and may enlarge the moment. It does not say, "I did not mean it like that, you know me." That can sound defensive. It says what may have landed poorly, what was meant, and where the clarification belongs. Specificity lowers drama.

A simple check-in can also be enough. Replay-prone minds often underestimate the power of light contact. They assume that repair must be elaborate because the internal experience is intense. But the other person may not be living the moment with the same intensity. A small, calm sentence can do more than a long explanation because it respects the scale of the exchange. "I hope that came across clearly earlier; I meant X rather than Y." "I noticed I jumped in quickly there. I did not mean to cut you off." "I think I may have sounded sharper than I intended. Sorry about that." These are not performances. They are bridges.

The danger is over-repair. Over-repair happens when you keep adding explanation after the necessary repair has already been made. You apologise, then apologise for apologising. You clarify, then clarify the clarification. You send one message, then another to adjust the tone of the first. You try to prevent every possible interpretation and end up creating more intensity than the original moment carried. Over-repair is usually not generosity. It is anxiety trying to secure a guarantee.

A useful way to detect over-repair is to ask, "Am I trying to help the situation, or am I trying to make them remove my discomfort?" This question may sting, but it is honest. Good repair is concerned with impact and clarity. Anxiety-driven repair is concerned with reassurance. It wants the other person to say, "No, you were fine," "I am not upset," "You did nothing wrong," "Please stop worrying." There is nothing shameful about wanting reassurance. It is human. But when reassurance becomes the hidden purpose of repair, the action may serve your anxiety more than the relationship.

Under-repair has its own cost. Some people avoid repair because they fear making things awkward. They replay for hours, but never send the simple acknowledgement that would help. They wait for the feeling to disappear. They hope the other person will forget. They tell themselves it was probably nothing, while continuing to monitor the relationship for signs of damage. Avoiding a needed repair does not always protect the connection. Sometimes it leaves the mind looping because the social loop remains incomplete.

The question is not whether repair feels comfortable. It often does not. The question is whether repair is appropriate. If there was clear impact, an ongoing relationship, and a feasible next step, discomfort alone is not a reason to avoid it. A clean repair may feel exposing for a moment and relieving afterwards, because it returns you to action instead of leaving you trapped in speculation.

Repair should also match the size of the harm or confusion. A small ambiguity needs a small clarification. A missed deadline needs a practical correction and, where appropriate, an apology. A hurtful comment needs acknowledgement of impact, not a lecture on your intention. A pattern needs changed behaviour, not only words. The larger the impact, the more repair must be grounded in action. Words matter, but repeated behaviour is the repair that carries weight over time.

This is why apology is not always the right repair. Sometimes the better action is correction. Sometimes it is a boundary. Sometimes it is asking a question. Sometimes it is waiting until the other person has space. Sometimes it is changing how you prepare before the next meeting. The mind often reaches for apology because apology feels like the universal solvent for social discomfort. But not every discomfort is guilt, and not every repair is an apology.

For example, if you suspect you were misunderstood, clarification may be more useful than apology. "I want to clarify what I meant earlier" is different from "I am sorry." If you made a practical mistake, correction may be more useful than emotional explanation. "I have attached the correct version now" may matter more than a long confession. If you crossed a boundary, apology may need to be paired with changed behaviour. "I am sorry I pushed after you said no. I will not do that again" is stronger than repeated remorse without adjustment.

Repair becomes cleaner when you separate the purpose from the feeling. The purpose might be clarity, acknowledgement, correction, reconnection, or changed behaviour. The feeling might be embarrassment, guilt, shame, anxiety, or fear. If you let the feeling decide the size of the repair, the action may become disproportionate. If you let the purpose decide, the action becomes more respectful.

There is also timing to consider. Some repairs are best made soon because delay allows confusion to harden. Others benefit from a short pause because immediate action would come from panic rather than steadiness. The difference lies in whether you can act cleanly. If you can send one clear sentence, do it. If you are activated and likely to over-explain, pause long enough to reduce the emotional charge. A repair made from panic may become another thing to replay.

A good pause has a boundary. "I will wait until I can write this in two plain sentences" is a useful pause. "I will think about this all evening until I feel certain" is rumination. The pause should prepare action or confirm no action, not create indefinite review. If the situation needs repair, choose a time and a form. If it does not, close it.

The tone of repair should be calm and unburdening. You are not asking the other person to manage your shame. You are not making your distress the centre. You are addressing the moment. This is especially important when you care deeply about being a good person. The temptation is to repair in a way that proves your goodness: too many words, too much explanation, too much visible remorse. But the other person may need clarity more than your emotional display. Let the repair serve them, not your self-image.

A useful repair sentence often has three parts: the moment, the impact or possible misunderstanding, and the next intention. "When I said X, I realise it may have sounded like Y. I meant Z, and I will be clearer next time." Or, "I interrupted you earlier. I am sorry; I will make sure I leave space next time." Or, "I sent that too quickly and it read abruptly. I meant to be concise, not dismissive." These sentences are plain because plainness builds trust. They do not dramatise the repair. They complete it.

After repair, the hardest part may be stopping. The mind wants to monitor the response. Did they accept it warmly enough? Did they use punctuation that suggests irritation? Did they reply too quickly or too slowly? Are they acting normal? The replay may simply move from the original moment to the repair itself. This is why repair needs closure. Once you have made a proportionate repair, your next task is not to control their response. It is to allow the relationship to receive the repair in its own time.

This can feel vulnerable. Repair places something into the open. The other person may respond warmly, briefly, later, awkwardly, or not at all. That uncertainty is real. But uncertainty after a clean repair does not mean the repair failed. It means you have done your part and the rest is no longer fully yours. If you keep chasing certainty, the repair becomes a new loop.

Sometimes the best repair action is behaviour over time. A person who repeatedly interrupts does not repair the pattern through one perfect apology. They repair it by pausing, listening, and changing the rhythm of future conversations. A person who often sends abrupt messages does not repair the pattern through long self-explanations. They repair it by adding clarity and warmth before sending. A person who avoids difficult conversations does not repair trust by promising to be different. They repair it by showing up more directly. Behaviour is the proof that the lesson has moved from mind to life.

This is where repair becomes liberating rather than punishing. The replay says, "Replay until you feel safe." Repair says, "Do the next clean thing." The replay keeps you inside imagined reactions. Repair returns you to reality. The replay seeks perfect emotional certainty. Repair accepts human uncertainty and acts with care anyway.

Not every repair will be received as you hope. That is part of the risk. You may clarify and the other person may still feel hurt. You may apologise and they may need time. You may try to reconnect and find that the relationship has changed. Repair is not control. It is an offer of responsibility. Its value is not measured only by whether it instantly restores comfort. Its value is that it aligns your action with your values.

There will also be moments when you choose not to repair because the criteria are not met. No clear impact. No meaningful ongoing relationship. No feasible next step. Or the only action available would be reassurance-seeking dressed as care. In those cases, not repairing is not avoidance. It is restraint. It says, "I have reviewed this fairly. I am not going to make another person responsible for settling a feeling that belongs to me." That restraint is a mature repair of a different kind: it repairs your relationship with your own attention.

The mind may object. It may say, "But what if they misunderstood?" Perhaps they did. But repair cannot be based on every imaginable misunderstanding. It must be based on reasonable evidence and proportionate responsibility. If later evidence appears, you can respond then. You do not need to pre-empt every possible interpretation before it exists.

Choosing repair actions is therefore an exercise in disciplined care. Care enough to look. Care enough to act when action is needed. Care enough not to over-act when anxiety wants relief. Care enough to let a small moment stay small. Care enough to let repair be simple.

The replay wants certainty, but repair requires judgement. The replay wants perfection, but repair requires proportion. The replay wants to keep asking whether you are safe, acceptable, forgiven, understood. Repair asks a cleaner question: "What, if anything, would help this situation now?"

Answer that question honestly. If there is clear impact, an ongoing relationship, and a feasible next step, take the step. Make it plain. Make it respectful. Make it no larger than it needs to be. Then stop repairing and let the action stand.

Simple Apology Language

A good apology is often much shorter than the replay wants it to be.

When the mind is looping, apology can become inflated. You do not simply want to acknowledge what happened; you want to remove every possible doubt about your intention, every possible negative impression, every trace of awkwardness, every risk that someone might still think poorly of you. The apology grows because the anxiety grows. A sentence becomes a paragraph. A paragraph becomes an essay. The repair becomes less about the other person's experience and more about trying to secure emotional relief.

This is why simple apology language matters. It protects the apology from becoming another form of rumination. A clean apology completes the social loop. It does not reopen the entire scene for another hearing. It says what needs to be said, owns what needs to be owned, and leaves room for the other person to receive it without being burdened by your panic.

The mind often distrusts simplicity after a mistake. It says, "That is not enough." It argues that a short apology will sound careless, cold, or insincere. It insists that you must add context, explain your intention, describe how bad you feel, prove that this is not who you are, promise that you have been thinking about it, and make sure the other person knows every detail of your internal remorse. Some of that may feel honest. Much of it may be unnecessary.

An apology is not measured by volume. It is measured by clarity, ownership, proportion, and follow-through.

The foundation is plain: name what you did, acknowledge the impact or possible impact, and state the repair or adjustment. That is enough for many ordinary situations. "I interrupted you earlier. I am sorry. I will slow down next time." This does not dramatise the moment. It does not ask the other person to reassure you. It does not explain at length why you interrupted. It owns the behaviour and points towards change.

Simple language works because it respects the other person's position. When someone has been affected, they do not usually need a tour of your inner courtroom. They need to know that you saw the behaviour, understood why it mattered, and intend to respond differently. Excessive explanation can shift the emotional labour onto them. They may feel pressed to say, "It is fine," not because they are ready, but because your distress has entered the room and now needs managing.

This is one of the hidden dangers of over-apologising. It can look humble while quietly seeking reassurance. The words may say, "I am sorry," but the emotional request underneath may be, "Please tell me I am not bad." That request is understandable. Shame is painful, and reassurance can feel like air. But if the apology is being used mainly to discharge your anxiety, it may stop serving the repair. The other person becomes a witness to your self-punishment rather than the receiver of your accountability.

A simple apology keeps the focus where it belongs. Not on your identity. Not on your suffering. Not on a long defence of your character. On the moment, the impact, and the next action.

There are times when intention should be named, but it must be named carefully. Intention can clarify without excusing. It can help close the gap between what you meant and what landed. The mistake is using intention as a shield: "I am sorry you felt that way, but I did not mean it like that." This wording often fails because it places the discomfort back on the other person and rushes to defend the speaker. It may be factually true that you did not intend harm, but the apology becomes weaker when the defence takes over.

A cleaner version would be: "I meant to be direct, but I can see it may have sounded dismissive. I am sorry for that." This sentence holds both truths. It names the intention without letting intention erase impact. It does not grovel. It does not deny. It does not turn the moment into a trial. It simply recognises the gap.

When your intent was good but the impact was off, the best language is steady and specific. "I was trying to help, but I realise I stepped in too quickly." "I meant the joke lightly, but I can see it may have landed badly." "I intended to be brief, but the message read colder than I wanted." "I wanted to solve the issue, but I did not make enough room for your view." These sentences are useful because they do not demand that good intention cancel the need for care.

The word "but" needs caution. It can either clarify or erase. "I am sorry, but I was tired" often sounds like a withdrawal of responsibility. "I was tired, and I still should not have spoken that sharply" holds responsibility more cleanly. In apologies, "and" often does better work than "but" because it allows complexity without turning complexity into an excuse. "I was under pressure, and I should have paused." "I misunderstood the situation, and I see why that created confusion." "I meant to support you, and I can see I took over."

A simple apology should avoid making the other person responsible for judging your worth. Phrases such as "I am such a terrible person," "I do not know why anyone puts up with me," or "I feel awful, please forgive me" may be emotionally sincere, but they can place pressure on the other person to comfort you. The apology becomes crowded. Instead of addressing the behaviour, it asks for rescue from shame.

A stronger apology stays adult. "I am sorry I spoke over you." "I am sorry I dismissed that too quickly." "I am sorry I did not reply sooner." "I am sorry my message was abrupt." These sentences are not grand, but they are clean. They do not collapse. They do not perform. They leave space for the other person's response.

It is also wise to avoid vague apologies when a specific one is available. "Sorry for everything" may sound intense, but it is often unclear. "Sorry if I was annoying" is usually too self-focused and uncertain. "Sorry if you were offended" can sound dismissive because it makes the other person's reaction the problem. A specific apology says, "Sorry I cut you off earlier." Or, "Sorry I made that comment before I had the full context." Or, "Sorry I put you on the spot." Specificity communicates attention. It shows that you are not trying to escape discomfort with a blanket statement.

At the same time, not every apology needs to become heavy. For minor social moments, lightness is appropriate. "I realised I interrupted you earlier - sorry about that." "That came out more bluntly than I meant. Sorry." "I sent that too quickly; I should have added more context." These are small bridges. They allow the relationship to continue without dragging the moment into unnecessary drama.

Proportion is essential. A small misstep needs a small apology. A larger impact needs more care. A repeated pattern needs behaviour change. The replay often struggles with proportion because the internal feeling may be much larger than the external issue. You may feel deep shame over a minor awkwardness. That does not mean the apology should match the shame. It should match the situation.

This is where simple language becomes protective. It stops shame from writing the apology. Shame writes long, apologetic, self-erasing messages because it wants to be absolved. Responsibility writes clear sentences because it wants to repair. There is a world of difference between "I am so, so sorry, I have been spiralling about this all day and I feel terrible because I never meant to make you uncomfortable" and "I realised my comment may have put you on the spot. I am sorry; that was not fair." The second sentence is stronger because it is less burdened.

A good apology also knows when to stop. Once you have named the behaviour, acknowledged impact, and stated the adjustment, do not keep adding layers unless the situation genuinely requires them. The urge to continue may be anxiety, not care. It may feel as if one more sentence will make the apology safer, but often it only makes it heavier. Stopping is part of the repair. It shows that you trust the other person to receive the apology without being managed.

After apologising, the replay may shift from the original mistake to the apology itself. "Was that too short?" "Did I sound cold?" "Should I have said more?" "Why have they not replied?" This is predictable. The mind is still looking for certainty. A simple apology needs a closing boundary: "I have apologised clearly. I do not need to revise it unless new information appears." Without that boundary, the apology becomes another object of mental rewinding.

Apology language should also be chosen according to the relationship. With a close friend, warmth may be natural. With a colleague, clarity and professionalism may matter more. With someone you have hurt more deeply, patience and openness may be needed. With a minor awkwardness, brevity may be kindest. The principle remains the same: say enough to own your part, not so much that the apology becomes a demand for reassurance.

There are situations where the best apology includes an invitation, but the invitation should not be manipulative. "I am sorry I spoke sharply earlier. I am open to talking about it if you would like." This gives the other person room. It does not force an immediate emotional resolution. It does not insist they respond in a way that soothes you. It simply keeps the door open.

There are also times when an apology should not include pressure for forgiveness. Forgiveness is not a receipt you are owed because you issued the correct words. The other person may need time. They may accept briefly. They may not respond as warmly as you hope. That uncertainty is uncomfortable, but it is part of real repair. Your task is to apologise well, not to control the emotional outcome.

When the replay demands perfect apology language, remember that perfection is not the aim. Sincerity and clarity are. A flawed but honest apology is often better than an endlessly polished one that never gets sent. The mind may spend hours trying to craft a sentence that cannot be misunderstood. Such a sentence does not exist. Human beings can misunderstand anything. The goal is not to remove all risk. The goal is to speak responsibly.

A simple apology might follow this pattern: "I am sorry I did X. I can see it may have affected Y. I will do Z next time." For example: "I am sorry I interrupted you in the meeting. I can see it made it harder for you to finish your point. I will pause next time." This is plain enough to use under stress. It is also complete enough to be meaningful.

For intent-impact gaps, the pattern can be: "I meant X, but I can see it landed as Y. I am sorry. I will Z." For example: "I meant to be concise, but I can see the message landed as abrupt. I am sorry. I will add more context next time." Again, no drama. No self-trial. No demand for comfort. Just ownership.

For small awkwardness, the pattern can be lighter: "That came out more sharply than I meant. Sorry about that." Or, "I realised I jumped in quickly there. Sorry." These apologies are useful because they do not inflate the moment. They show awareness without making the other person responsible for reassuring you.

For practical errors, apology should be paired with correction: "I am sorry I sent the wrong version. I have attached the correct one now." Or, "I am sorry I missed that detail. I have updated it." In practical situations, repair often matters more than emotional explanation. Fix the issue. Keep the apology clean. Do not make the recipient wade through your guilt before they get the solution.

For repeated behaviour, apology must not be used as a substitute for change. "I am sorry I keep cancelling late" is weaker if nothing changes. A stronger version is: "I am sorry I cancelled late again. I know that affects your planning. I am going to stop agreeing to times until I know I can make them." Here the apology becomes credible because it includes a behavioural boundary.

Simple apology language also helps you avoid the trap of apology as self-punishment. You are not apologising to prove you are ashamed enough. You are apologising to acknowledge reality and repair trust where possible. Once that has been done, further punishment does not improve the apology. It only extends the replay.

The most effective apologies often leave dignity intact on both sides. You do not grovel. You do not defend. You do not minimise. You do not dramatise. You stand in the truth of the moment and speak from there. This steadiness can feel unfamiliar if you are used to replaying mistakes as moral emergencies, but it is a more respectful way to relate.

The person receiving the apology should not have to rescue you from your own words. They should be free to accept, discuss, decline, or take time. A clean apology gives them that freedom. It does not crowd the space with your fear of being seen badly.

After the apology, return to closure. "Apology made. My part is handled." That sentence may feel uncomfortable if the other person has not replied yet. Still, it matters. Without closure, the mind will keep monitoring for proof that the apology worked. You may reread it, revise it mentally, imagine their reaction, and begin another loop. The social loop has been completed as far as your part allows. The emotional loop must not be allowed to take its place.

Simple apology language is not simple because the situation is always simple. It is simple because clarity is kind. It lets responsibility speak without panic. It gives repair a clean shape. It reduces the chance that shame will turn an apology into a performance. It helps the mind stop rehearsing and complete the human task in front of it.

When a repair is needed, do not ask, "How can I say this so perfectly that I never feel uncertain again?" Ask, "What is the clearest honest sentence that owns my part and respects the other person?" Say that. Then let the apology stand.

Accepting No Action

Sometimes the most responsible response is not to send the message, not to clarify, not to apologise, not to reopen the conversation, not to check the thread again. Sometimes the healthiest move is to let the moment remain slightly unfinished in your feelings while being complete in reality. This can feel deeply uncomfortable to a replay-prone mind because anxiety often mistakes discomfort for duty. It says, "If I still feel uneasy, there must be something left to do."

But unease is not always unfinished business. It may be embarrassment moving through the body. It may be the ache of uncertainty. It may be the mind adjusting to the fact that you cannot know exactly what another person thought. It may be the residue of shame after a small social awkwardness. If you treat every trace of discomfort as a command to act, life becomes crowded with unnecessary repairs. You begin managing feelings by managing other people, and that is a heavy, unstable way to live.

Accepting no action does not mean ignoring a real impact. It does not mean becoming careless, cold, proud, or avoidant. It means making a clear distinction between a situation that requires response and a feeling that requires tolerance. There are moments when repair is needed. There are moments when apology is right. There are moments when clarification protects trust. But there are also moments when action would not serve the situation; it would only serve the urgent wish to feel certain, liked, forgiven, or safe.

This is where many replays become deceptive. The mind presents action as care. "Send one more message." "Explain what you meant." "Check whether they are annoyed." "Apologise just in case." These suggestions can sound considerate, but the motive matters. Are you acting because there is clear impact and a feasible next step, or because you cannot bear not knowing what someone thinks? Are you repairing a relationship, or trying to extract reassurance from it? Are you making something clearer, or trying to make yourself feel less exposed?

No action becomes appropriate when the replay has no new information, no clear evidence of harm, and no useful step that would improve the situation. Perhaps the conversation was mildly awkward, but not damaging. Perhaps the message was imperfect, but understandable. Perhaps your joke did not get the reaction you hoped for, but there is no sign anyone was hurt. Perhaps someone replied briefly, but there is no actual indication of anger. In these cases, another message may not repair anything. It may simply transfer your anxiety into the interaction.

This is especially true when the desired action is designed to close a gap that cannot be closed by you alone. You cannot force someone to reveal their private interpretation. You cannot make a delayed reply arrive faster by rereading the thread. You cannot guarantee that your tone was received exactly as intended. You cannot control whether another person remembers a moment that you are still mentally replaying. Accepting no action means accepting the boundary between your responsibility and another person's mind.

That boundary is not easy. A replay often tells you that if you care, you should keep checking. But care without boundary becomes intrusion, over-explanation, or self-abandonment. You may begin treating every silence as something you must fix, every small awkwardness as a debt, every possible misunderstanding as an emergency. Over time, this can make relationships feel fragile, as though they cannot survive ordinary human imperfection. Strong relationships often need repair, yes, but they also need room. Not every moment has to be processed aloud.

There is a quiet dignity in letting a small thing be small. If you slightly stumbled over your words, the next right action may be to continue speaking normally in future interactions. If you sent a message that was adequate but not beautifully phrased, the next right action may be to stop reopening it. If a conversation ended without perfect warmth, the next right action may be to allow the next natural contact to arrive. No action, when chosen clearly, is not passivity. It is restraint.

The mind may resist restraint because restraint leaves uncertainty alive. That is the real difficulty. If you apologise, you may get reassurance. If you clarify, you may feel briefly safer. If you check, you may gain a moment of relief. No action asks you to remain with the unanswered question. Did they notice? Did it matter? Are we fine? Was that awkward only to me? These questions may not settle immediately. Accepting no action means refusing to build a behaviour around the demand for instant settlement.

A useful test is to ask, "Would I still take this action if I already felt calm?" If the answer is yes, the action may be genuinely needed. If you would still apologise because you clearly interrupted, still clarify because the message genuinely lacked necessary context, still correct the practical mistake because it affects someone else, then the action has a real purpose. But if the action only seems necessary while your body is flooded with shame or anxiety, pause. The urgency may belong to the feeling, not the facts.

Another useful test is to ask, "What would this action ask of the other person?" A brief, appropriate apology asks little. A clear clarification asks little. But an anxious follow-up may ask the other person to soothe you, reassure you, confirm that you are still acceptable, or participate in a problem they did not experience as a problem. This does not make you bad for wanting comfort. It simply helps you see whether the proposed action is relationally fair.

No action can also be the correct choice when the moment has already been repaired enough. Many people continue acting after the repair is complete because the feeling has not gone away. They apologise, receive a neutral or kind response, then feel tempted to apologise again. They clarify, then want to clarify the clarification. They send the follow-up, then worry about the tone of the follow-up. At that point, action has stopped serving repair and started feeding the loop. The social task is done; the emotional residue remains. The next work is internal closure.

Accepting no action requires a sentence strong enough to hold the boundary. "No further action is needed." "This is discomfort, not a task." "I have reviewed this fairly." "I am not going to make another person manage my uncertainty." "The lesson is taken; the scene can close." The exact wording matters less than its honesty. The sentence should not deny concern. It should name completion. It should tell the mind that the absence of action is not neglect, but a deliberate decision.

The body may not believe this immediately. You may still feel the pull to check. Your hand may reach towards the phone. Your mind may produce another argument: "Just one short message." "Just one more look." "Just to be sure." This is the moment where no action becomes active. You are not merely failing to act; you are choosing not to feed the loop. You are practising the ability to feel uncertainty without converting it into behaviour.

This skill is vital because the replay system often learns through repetition. If every discomfort is answered with checking, apologising, clarifying, or reassurance-seeking, the mind learns that discomfort is dangerous and must be solved externally. If some discomfort is met with grounded restraint, the mind learns a different lesson: unease can be tolerated, and not every alarm requires response. That learning may be slow, but it is powerful.

There is a difference between avoidance and chosen no action. Avoidance is vague, tense, and unexamined. It refuses to look because looking feels threatening. Chosen no action is clear, reviewed, and bounded. It looks at the facts, considers impact, checks the controllable part, and decides that further response would not help. Avoidance says, "I do not want to deal with this." Chosen no action says, "I have dealt with this enough, and more action would be rumination in disguise."

The emotional texture is different too. Avoidance often leaves a sense of hiding. Chosen no action may still feel uncomfortable, but it has steadiness underneath it. You can say why you are not acting. You can name the evidence. You can identify the lesson. You can explain, at least to yourself, that the proposed action would be disproportionate. This clarity matters because the mind will try to accuse restraint of being neglect. You need to know the difference.

For example, suppose you made a comment in a group conversation and later worry it sounded less polished than you intended. No one reacted negatively. The conversation continued. There is no person to repair with, no clear impact, and no practical consequence. The replay may still insist that you looked foolish. Sending a message to someone afterwards saying, "Sorry if I sounded strange earlier," may not serve the group or the relationship. It may only export your embarrassment. The wiser action may be no action: take the lesson if there is one, then let the moment pass.

Or suppose a friend replies to your message with a brief "okay". Your mind hears coldness. You reread your message, searching for what you did wrong. There is no clear conflict, no question unanswered, no obvious harm. You could send, "Are you annoyed with me?" but that may be asking your friend to manage a fear created by ambiguity. No action might mean waiting, allowing the next natural exchange, and refusing to assign meaning to one short word. That is not indifference. It is proportion.

No action is hardest when your identity feels at stake. If you fear you appeared unkind, foolish, needy, blunt, or incompetent, the urge to repair may be intense because you are not only trying to fix the moment; you are trying to restore the image of yourself you prefer. This is human. But it is also risky. Actions taken to restore self-image often become excessive. They are driven less by the needs of the situation and more by the need to escape shame. Accepting no action means allowing your image to feel temporarily imperfect without rushing to polish it in someone else's eyes.

This is a mature form of self-respect. You are allowed to be imperfectly seen. You are allowed to have moments that are not beautifully explained. You are allowed to let other people think whatever they think, especially when there is no clear harm and no reasonable repair. This does not mean you stop caring. It means you stop trying to control every private interpretation of your existence.

A practical way to choose no action is to complete a short internal review. What happened, in observable terms? What do I know about the impact? What am I imagining? Is there an ongoing relationship that needs a bridge? Is there a feasible step that would serve the situation? If the answers point to no useful action, then the decision is made. Not because the feeling has disappeared, but because the facts do not justify further intervention.

Then pair the decision with a behavioural boundary. Do not leave "no action" as an abstract idea while continuing to reread, check, draft, delete, and mentally rehearse. No action means no further feeding of the loop. Close the thread. Put the phone down. Return to the task. Stand up. Wash the cup. Write one line of lesson if needed. Give the mind and body evidence that the scene has been closed.

The replay may return. When it does, do not reopen the full review. Repeat the decision: "No new evidence. No further action." This is not suppression. The thought may be present. The feeling may be present. But the behaviour is no longer being directed by the loop. The mind is being trained that repeated discomfort does not automatically reopen a settled decision.

There will, of course, be cases where new information arrives. Someone later says they were hurt. A misunderstanding becomes clear. A practical consequence appears. In that case, no action can change into action. That is not failure; it is responsiveness. The point is not to become rigid. The point is to stop acting on imagined evidence as if it were confirmed reality. New facts deserve attention. Old anxiety dressed as new urgency does not.

Accepting no action is also an act of trust in ordinary repair over time. Not every relational awkwardness needs a formal conversation. Sometimes warmth returns through the next normal interaction. Sometimes trust is maintained by behaving steadily rather than making the awkwardness larger. Sometimes the best evidence that a moment is over is that life continues. The replay may demand a special resolution, but the relationship may only need ordinary continuity.

This is important in close relationships. Constant repair attempts can make a bond feel permanently under review. If every small misstep becomes a discussion, every slight tension becomes a check-in, and every delayed response becomes a reassurance ritual, the relationship may begin to carry the weight of your rumination. Healthy connection needs honesty, but it also needs space to breathe. Letting small things pass is part of relational resilience.

In work settings, accepting no action can protect professionalism. A minor stumble in a meeting may not need a follow-up email. A slightly imperfect sentence may not need public correction. A moment of uncertainty may not need to be turned into a performance of apology. Sometimes the most professional move is to absorb the lesson privately and show the adjustment next time. Competence is not proven by explaining every imperfection. Often, it is proven by moving forward steadily.

The fear, of course, is that doing nothing means you are missing something. That fear cannot always be fully removed. You may have to live with a small possibility that someone interpreted the moment differently from how you intended. This is not a flaw in the method; it is the condition of human communication. There is no life in which every possible misunderstanding is prevented. There is only the practice of responding when there is enough reason to respond, and releasing when there is not.

No action becomes easier when you stop treating uncertainty as a debt. You do not owe the world a clarification for every possible interpretation. You do not owe anxiety a behaviour every time it produces a theory. You do not owe shame a performance of remorse when no clear harm has occurred. Your responsibility is to be honest, attentive, and willing to repair when repair is called for. It is not to chase every imagined reaction until you feel safe.

A helpful closing line is: "If real information appears, I can respond then." This sentence reassures the responsible part of the mind without feeding the loop. It does not say, "Nothing could be wrong." It says, "I do not need to act before the evidence exists." That is a strong boundary. It allows you to remain open without remaining entangled.

Accepting no action is therefore not the absence of skill. It is a skill. It is the ability to leave a scene alone after fair review. It is the ability to tolerate not knowing. It is the ability to choose restraint when anxiety wants performance. It is the ability to let a feeling pass through you without turning it into another message, another apology, another check, another attempt to control how you are seen.

The next time your mind says, "Do something," pause before obeying. Ask whether the situation needs action or the feeling wants relief. Ask whether the facts support repair or the replay is manufacturing urgency. Ask whether your proposed step would serve clarity, kindness, and responsibility, or merely ask someone else to soothe uncertainty that belongs inside you.

If action is needed, take it cleanly.

If no action is needed, let that be the action.

Handling Unresolved Responses

Few things feed a replay as efficiently as an unresolved response. You send a message, make an apology, offer a clarification, or ask a careful question, and then nothing comes back. Or something comes back, but it is brief, neutral, delayed, or hard to read. The mind moves quickly into the open space. It starts interpreting the silence, rereading the words, measuring the timing, imagining tone, and searching for proof that the social loop is complete.

Waiting is difficult because it removes the illusion of control. Before you send the message, the words are still yours. You can draft, edit, soften, clarify, delete, delay, or perfect. Once it is sent, the message belongs partly to the other person's world. They may read it while tired, busy, distracted, annoyed, calm, caring, indifferent, thoughtful, or overwhelmed. They may respond quickly, slowly, warmly, briefly, awkwardly, or not at all. The mind dislikes this transfer of control, so it tries to take control back through analysis.

This is why unresolved responses create such a strong urge to reread. Rereading feels like doing something. It gives the mind a task while you wait. You open the thread and inspect your wording. You notice one phrase that now seems too formal. Another that seems too casual. A line that could be misread. A punctuation mark that suddenly looks colder than you intended. The same message that seemed adequate when you sent it now appears full of hidden risk. The message has not changed. Your state has.

The danger is that the mind treats waiting as evidence. A slow reply becomes possible rejection. A short reply becomes possible irritation. A neutral phrase becomes possible distance. An unread message becomes possible avoidance. None of these meanings may be true. They are stories built in the absence of information. The less you know, the more the mind may invent. This is story-building: the attempt to fill the gap between fact and certainty with imagined explanation.

Story-building usually begins with a fact and then quietly adds fiction. Fact: they have not replied yet. Story: they are upset. Fact: their response was brief. Story: they are being cold. Fact: they said, "Okay." Story: they are disappointed and do not want to say it. Fact: they have read the message. Story: they are choosing to punish you with silence. The problem is not that these stories are impossible. The problem is that the mind often treats them as if they are already confirmed.

A waiting plan interrupts this process by deciding in advance how you will behave while the response remains unresolved. Without a plan, the mind keeps negotiating. Check now? Wait five more minutes? Reread once? Send another message? Ask if everything is all right? Delete the thread? Look again? Each decision becomes a fresh point of anxiety. A waiting plan removes repeated negotiation. It says, "This is what I will do, this is when I will check, and this is what I will not assume in the meantime."

The plan does not need to be complicated. In fact, it should not be. The more elaborate it becomes, the more it resembles rumination in a different outfit. A clean waiting plan has three parts: the next action, the checking boundary, and the meaning boundary. The next action is what you will do instead of hovering over the thread. The checking boundary is when, or how often, you will look. The meaning boundary is the story you refuse to assign without evidence.

For example, after sending a clarification, the plan might be: "I will put the phone down and work on the next task. I will check after I finish this task, not before. I will not decide that silence means anger." That is enough. It gives the body and mind a direction. It does not promise that the waiting will feel easy. It simply prevents waiting from becoming a continuous act of checking.

The meaning boundary is the most important part. Replays thrive when the mind is allowed to convert delay into interpretation. A slow reply does not automatically mean rejection. A brief reply does not automatically mean annoyance. A lack of warmth does not automatically mean the relationship is damaged. A message left unanswered does not automatically mean you have done something wrong. These statements are not forced reassurance. They are protection against false certainty.

There is a difference between saying, "Everything is definitely fine," and saying, "I do not have enough evidence to assign a negative meaning." The first may feel unbelievable. The second is disciplined and honest. You do not know yet. That is the truth. The mind may hate the truth because it leaves uncertainty in place, but uncertainty is still cleaner than a frightening story pretending to be knowledge.

Rereading often becomes the behaviour that keeps the loop alive. Each reread strengthens the idea that there is something hidden in the message to find. You may feel a brief moment of relief when the wording looks acceptable, but the relief rarely lasts. Soon the mind returns with a new concern. What about the tone? What about the timing? What about how they might read that one phrase? Checking trains the mind to seek reassurance from the same material that is making it anxious.

A better rule is to reread only for a clear purpose. If you are checking whether you included the correct information, that is practical. If you are checking because you hope the message will finally feel safe, that is rumination. Practical checking has an end. Reassurance checking usually asks for another round. When you notice that the purpose is emotional relief rather than useful information, the waiting plan should take over.

Unresolved responses are also hard because they awaken the desire to send one more message. The mind argues that a follow-up will settle everything. Sometimes a follow-up is appropriate. If essential information was missing, send it. If your wording was genuinely unclear, clarify once. If a repair was incomplete, complete it cleanly. But if the follow-up is designed to ask, indirectly, "Are we okay?" then pause. That may be reassurance-seeking rather than repair.

One follow-up can clarify. Repeated follow-ups often intensify. They may make the situation feel larger to the other person than it was. They may shift the focus from the original issue to your anxiety about the issue. They may create the very awkwardness you were trying to prevent. A useful follow-up should serve the situation. It should not merely serve the panic of waiting.

A clear waiting plan protects the relationship as well as the mind. It prevents anxious behaviour from entering the space where patience would have been better. It stops the phone from becoming a measuring device for your worth. It allows the other person time to respond from their own life, not according to the emergency your nervous system has created. This is not easy, especially when the relationship matters. But respect includes allowing other people to have their own timing.

Slow replies have many possible meanings. People are busy. They need time to think. They do not know what to say yet. They are dealing with something unrelated. They saw the message at an inconvenient moment. They intend to reply later. They are tired. They are avoidant. They are upset. Any of these may be possible in a given situation. The replay selects the one that feels most threatening and calls it intuition. Sometimes intuition is useful. Sometimes it is anxiety with a confident voice.

The way to test it is not by replaying harder. Ask what is factually known. Has the person said they are upset? Has there been a clear change in behaviour beyond this delay? Is there a practical reason they may not have replied? Is the issue urgent, or merely uncomfortable? What would a proportionate person do with the information available? These questions bring the mind back to facts without demanding instant certainty.

Ambiguous replies need the same discipline. A response such as "Fine," "Okay," "No worries," or "Sure" can become a replay trigger because tone is missing. The mind supplies tone according to fear. It hears coldness, irritation, dismissal, distance. Sometimes that may be accurate; often it is unknown. Before responding to the imagined tone, check the actual content. What did they say? Did they ask for anything? Did they set a boundary? Did they invite further discussion? Did they give evidence of harm? If not, the next step may be no step.

This is difficult because the body may already be reacting as if the worst interpretation is true. You may feel heat, pressure, agitation, or a strong urge to repair. That bodily urgency does not have to decide the meaning. A useful sentence is: "My body is reacting to uncertainty; uncertainty is not evidence." This keeps the feeling in view without allowing it to write the story.

A waiting plan should also include what you will do with your body. Waiting cannot remain purely mental, because the loop will keep pulling attention back to the thread. Put the phone somewhere less reachable. Turn it over. Close the app. Stand up. Return to a task with a defined endpoint. Make tea. Walk to another room. Write the next paragraph. Finish the practical thing already in front of you. The body needs evidence that life has not paused until the response arrives.

Choose a task that is concrete, not vague. "I will distract myself" is weak because the replay can travel inside distraction. "I will wash the dishes and then check once" is stronger. "I will finish this document section before looking again" is stronger. "I will go for a walk without opening the thread" is stronger. The task gives attention somewhere specific to land, which reduces the mind's tendency to drift back into imagined meanings.

The checking boundary must be realistic. If you set an impossible boundary, such as never checking again when the matter genuinely matters, the mind may rebel. If you set no boundary, the mind may check compulsively. A balanced plan might be, "I will check after lunch," "I will check when I finish this work block," or "I will not check again tonight." The precise timing depends on the situation, but the principle is the same: checking should be chosen, not compulsive.

For emotionally charged messages, it can help to decide beforehand what would justify another action. For example: "If they ask a question, I will answer. If they say they were hurt, I will respond with care. If they do not reply tonight, I will not send another message. If the issue still matters tomorrow, I will review it once in daylight." This reduces the mind's tendency to invent new rules while activated.

Daylight matters more than people admit. At night, unresolved responses can feel larger because fatigue weakens proportion. The mind may treat silence as urgent simply because there are fewer distractions and the body is tired. A good waiting plan may include a night boundary: "No interpretation after bedtime." This is not denial. It is respect for the fact that a tired mind is often a poor judge of social meaning.

When the reply finally arrives, the replay may not end immediately. The mind may begin analysing the response. Was it warm enough? Why that wording? Why no emoji? Why only one sentence? Why did they take that long? This is the loop relocating. The waiting plan should extend into receiving. Read the response for content before tone. What is being communicated? Is there a request? Is there a repair to continue? Is there evidence of concern? Or is the mind searching for emotional certainty that no reply can fully provide?

A response does not need to feel perfectly reassuring to be sufficient. People often reply in ordinary, imperfect ways. They may be brief because they are busy, not because they are cold. They may not match your emotional intensity because they were not living inside the same replay. This can feel disorientating. You have spent hours in the scene; they may have spent seconds. Their reply may seem too small for the size of your anxiety. That does not mean it is inadequate. It may mean the replay inflated the event.

There are, of course, times when an unresolved response genuinely signals something that needs attention. Someone may be upset and not yet ready to say so. A relationship may be strained. A work issue may need follow-up. A silence may matter in context. The point is not to deny this. The point is to avoid acting as though every silence already means the worst. If real evidence appears, respond to it. Until then, do not make imagined evidence your master.

Handling unresolved responses also requires tolerating the discomfort of being unable to complete the social loop alone. This is hard for responsible people. They want closure. They want mutual understanding. They want the other person to confirm that the bridge is intact. But closure sometimes arrives slowly, indirectly, or not in the form you prefer. You may need to complete your part before the whole exchange feels complete.

That means saying, "My message was clear enough." "My apology was made." "My clarification was sent." "My part is complete for now." These statements are not attempts to control the other person's response. They are boundaries around your own behaviour. They remind you that you are not required to keep working on something that is no longer fully yours to work on.

The mind will still offer stories. It may say the delay is meaningful. It may say the short reply proves distance. It may say the silence is punishment. Treat these as stories, not instructions. A story is allowed to appear. It is not allowed to decide your next behaviour without evidence. Return to the facts. Return to the plan. Return to the next concrete task.

A useful formula is: fact, story, boundary. Fact: "They have not replied." Story: "My mind says they are annoyed." Boundary: "I will not assign that meaning without evidence; I will check after I finish this task." This formula is plain enough to use when activated. It prevents the replay from pretending that its interpretation is the same as reality.

If the waiting becomes intense, bring attention back to the body. Unresolved responses often create physical agitation: tight chest, restless hands, shallow breathing, a pull towards the phone. Name the sensation before obeying it. "This is waiting anxiety." "This is uncertainty in my body." "This is the urge to check." The urge may rise and fall. You do not have to treat it as a command. An urge is a wave, not a law.

The deeper lesson is that uncertainty after communication is not a failure. It is part of communication. Once words leave you, they enter another person's timing, attention, and interpretation. You can make your words respectful, clear, and proportionate. You can repair when needed. You can ask when asking is appropriate. You cannot remove every gap. The replay wants a world without gaps. Real relationships have gaps, and maturity includes not filling all of them with fear.

A good waiting plan turns passive waiting into active steadiness. You are not helplessly suspended until the reply arrives. You are choosing how to behave while you do not know. You are deciding when to check. You are refusing to assign meanings prematurely. You are keeping your body and attention connected to the present. You are letting the other person have their response without forcing your anxiety into the space between you.

The next time a message remains unanswered or a reply arrives with ambiguous tone, do not hand the silence a script. Write the plan before the story writes itself. What will you do now? When will you check? What meaning will you refuse to assign without evidence? Those three decisions may not remove the discomfort, but they will stop the discomfort from becoming the author of the next scene.

Chapter 8
Night-Time Replays and Sleep

At 2am, an ordinary mistake can acquire the weight of a verdict. The house is quiet, the room is dark, and the mind returns to a moment from earlier: a rushed answer, a message that now seems too blunt, a passing comment that might have sounded careless. In daylight, the scene had edges. It was awkward, perhaps, but manageable. In the dark, it expands. The sentence repeats. The possible meanings multiply. The body tightens under the duvet as if the conversation is happening again.

Nothing new has occurred. No one has appeared at the door with evidence. No fresh information has arrived. Yet the mind begins its hearing. It replays the tone, then edits the wording, then imagines the other person's reaction, then rehearses a repair that cannot reasonably be sent at this hour. The bedside table becomes the edge of a small courtroom. You are tired, but the mind is suddenly alert, convinced that the scene must be solved before sleep can return.

Night has a strange talent for enlarging unfinished material. During the day, attention is held by movement, noise, light, tasks, people, decisions, and practical demands. At night, much of that scaffolding falls away. There is less to interrupt the loop, less present-time evidence to balance the story, less energy for perspective. Fatigue does not make the replay wiser. It often makes it more convincing. The mind, deprived of ordinary anchors, treats old discomfort as if it has become newly urgent.

The central tension is that bedtime is meant to be a descent into rest, but it can become an opening for review. The mind uses quiet as processing space. That is not wrong in itself. Many people naturally sort the day when the day stops moving. The difficulty begins when processing turns into rumination, when the mind does not simply place the day in order but reopens the same scene again and again, demanding certainty at the very time you have the least capacity to judge clearly.

The cost is not only lost sleep. Night-time replays can change the emotional memory of the event itself. A minor mistake reviewed in a tired, activated state can feel more serious the next morning because it has been rehearsed with fear. The body remembers the night's alarm and attaches it to the scene. What was once a small discomfort becomes a familiar threat. This is how a loop can become chronic: not because the original event deserves endless review, but because the mind repeatedly practises treating it as unfinished.

There is also a cruel secondary loop. You replay, then you worry that you are not sleeping. You worry that tomorrow will be harder. You become frustrated with yourself for still thinking. Then the body becomes more alert because frustration is arousing. The original scene now has company: anxiety about sleep itself. The harder you fight for instant calm, the more awake you may become. The problem is no longer only the replay; it is the struggle around the replay.

A better night begins before the difficult hour arrives. The mind needs a way to put the day down deliberately, not vaguely. A short evening shutdown can give unfinished material a place to land: capture what needs remembering, close what has already been reviewed, and cue the body towards sleep. A brief parking note can be enough to reassure the mind that it does not need to keep holding the same concern in active memory. The note is not a diary for rumination. It is a small shelf for tomorrow's legitimate tasks and today's completed lessons.

When the replay has already started in the dark, the task changes. Debate is rarely the best tool at 3am. The tired mind is too easily persuaded by fear, and the body may be too activated to benefit from another round of analysis. The wiser movement is smaller: label the replay, soften the body where possible, and redirect attention gently towards present safety. A low-light action may help when lying still has become a battleground. The aim is not to force sleep as proof of success. The aim is to stop feeding the fight that keeps sleep away.

So the question at night is not, "Can I solve this perfectly before morning?" It is more practical and more merciful: "Is this a real task for now, or is my tired mind trying to process discomfort in the dark?" The answer will determine whether the night becomes another courtroom, or whether the scene can be parked, closed, and left outside the bedroom door.

Why Replays Worsen at Night

Night changes the scale of things. A moment that seemed mildly uncomfortable at lunchtime can feel severe in the dark. A sentence you barely noticed while the day was moving can return with a sharper edge. A reply you were waiting for can seem colder, slower, more meaningful. The mind that could hold proportion at four in the afternoon may struggle to hold it at two in the morning.

This does not mean the night has revealed the truth. It often means the night has removed the ordinary supports that helped you stay balanced.

During the day, attention is carried by structure. There are conversations, tasks, meals, noise, light, movement, obligations, and practical interruptions. Even if a replay starts, something may pull you back: a person asking a question, a message requiring an answer, a bus arriving, a kettle boiling, a meeting beginning. The world keeps providing evidence that life is larger than the scene in your head.

At night, much of that evidence disappears. The room is quiet. The body is still. The phone may be close. There is less external input to compete with the replay. The mind has more open space, and open space can be useful when it leads to calm processing. But when the mind is carrying unresolved social discomfort, that space can become a stage. The old sentence walks back on. The silence returns. The imagined reaction appears. The scene begins again.

Fatigue makes this worse. A tired mind is not usually a fair judge of emotional meaning. It has less patience, less perspective, and less ability to hold complexity. During the day, you may be able to say, "That was awkward, but probably not serious." At night, the same event may become, "What if I have damaged the relationship?" Fatigue narrows the mind's range. It makes the most threatening interpretation feel strangely plausible.

This is why night-time replays often sound more absolute than daytime reflections. The mind becomes less interested in nuance. It is more likely to collapse uncertainty into danger, awkwardness into failure, delay into rejection, and regret into self-criticism. The replay does not become more accurate because it is louder. It becomes louder because the system is tired, under-stimulated, and searching for resolution without the resources needed to assess the situation well.

Quiet also changes the body. During the day, bodily signals may be absorbed into movement and activity. At night, every sensation can feel amplified. A tight chest, a warm face, a restless stomach, a quickened pulse, or a general sense of unease may become difficult to ignore. The mind then tries to explain the sensation. It looks backward through the day and finds a possible cause: the awkward comment, the meeting, the message, the disagreement. The body says, "I am activated," and the mind translates it as, "Something must be wrong."

That translation can start the loop. You wake with discomfort, then search for a story. Once the story is found, the replay gives the discomfort a target. Now the body and mind begin feeding each other. The thought creates more tension. The tension makes the thought feel more serious. The seriousness demands further review. The review keeps the body awake. What began as a sensation becomes an investigation.

Bedtime also has a natural tendency to gather unfinished material. When activity stops, the mind may attempt to sort what has been left open. This can be helpful when the day contains practical loose ends: something to remember, a task to complete, a message to send later. But a replay-prone mind often treats emotional uncertainty as if it were an unfinished task. It says, "We cannot sleep until this is understood." The problem is that some of what it wants to understand cannot be fully known, especially at night. You cannot know exactly what someone thought. You cannot repair a relationship by mentally rewriting a conversation in the dark. You cannot force tomorrow's reply to arrive by rehearsing what you will say if it does not.

The mind still tries.

A small mistake becomes the perfect night-time object because it is unfinished enough to invite thought and painful enough to hold attention. Imagine a minor workplace moment. Earlier in the day, you answered a question more sharply than you intended. No one complained. The meeting continued. You made a note to be warmer next time and carried on. Then, in the middle of the night, the sentence returns. It sounds harsher now. You remember one person looking down. You wonder whether that look meant discomfort. You imagine them repeating your words later. You draft a message in your head, then reject it as too much. You decide no action is needed, then doubt the decision. Sleep becomes impossible because the mind has mistaken a small uncertainty for an urgent assignment.

The night gives the replay ideal conditions: stillness, darkness, tiredness, and the absence of fresh evidence. There is nothing new to learn, so the mind manufactures new angles. Perhaps it was not only what you said, but how you said it. Perhaps the timing was worse than you realised. Perhaps your apology, if you sent one, sounded awkward. Perhaps saying nothing looks careless. Each possibility feels like progress because it is new to the loop, but it is not new information. It is only another shape of uncertainty.

This is one reason night-time analysis so often backfires. The mind believes it is solving, but it is usually rehearsing. It returns to the same facts with less energy and more fear. It asks for decisions at a time when the body needs safety, not strategy. It demands moral clarity when the nervous system is already strained. The result is rarely a clean answer. More often, the result is a longer night and a heavier morning.

The fight against the replay can become as wakeful as the replay itself. You notice the thought and become irritated. You tell yourself to stop. You worry that you will be tired tomorrow. You calculate how much sleep you are losing. You judge yourself for still caring. Now there are two problems: the original scene and the anxiety about being awake with it. The mind becomes caught between replay and resistance. Both keep the system alert.

This secondary struggle matters. Many people believe the goal at night is to force the replay away so sleep can return immediately. But force creates monitoring. You check whether the thought has gone. You check whether you feel sleepy. You check whether your body is relaxing. Each check wakes the system a little more. Sleep does not respond well to being chased. It usually comes more easily when the mind stops treating wakefulness as an emergency.

Night-time replays can become chronic when the mind learns that bed is the place where unresolved material gets unlimited attention. If you repeatedly conduct emotional investigations in the dark, the body may begin to associate night with review. The bed becomes not only a place of rest, but a place of mental hearings. The mind lies down and begins scanning: What have we not solved? What could go wrong? What did we miss? What still feels unfinished?

This pattern is not a personal failure. It is a learned association. The mind has practised turning quiet into review. The body has practised becoming alert in response. The good news is that learned associations can be retrained, but not through self-attack. Telling yourself that you are ridiculous for replaying at night only adds more threat. The system needs a different message: night is not the time for full investigation.

This does not mean concerns must be ignored. Some worries are real. Some lessons matter. Some repairs need to be made. The point is timing. A tired mind in a dark room is rarely the best place to decide the meaning of a socially charged moment. If something genuinely needs attention, it can be captured for daylight. If no action is available until morning, the night does not become more useful by being sacrificed to rehearsal.

A useful distinction is between processing and solving. At night, the mind may process fragments of the day. That is normal. A memory may drift through. A feeling may rise. A loose end may appear. Solving is different. Solving demands a verdict, a plan, a perfect wording, a final interpretation. Night-time solving often turns into rumination because the conditions are poor for clear judgement. The mind is tired, the body is still, and the evidence is incomplete.

When a replay worsens at night, it is often because the mind is trying to achieve daytime certainty with night-time resources. It wants the clarity of a calm conversation, the steadiness of a rested body, and the information that only time or another person can provide. None of these is available at two in the morning. So the mind uses what it does have: memory, imagination, fear, and repetition. That combination feels productive, but it is usually circular.

The physical stillness of bed can also make the replay feel inescapable. During the day, you can stand up, walk, wash a cup, step outside, begin a task, or speak to someone. At night, you may remain still, hoping sleep will arrive, while the mind continues moving. The body becomes passive while attention becomes frantic. This mismatch can make the replay feel more powerful than it is. Sometimes a small, gentle physical reset is needed, not to "solve" the replay, but to remind the body that the present is safe and that the scene is not happening now.

Another reason replays worsen at night is that darkness reduces perspective. This is not mystical; it is practical. In darkness, the world is smaller. The ceiling, the pillow, the sound of breathing, the glow of a screen if you reach for it. There are fewer cues of ordinary life. The mind can mistake this smallness for importance. The replay fills the available mental room. A thought that would have occupied one corner of the day now seems to occupy everything.

Screens can intensify the pattern. When a replay involves a message, the urge to check at night is especially strong. The phone offers the illusion of control: reread the thread, inspect the wording, see whether a reply has arrived, search for a clue. But checking wakes the mind further. It reintroduces the social world at the very moment the body needs to disengage from it. It also teaches the loop that night-time discomfort should be answered with digital investigation. That lesson is costly.

A night replay often requires less content work and more boundary work. The boundary is simple: not now, not here, not by rumination. This does not deny the issue. It places it in time. If there is a lesson, capture it briefly. If there is a task, park it for morning. If there is only anxiety, label it as anxiety. The bedroom does not need to become a planning room, a courtroom, a confessional, and a rehearsal space all at once.

Normalising night-time replays is important because shame makes them worse. Many people feel embarrassed by how irrational their thoughts seem at night. They may wake in the morning and wonder why the issue felt so enormous. This does not mean they are unstable or weak. It means the conditions of the night distorted the scale. A thought can feel convincing in one state and exaggerated in another. The wise response is not to obey every night thought, but to understand the state in which it appeared.

A helpful rule is to mistrust the urgency of night-time conclusions. Not every night thought is false, but many are poorly timed. "I must send a message now." "I have ruined everything." "They definitely think badly of me." "I will never fix this." These conclusions often carry the stamp of fatigue. They may not deserve action. They may deserve noting, softening, and revisiting in daylight if they still matter.

The aim is not to make the night perfectly thought-free. That is unrealistic and would create another pressure. The aim is to stop the mind from turning every thought into a case. A memory can appear without being analysed. A feeling can rise without being justified by a replay. A concern can be parked without being solved. Wakefulness can be uncomfortable without becoming a battle.

There is mercy in postponement when postponement is honest. "This is not for now" is not avoidance if no useful action can be taken in the dark. It is respect for timing. Many things that feel urgent at night become clearer after rest, food, daylight, movement, and ordinary contact with the world. The mind may object that waiting is dangerous. Usually, waiting is what allows proportion to return.

The next time a replay worsens at night, notice the conditions before trusting the conclusion. You are tired. It is quiet. The world is small. The body may be activated. There is little new evidence. The mind is trying to process unfinished material with limited resources. That does not make the feeling unreal, but it does make the interpretation suspect.

Night does not always reveal what matters most. Sometimes it simply turns down the world until one thought sounds like the only voice left. The task is to recognise the acoustics of the dark, not mistake the echo for truth.

A Shutdown Routine

Sleep rarely begins at the pillow. It begins with the way the day is put down.

For a mind that replays, bedtime can become a doorway into unfinished material. The body is ready to stop, but the mind is still carrying loose threads: a conversation that felt slightly off, a message that has not been answered, a task that was not completed, a sentence that now seems poorly chosen. If those threads are not placed somewhere, the mind may try to hold them through the night. It does not trust that they will be remembered, resolved, or handled later, so it keeps them active. What looks like overthinking is often the mind refusing to drop what has not been clearly stored.

A shutdown routine gives the mind a different instruction. It says, "The day has been reviewed enough. Anything that needs tomorrow has been captured. Anything that is already complete is closed. The body can now move towards sleep." This does not need to be elaborate. In fact, it should not be. A bedtime routine that becomes complicated will be abandoned when you are tired, and the whole point is to create something simple enough to repeat when your energy is low.

The mistake many people make is trying to solve the day at night. They lie down and begin sorting everything mentally: what happened, what went wrong, what needs doing, what someone meant, what should be said tomorrow, what could have been handled better. But the bed is a poor office and a worse courtroom. Once you are under the duvet, the mind has too much quiet and too little structure. Thoughts that would have been manageable on paper become circular in the dark. The shutdown routine prevents this by moving the sorting process earlier, before the bedroom becomes the place where the mind conducts its late hearing.

The routine has three movements: capture, close, and cue sleep.

Capture means writing down what the mind might otherwise try to hold. This is not journalling in the deep, reflective sense. It is not an invitation to analyse your childhood, diagnose every feeling, or write a full account of the day. It is a brief parking note. The purpose is to give unfinished material a place outside your head. The mind is more willing to release a concern when it trusts that the concern has been recorded somewhere visible and retrievable.

A useful parking note is plain. "Email Sam tomorrow about the meeting time." "Check invoice." "Clarify the handover point." "Buy milk." "Ask whether the deadline has moved." "Reply to the message after breakfast." These are not emotional essays. They are anchors for tomorrow. The mind does not need to keep repeating them at 2am if they have already been put somewhere reliable.

A replay-prone mind may try to turn the parking note into a full review. It may begin with "Clarify the handover point" and then drift into, "Why did I sound so abrupt? Did they think I was difficult? Should I have said it differently?" That is not capture. That is rumination with a pen. The parking note should be kept short enough that it cannot become another loop. If the issue needs a future action, write the action. If it needs no future action, do not give it a page.

Close means marking what has already been processed. Some moments return at night not because they need action, but because the mind has not received a clear ending. A conversation may have been reviewed. The lesson may already be obvious. The repair may already be done. Yet the mind keeps presenting it as unfinished. Closure gives that moment a boundary.

A closing note might be one line: "Meeting comment reviewed: next time, add warmth before critique. No action needed." Or, "Message sent clearly enough. No more checking tonight." Or, "Apology made. My part is complete for now." These statements are not forced reassurance. They are records of completion. They tell the mind that the concern has passed through a fair process and does not need to be re-litigated in bed.

This is especially useful after small social discomforts. Suppose you made a slightly blunt comment in a meeting and spent part of the evening replaying it. If there is no clear harm and no useful repair, the shutdown note might read, "Blunt comment: lesson is to pause and soften next time. No further action." That line is modest, but it does important work. It captures the lesson without opening the whole scene again. It gives the mind enough structure to stop claiming the event is still unhandled.

Cue sleep means creating a repeated signal that the day's mental work is finished. The body learns through repetition. If every night ends with checking messages, rereading threads, mentally reviewing mistakes, and scanning for unresolved tension, the body learns that bedtime is a time for vigilance. If every night ends with a brief capture, a clean closure, and a steady shift into low-stimulation activity, the body begins to associate the routine with release.

The cue should be ordinary and repeatable. Close the notebook. Put the pen down. Place the phone away from the bed. Wash your face. Turn down the light. Make a warm drink if that suits you. Stretch gently. Read something undemanding. Sit quietly for a few breaths. The details matter less than the sequence. The same small actions, repeated in the same order, tell the body that no more mental investigation is required tonight.

The phone deserves particular attention because it can undo the shutdown in seconds. A parking note cannot do its work if you immediately reopen the message thread that triggered the replay. A closing statement cannot settle the mind if you then check whether someone has replied, inspect their punctuation, or reread your own wording. The shutdown routine should include a digital boundary. Not because phones are evil, but because they are portals back into unresolved loops. If the mind is trying to sleep, it does not need fresh social evidence to interpret.

A useful digital boundary is concrete. "No rereading messages after the shutdown note." "No checking for replies in bed." "Phone charges outside arm's reach." "If I remember something important, it goes on the parking note, not into the thread." Vague intentions are weak at night. Clear rules reduce negotiation. The tired mind should not have to decide, over and over, whether to check.

The routine should also distinguish between genuine tasks and emotional noise. A genuine task can be written down and handled later. Emotional noise keeps asking for certainty. "What if they were annoyed?" is not a task. "Send one clarification tomorrow if still needed" is a task. "Why did I say it like that?" is usually not a bedtime task. "Pause before answering in tomorrow's meeting" is a usable lesson. The shutdown routine trains the mind to translate concern into either action, lesson, or closure.

There will be nights when the mind refuses to cooperate. You may write the note, close the day, move towards sleep, and still feel the replay tugging. This does not mean the routine has failed. It means the nervous system is still activated. The aim is not to guarantee instant sleep. The aim is to stop feeding the loop. Even if sleep takes time, you are no longer giving the replay unlimited material.

When the mind returns to a closed item, respond with the same boundary rather than reopening the review. "This is parked." "This is closed for tonight." "The action is written down." "No new thinking now." These sentences may need repeating. Repetition is part of training. The old pattern has been practised many times; the new one will need practice too.

A shutdown routine should be brief enough to feel almost boring. That is a virtue. Rumination loves intensity. It wants late-night revelations, emotional investigations, perfect conclusions, dramatic self-correction. Sleep prefers boring. Sleep prefers predictability, low stakes, low light, familiar actions, and a mind that has been told, clearly and repeatedly, that the day is not available for further debate.

A simple version might look like this. Sit somewhere other than the bed. Write down any task that genuinely needs tomorrow. Write one closing line for any replay that has already been reviewed. Choose the next day's earliest sensible action if one is needed. Put the note away. Say a closing statement: "Captured, closed, done for tonight." Then begin the same quiet sleep cue you use each evening.

The words "for tonight" are important. They reduce resistance. The mind may not be ready to believe that the issue is closed forever. It may argue that more thinking will be needed. Fine. The boundary does not have to be eternal. It only has to hold the night. "Not now" can be enough. If the issue truly matters, it will still be available in daylight, when your mind is more capable of handling it with proportion.

The shutdown routine also protects the bed. Over time, the bed should become less associated with solving and more associated with release. If you repeatedly process difficult material under the duvet, the body may begin to expect alertness there. Keeping the capture-and-close process outside the bed helps preserve the bedroom as a place of rest rather than review. The mind should not learn that lying down is the signal to begin the investigation.

This does not need to be perfect. Some nights will be messy. Some concerns will still intrude. Some feelings will remain unfinished. The routine is not a performance of control. It is a practice of direction. Each evening, you are teaching the mind that unfinished material has a place, lessons have a boundary, and sleep does not require every uncertainty to be solved.

The deepest value of the routine is trust. The mind replays when it does not trust that important material will be handled. Capture builds trust: tomorrow's tasks will not be forgotten. Closure builds trust: completed reviews will not be endlessly reopened. Sleep cues build trust: the body can shift out of vigilance. Over time, the mind has less reason to keep the day alive in the dark.

A shutdown routine is not about becoming someone who never thinks at night. It is about refusing to let night become the default storage room for every unresolved feeling. The mind needs somewhere to put things. Give it a small, reliable place before sleep, and it may stop trying to use the pillow as a filing cabinet.

What to Do at 3am

At 3am, the mind should not be trusted with a courtroom.

This is not because your concerns are foolish. It is because the conditions are poor. You are tired. The room is dark. The body is more sensitive to discomfort. There is little fresh evidence. There is usually no one to ask, no repair to make, no useful message to send, and no reliable way to judge the true size of the problem. Yet this is exactly when the replay often speaks with its strongest confidence. It says, "Now we must solve it."

The first task is to refuse the invitation to conduct a full investigation in the dark. A replay at this hour will usually claim urgency, but urgency is not the same as importance. The mind may insist that if you do not solve the moment now, you will forget something crucial, miss your chance to repair it, or wake to a worse situation. Most of the time, the night is not offering wisdom. It is offering tired interpretation.

The aim at 3am is not to win an argument with the replay. It is not to prove that everything is fine. It is not to force yourself to sleep immediately. Those goals often create more pressure, and pressure keeps the body awake. The aim is simpler and more practical: stop feeding the loop, signal safety to the body, and return attention gently to the present.

Begin by labelling what is happening. Keep the words plain. "This is a night-time replay." "This is my tired mind reviewing." "This is uncertainty in the dark." "This is not the time to solve." The label matters because it separates the process from reality. Without a label, the replay feels like a genuine emergency. With a label, it becomes a mental event occurring under difficult conditions.

Do not make the label too clever or too long. At 3am, the mind does not need a speech. It needs a boundary. "Night replay" may be enough. The shorter the phrase, the easier it is to use when the body is already tense and the mind is pulling hard towards the scene.

After labelling, soften the body before you try to think differently. A tired, activated body will keep making the replay feel important. If your jaw is clenched, let it loosen slightly. If your shoulders are raised, allow them to drop by a small amount. If your hands are tight, let the fingers uncurl. If your breathing is shallow, lengthen the exhale without forcing it. Do not demand total relaxation. At this hour, even a small softening is useful.

The body does not need to be bullied into sleep. It needs evidence that there is no present emergency. That evidence can be quiet and physical. Feel the weight of the duvet. Notice the support of the mattress. Let the back of the head rest into the pillow. Feel one point of contact: heel, hand, shoulder, hip, cheek. Give attention to contact rather than content. The replay says, "Go back to the scene." The body practice says, "You are here."

This is not avoidance. It is sequencing. If the body is alarmed, analysis will usually intensify the alarm. You can review the issue in daylight if it still matters. At 3am, the useful task is to lower activation enough that the mind stops treating thought as threat management.

The next step is to redirect gently. Choose a present-time anchor that does not require much effort. You might listen for a distant sound, then a nearer sound. You might feel the texture of the sheet against your hand. You might notice the darkness behind closed eyes without trying to make anything happen. You might count slow exhales, not as a performance, but as a way of giving attention a simple rhythm.

The word gently is important. A replay-prone mind often turns every technique into a test. "Is this working? Am I calmer? Am I falling asleep yet? Why am I still awake?" That monitoring becomes another loop. Instead, treat the redirection as placing attention down softly, again and again, rather than forcing it to stay. The mind will wander back. That is expected. Each return to the anchor is the practice.

If the replay keeps demanding that something must be remembered, use a parking note. Keep it brief and low-stimulation. Do not turn on bright lights. Do not open messages. Do not reread threads. Do not begin drafting a long apology. If needed, write one line on paper: "Tomorrow: review whether clarification is needed about the meeting comment." Or, "Tomorrow: reply after breakfast." Or, "Lesson: pause before sending when tired." Then stop. The note is a shelf, not a doorway into more analysis.

The parking note should never become a night-time essay. The purpose is to reassure the mind that the concern has been captured, not to solve the concern in bed. If you find yourself writing explanations, defences, imagined replies, or emotional arguments, the note has turned into rumination. Return to one line. Tomorrow can hold more detail if more detail is genuinely needed.

Sometimes lying still becomes part of the struggle. You remain in bed trying to sleep, but the bed has become a place of effort. In that case, a small low-light action can help reset the body. Sit up. Take a sip of water. Touch the floor with your feet. Adjust the blanket. Stand briefly and return. Keep the action dull, quiet, and ordinary. You are not starting the day. You are signalling present time.

Avoid anything that reopens the social world. Checking your phone is particularly risky because it gives the replay new material. You may see that there is still no reply. You may reread the message. You may notice a phrase that now looks wrong. You may be pulled into other people's lives, other cues, other comparisons. The mind will call this checking for safety. In practice, it often teaches the body that night-time unease should be answered with investigation.

If you feel the urge to check, label the urge separately. "This is the urge to check." "Checking will feed the loop." "No new evidence is needed tonight." Then return to the body. The urge may rise sharply and then soften. You do not need to obey it at its peak. An urge is uncomfortable, but it is not an instruction.

The replay may try to persuade you through moral language. It may say, "If you cared, you would think about this." "If you sleep, you are avoiding responsibility." "If you wait until morning, it will be too late." Treat these statements with caution. Responsibility at 3am often looks different from responsibility in daylight. At night, responsibility may mean not sending the anxious message, not reopening the apology, not trusting the harsh verdict, and not turning tired fear into a decision.

A useful sentence is: "If this matters, it will still matter in the morning." This is not a dismissal. It is a timing boundary. Real issues survive daylight. Rumination often loses some of its authority once the body has rested and the ordinary world has returned. If an apology is needed, it can be made more cleanly after sleep. If a clarification is needed, it can be written with better judgement. If no action is needed, that will often be easier to see when the mind is not half-submerged in fatigue.

Do not debate the replay in the dark. Debate is one of rumination's favourite traps. The thought says, "You ruined that." You answer, "No, I did not." The thought says, "But what about their expression?" You answer that. The thought says, "But what if they tell someone?" You answer that too. Soon you have spent another hour inside the scene, even though you were technically arguing against it. The content changes, but attention remains captured.

Instead of debating, return to process. "This is the replay asking for debate." "No courtroom tonight." "Parked for morning." These phrases are deliberately firm. They do not try to settle the question. They refuse the method. You are not saying the issue is meaningless. You are saying that 3am rumination is not the way to handle it.

If shame is present, name it as shame. "This is shame in my body." Shame often makes night replays feel urgent because it creates the sensation of exposure. The mind then tries to cover that exposure by finding a repair, an explanation, a perfect alternate version. At 3am, this usually makes things worse. Shame needs softening before strategy. Feel where it sits: face, throat, chest, stomach, hands. Let it be sensation before it becomes story.

If anxiety is present, name it as anxiety. "This is waiting anxiety." "This is uncertainty." "This is the body asking for certainty." Anxiety often demands action, but not all action is wise. The action at 3am may be internal: stay with the body, keep the phone down, postpone interpretation, return to the anchor. This may feel like doing nothing, but it is active restraint.

If regret is present, name it as regret. "This is regret about the earlier moment." Regret wants to rewrite the past. It will produce better lines, better timing, better facial expressions, better messages. One usable lesson can be parked for morning. The rest is rehearsal for a scene that has ended. At 3am, alternate scripts are especially punishing because they make your tired mind compare reality with an impossible edited version.

A short 3am protocol can be simple enough to remember. Label the replay. Soften one part of the body. Park one task if necessary. Choose one anchor. Return to it without argument. The sequence is plain because the night is not the time for complexity. Complexity belongs to rumination. Simplicity belongs to sleep.

There will be nights when this does not produce sleep quickly. That does not mean the practice has failed. Measuring success only by instant sleep creates pressure, and pressure can keep the nervous system alert. A better measure is whether you stopped adding fuel. Did you avoid rereading the thread? Did you refuse the debate? Did you write one parking note instead of a long analysis? Did you soften the body rather than punish yourself for being awake? These are real wins, even if sleep comes slowly.

The fight against wakefulness can be more activating than wakefulness itself. You may notice yourself calculating how much rest remains, worrying about tomorrow, resenting the replay, blaming your mind. This is another loop. Label it: "Now I am replaying being awake." Then soften again. The body is more likely to settle when wakefulness is treated as uncomfortable but not catastrophic.

A small phrase can help: "Rest is still useful." Even if sleep has not returned, lying quietly without feeding the replay is better than conducting a night-long investigation. This phrase reduces the all-or-nothing pressure that says the night is ruined unless you sleep immediately. The less you treat wakefulness as disaster, the less the body has to defend against it.

Be careful with problem-solving plans made in the dark. The mind may design dramatic solutions: send a long message, apologise intensely, cancel something, confront someone, withdraw, make a promise, change a decision. Unless there is a genuine urgent matter that cannot wait, do not act on night-time intensity. Write the basic concern down and review it later. The night is allowed to produce notes. It is not allowed to make major social decisions on a tired nervous system.

If the replay is about an apology already sent, remind yourself: "My part is complete for now." If it is about a message unanswered, say, "No meaning assigned until evidence appears." If it is about an awkward moment, say, "Lesson can be reviewed in daylight." If it is about a mistake, say, "Correction tomorrow if needed." These statements are not meant to be comforting in a sugary way. They are meant to be operational. They tell the mind what category the concern belongs to.

The low-light action is especially helpful when the body feels trapped. Keep it brief and boring. Sit on the edge of the bed and feel your feet. Drink water. Stretch the neck gently. Walk slowly to the doorway and back. Adjust the room temperature if needed. Write the parking note. Then return. Do not make the action interesting enough to wake the mind further. You are not rewarding the replay with stimulation. You are interrupting the physical freeze around it.

If a thought returns repeatedly, answer it with the same boundary rather than a new analysis. The thought says, "What if they are upset?" You answer, "No evidence tonight." It returns: "But what if?" You answer, "No evidence tonight." This repetition may feel dull, but dullness is useful. Rumination wants novelty: new angles, new fears, new imagined scenes. A consistent boundary gives it less to work with.

The dark can make a thought sound profound simply because it is the only voice in the room. Remember this. Night-time thoughts often have dramatic acoustics. They echo. They seem larger than they are. The task is not to silence every echo, but to stop mistaking the echo for a command.

Morning will have more information. Morning will have light, movement, food, contact, proportion, and better judgement. The concern may still need attention. If so, you can give it attention then. But attention in daylight is different from attention in the dark. Daylight review can ask for facts, controllable parts, proportionate repair, or closure. Night-time replay usually asks only for another loop.

The deeper skill is learning that the mind can be unsettled without being obeyed. You can wake with a replay and not turn the bed into a courtroom. You can feel urgency and still postpone interpretation. You can write one line and refuse the essay. You can soften the body before solving the story. You can be awake without making wakefulness another failure.

At 3am, do not aim for brilliance. Aim for steadiness. Label what is happening. Lower the fight in the body. Keep the light low. Keep the phone out of the loop. Park only what genuinely needs daylight. Return attention to one simple anchor. Let sleep come when it comes, without demanding that the mind produce perfect peace first.

The night does not need your best argument. It needs your refusal to keep the replay alive.

Chapter 9
Attention Training for Real Life

Attention is not simply where your mind happens to go. It is where your life is being spent.

A replay steals attention by making the past feel more urgent than the present. One message, one sentence, one look, one mistake becomes the centre of the room, even when nothing in the room is asking for your response. You may be making breakfast, sitting in a meeting, walking down the street, or trying to read, yet part of you remains elsewhere, watching the old scene again. The body is here. The mind is back there.

This is why stopping mental rewinds cannot depend only on insight. Understanding the loop matters, but understanding alone does not always return attention when the replay has momentum. A mind that has practised going back will go back quickly. It needs another route. Not a grand practice that requires perfect calm or long stretches of silence, but small, repeatable moments of attentional strength built inside ordinary life.

Attention training is often misunderstood. It is not about emptying the mind. It is not about becoming serene, detached, or untouched by discomfort. It is not about forcing every thought to behave. A trained attention is not a silent attention. It is a returnable attention. It wanders, notices, and comes back. It gets hooked, recognises the hook, and chooses the next anchor. It does not demand perfection. It builds reliability.

This matters because replays thrive in the gap between intention and placement. You intend to move on, but attention remains fused with the scene. You intend to work, but attention keeps checking the message. You intend to rest, but attention keeps rehearsing the apology. Without training, attention follows emotional intensity. With training, attention can be guided by choice. That shift is quiet, but it changes the architecture of a day.

The aim is practical strength. A few seconds of returning to sound after a replay begins. A moment of feeling your feet before opening a message. A deliberate look around the room after sending an email. A brief anchor before entering a meeting, after leaving one, before replying, after speaking, while waiting. These small returns teach the mind that the replay is not the only available destination. They also teach the body that discomfort can exist without becoming the centre of attention.

Micro-anchors become especially important because real life rarely gives ideal conditions. You will not always have a quiet room, a clear schedule, or a calm nervous system. Replays often begin in the middle of things: after a conversation, during a commute, between tasks, while standing in a queue, just after pressing send. A useful practice must fit those moments. It must be brief enough to use before the mind builds a full story and concrete enough to compete with the pull of the past.

The path here is to strengthen attention in small repetitions, then place anchors where replays most often begin. Attention is trained like a practical capacity, not a moral virtue. You are not failing when the mind wanders; you are practising when you return. The more often attention comes back to the present through sound, touch, sight, movement, or task, the less authority the replay has when it calls.

The question is not whether your mind will wander. It will. The sharper question is whether you can catch the moment it has been taken, and bring it back before the old scene becomes the whole world again.

Building Attentional Strength

Attention is often treated as if it should obey automatically. You decide to stop replaying, so attention should return to the present. You decide the conversation is over, so the mind should stop revisiting it. You decide the message was clear enough, so the urge to reread should fade. When this does not happen, it can feel like a personal failure, as though you lack discipline or emotional maturity.

But attention is not strengthened by disappointment. It is strengthened by training.

A replay-prone mind has usually practised returning to certain scenes many times. After a meeting, it reviews. After a message, it checks. After a tense exchange, it scans for damage. After a mistake, it prosecutes. These routes become familiar because attention has travelled them repeatedly. The mind does not choose them because they are wise; it chooses them because they are well-worn. Building attentional strength means creating new routes back to the present, often through small, ordinary acts repeated with patience.

This is not about emptying the mind. A blank mind is not the goal. The goal is a mind that can return. Thoughts will appear. Memories will surface. Feelings will rise. The replay may begin before you notice it. Attentional strength is the ability to recognise that attention has been taken and then place it somewhere chosen. Not once, perfectly, but again and again.

This matters because rumination feeds on unattended drift. The mind slides from a cue into a thought, from a thought into a feeling, from a feeling into a full replay. Before long, the scene feels immersive. You are not choosing to think about it; you are inside it. Attention training interrupts that slide earlier. It gives you a moment of recognition before the replay becomes the whole room.

The practice should be modest enough to live inside a real day. Many people imagine attention training as something that requires silence, time, stillness, and perfect commitment. That is one reason they do not practise it. Real life is noisier. You may need to train attention while walking to the kitchen, waiting for a meeting to begin, standing outside a door, closing a laptop, or placing your phone face down after sending a message. The training that matters most is the training you can actually use when a loop begins.

Start with the simplest unit: notice and return. Notice where attention has gone. Return it to a chosen point. That point might be the sound in the room, the pressure of your feet, the object in your hand, the next sentence you are reading, the movement of your body, or the task directly in front of you. The return should be firm but not harsh. If you scold yourself each time attention wanders, you create another threat. Threat feeds rumination. A cleaner response is, "Attention went back. Bring it here."

This return may last only a few seconds at first. That is still training. The mind may go back to the replay almost immediately. Bring it here again. The value is not in how long you stay present on the first attempt. The value is in the repetition of returning. Each return teaches the mind that the replay is not the only available destination.

Think of attention as a muscle only in the practical sense: it strengthens through use, not through wishing. A person does not become stronger by criticising their current strength. They become stronger by repeating manageable movements. The same principle applies here. A few seconds of chosen attention, repeated often, can matter more than one ambitious practice that collapses under pressure. Heroic effort is less useful than reliable contact.

The first kind of exercise is sensory placement. Choose one sense and place attention there deliberately. Listen to the nearest sound. Feel the texture of your sleeve. Look at the outline of an object. Notice the temperature of the air on your hands. This is not decorative mindfulness. It is attentional redirection. The replay pulls attention towards mental reconstruction. Sensory placement pulls attention towards present evidence.

The second kind is task placement. Give attention a small job. Not "focus on work" in a vague way, but "write the next line," "open the document," "rinse this cup," "read this paragraph," "fold this shirt," "walk to the end of the street." A specific task gives attention a defined channel. Rumination thrives when attention is loose. A small task gathers it.

The third kind is transition placement. Replays often start in the spaces between things: after the call ends, after the message is sent, after you leave the room, after the conversation pauses, after the day quietens. These gaps are vulnerable because attention has not yet been assigned. A transition practice closes the gap. When the meeting ends, feel both feet and write one factual note. When the message sends, place the phone down and touch the desk. When you leave a conversation, name the next physical action. The goal is to stop attention from automatically falling backwards.

Attentional strength also requires learning the difference between returning and suppressing. Suppression says, "Do not think about it." Returning says, "Place attention here." Suppression remains organised around the unwanted thought. Returning is organised around the chosen anchor. This difference may seem small, but it changes the emotional tone. Suppression tightens. Returning directs. Suppression keeps checking whether the thought has disappeared. Returning gives attention another place to stand.

The practice becomes more effective when paired with process labelling. Before returning, name what is happening: "This is a replay." "This is checking." "This is story-building." "This is the post-message loop." The label prevents you from treating the thought as an emergency. Then return attention to the chosen point. Label, place, return. The sequence is short because the moment of intervention is often short.

There will be resistance. The replay will argue that it deserves attention because the issue is important. Sometimes it will be right. Some issues do deserve a proper review. But proper review is not the same as being dragged through the same scene without boundary. Attentional strength includes the ability to say, "I will review this at a set time if needed. I will not review it through uncontrolled replay now." This is not avoidance. It is governance.

One useful practice is the timed return. Choose a small period of present attention and make it deliberately manageable. For example, while washing your hands, give full attention to the water, the pressure, the movement, and the towel. While walking from one room to another, give attention to the contact of your feet. While waiting for a kettle, listen to the sound instead of entering the replay. These moments are brief, but they train the same skill you need when the mind is pulled backwards: notice, place, return.

Another practice is the single-task reset. When you catch a replay, choose one small task and complete it with as much attention as you can. The task should have a clear beginning and end. Make the bed.

Clear the desk. Reply to one ordinary email. Put three items away. Write one sentence. The purpose is not productivity for its own sake. The purpose is to restore confidence that attention can move from the old scene into present action.

Do not turn this into a performance metric. The mind may try to evaluate whether you are doing attention training well enough. It may say, "You failed because you went back to the replay." That is another harsh script. Wandering is part of the practice. The moment you notice the wandering is the moment training becomes possible. A return after ten seconds and a return after ten minutes are both returns. Earlier is useful, but later still counts.

Attentional strength is built through friendliness as much as firmness. If your inner tone becomes punitive, attention training becomes another courtroom. "Why cannot I focus?" "I am terrible at this." "I should be over it." These sentences add shame, and shame gives the replay more material. A more useful tone is plain and steady: "Back here." "Again." "This is the practice." "Attention returns now." The words are short because the goal is not to discuss the practice. The goal is to do it.

The body is a powerful ally because it always exists in the present. The replay may travel through memory and imagination, but the body remains here: breathing, touching, standing, sitting, hearing, seeing. When the mind feels unreachable, return through the body. Feel the soles of the feet. Press the thumb and fingers together. Notice the weight of the hands. Turn the head and look at the room. These are not grand solutions. They are entry points back into now.

Over time, these small returns create a different kind of trust. You stop needing the replay to disappear before you act. You learn that attention can move even while discomfort remains. You can feel a residue of embarrassment and still finish the task. You can feel uncertainty and still stop checking. You can feel regret and still bring your mind back to the cup, the page, the floor, the person in front of you. This is how mental freedom often begins: not with the absence of feeling, but with the ability to place attention while feeling is present.

Attentional strength also changes your relationship to urgency. A replay says, "Think about this now." Training allows you to ask, "Is now the right time, and is this the right method?" If the answer is no, attention can be moved. The urge may remain for a while, but it no longer decides automatically. This is the difference between being pulled by the mind and leading the mind.

Use ordinary moments as practice ground. Do not wait for a severe replay. Train during small gaps. When you open a door, feel the handle. When you sit down, feel the chair. When you drink, taste the first sip. When you hear a notification, pause before reaching. When you send a message, breathe once and place the phone down. These small acts may seem too minor to matter, but they teach attention to return before crisis makes returning harder.

A replay-prone mind often lives in afterthought. Attention training brings you back into contact. The work in front of you becomes more available. The person speaking becomes easier to hear. The room becomes less distant. The body becomes less like a vehicle carrying a mind trapped elsewhere. Life regains texture because attention is no longer being donated so freely to scenes that have already ended.

This does not mean every past thought is an enemy. Reflection still has its place. Learning still has its place. Repair still has its place. But attention training gives you the ability to choose when and how the past receives attention. Without that ability, every trigger can become a summons. With it, the past must wait its turn.

The next time attention is pulled into a replay, treat the moment as a training repetition rather than a failure. Name the loop. Choose one anchor. Return to it. Choose one small task. Place attention there. When the mind goes back, return again. Not dramatically. Not perfectly. Reliably.

The strength you are building is not the strength to never wander. It is the strength to come back.

Using Micro-Anchors

A micro-anchor is a small point of contact with the present moment. It is not a grand practice. It does not require a silent room, a cushion, a long ritual, or a perfectly calm mind. It is brief, physical, and available inside ordinary life. A sound. A texture. A breath. A foot on the floor. A hand on a door handle. The weight of a mug. The sight of a familiar object. These small anchors matter because replays often begin in small spaces.

After sending a message, there is a space. After leaving a meeting, there is a space. After speaking in a group, there is a space. After noticing a delayed reply, there is a space. The mind can use that space to return to the past, inspect the wording, imagine reactions, and build a story. A micro-anchor gives attention somewhere else to land before the replay claims the gap.

The value of a micro-anchor lies in its immediacy. A replay is usually made from memory and imagination. It pulls attention towards what was said, what might have been meant, what someone could be thinking, what you should have done, what may happen next. A micro-anchor is made from direct contact. It says, "Here is the desk. Here is the floor. Here is the sound in the room. Here is the body breathing now." It does not answer every question the replay raises. It changes the location of attention.

This is important because attention does not need a perfect argument before it moves. You do not have to convince the mind that the replay is irrational. You do not have to prove that everything is fine. You do not have to settle the meaning of the moment before returning to the present. A micro-anchor works at a more basic level. It gives attention a concrete assignment. Not "stop thinking," but "feel this." Not "calm down," but "listen here." Not "move on forever," but "come back for one breath."

The anchor should be simple enough to use under pressure. If it requires too much explanation, it will not help when the mind is already activated. "Feel both feet" is usable. "Listen for the nearest sound" is usable. "Touch the edge of the table" is usable. "Look at one fixed object and name its colour and shape" is usable. A micro-anchor should be so ordinary that it almost feels unimpressive. Its strength is not in drama, but in repeatability.

Sound is one of the easiest anchors because it is usually available without effort. After a replay begins, pause and listen. Notice one sound close to you: the hum of an appliance, a chair shifting, the movement of your own breath, a keyboard, a clock, a distant car, the faint noise outside a window. Do not analyse the sound. Do not turn it into a relaxation exercise that must succeed. Simply let attention rest there for a moment. The replay asks you to listen again to the past. The anchor asks you to listen to what is actually present.

Touch is often even stronger because it gives the mind a clear physical boundary. Feel the soles of your feet inside your shoes. Press your fingertips gently together. Notice the fabric of your sleeve. Hold a mug and feel its temperature. Let your palm rest flat on the desk. Feel the chair supporting your body. Touch interrupts the floating quality of rumination. It brings attention out of imagined conversations and into contact with matter.

Sight can widen the mind when the replay has narrowed it. Choose one object in the room and look at it carefully for a few seconds. Not symbolically. Not sentimentally. Just visually. Notice its edges, colour, position, shadow, surface, size. A replay often makes one mental image too bright: the person's face, the text on the screen, the meeting room, the moment of awkwardness. Visual anchoring reminds attention that the current field is wider than the scene being replayed.

Breath can be useful, but it should be handled gently. Some people become more anxious when they monitor breathing too intensely. The aim is not to control the breath perfectly. It is enough to notice one exhale. Let it lengthen slightly if that feels natural. Then return to a point of contact, such as the feet or hands. Breath is a door, not a performance. If it becomes another thing to do correctly, choose touch or sound instead.

The best time to use a micro-anchor is before the replay has fully formed. This is why transitions matter. After sending a risky email, do not wait until you have reread it five times. Place the phone down, feel your feet, and look at the room. After leaving a conversation, do not let the first quiet corridor become a theatre for analysis. Notice the sensation of walking, the sound of your steps, the door handle in your hand. After a meeting, touch the notebook, write one factual next step, and stand up. The anchor catches the mind before it drops into the old groove.

Micro-anchors are especially useful after digital actions. Pressing send can create a strange little vacuum. The message is gone, but the response has not arrived. The mind rushes to fill the gap. It wants to reopen the thread, inspect the wording, and prepare for possible judgement. A micro-anchor creates a deliberate ending. Send. Put the device down. Feel the surface beneath your hand. Look away from the screen. Move into the next task. This sequence teaches the mind that sending is followed by present action, not by immediate self-audit.

They are also useful before social exposure. Before speaking in a meeting, answering a difficult question, entering a conversation, or opening a message that may carry emotional weight, use a small anchor. Feel the chair. Notice the breath once. Touch the pen. Look at one point in the room. This does not guarantee that you will speak perfectly, and that is not the aim. The aim is to enter the moment from the present rather than from a cloud of imagined judgement.

After public speaking, a micro-anchor can prevent the post-performance audit from taking over. The mind may immediately select one imperfect sentence and begin replaying it. Instead, give the body a closing cue. Feel your hands. Close the notebook. Stand with both feet on the floor. Take one sip of water. Name the next practical action. These tiny gestures matter because they move you from performance into completion. Without them, the mind may treat the event as still open.

In moments of interpersonal tension, micro-anchors help you stay with what is actually happening rather than what the mind fears is happening. If someone's tone changes, if a reply seems brief, if a conversation becomes slightly strained, attention may race ahead into interpretation. Feel your feet. Notice the sound of their actual words, not the imagined meaning behind them. Touch the chair. Let your body arrive before your mind builds a verdict. The anchor does not make you passive. It makes you less reactive.

A micro-anchor should usually be paired with one small next action. Anchoring alone can create a pause, but action gives attention direction. After feeling your feet, write the next sentence. After listening to a sound, return to the task. After touching the mug, take it to the sink. After looking around the room, open the document you meant to work on. The anchor is the bridge; the task is the landing place. Without a landing place, attention may drift back to the replay.

This is why vague distraction often disappoints. "I will distract myself" gives the mind too much room. The replay can follow you into scrolling, watching, tidying, or half-working. A micro-anchor plus a specific task is stronger. "I will feel my feet, then write the next three lines." "I will touch the desk, then close the message thread." "I will listen for one sound, then wash the cup." The specificity gives attention a route.

The practice should remain small. Do not turn micro-anchors into a new perfection project. The aim is not to become beautifully mindful at every moment. The aim is to interrupt the replay often enough that the mind learns another pattern. A few seconds count. One return counts. Noticing that you forgot and beginning again counts. This is training, not performance.

There will be times when the anchor feels weak compared with the replay. The old scene may still pull hard. The body may still feel charged. The mind may say, "This is not working." That judgement is premature. A micro-anchor is not meant to erase the replay instantly. It is meant to stop giving the replay complete ownership of attention. Even a small shift matters. Attention placed on the floor for three seconds is attention not fully surrendered to the loop.

The anchor can be repeated without becoming mechanical. Return to the same point if it helps. Feet. Sound. Hands. Sight. Task. Feet again. The repetition should be calm, not desperate. If you use the anchor as a way to force the thought away, you may create another struggle. Use it instead as a direction: attention belongs here now. The replay may speak in the background, but it does not get the whole stage.

Different anchors suit different situations. If you are in a public place, touch may be discreet: fingertips together, feet on the floor, thumb against the side of a cup. If you are alone, sight or movement may work better: look around the room, stand up, place an object away. If you are in bed, keep anchors low-stimulation: the weight of the blanket, the pillow under your head, one slow exhale, the sound of the room. If you are at work, pair the anchor with a practical next step: write a note, open a file, answer the next straightforward message.

The most powerful micro-anchors are often attached to existing habits. After pressing send, feel the phone leave your hand. Before opening a reply, feel both feet. When a meeting ends, touch the notebook and write one factual next step. When you enter your home, notice the door handle. When you make tea, listen to the kettle. When you sit at your desk, feel the chair before checking messages. Existing habits become hooks for present attention.

This reduces the need for willpower. You do not have to remember a whole system. The day itself reminds you. Door handle: return. Phone down: return. Mug in hand: return. Feet on floor: return. The anchor becomes woven into ordinary movement, which is exactly where replay often tries to begin.

Micro-anchors also help you separate discomfort from danger. You may still feel embarrassed after anchoring. You may still wish you had phrased something differently. You may still dislike waiting for a reply. But the anchor teaches the body that discomfort can be present while life continues. You do not have to stop everything and investigate. You can feel the feeling and still return to the next moment.

This is particularly important for people who believe they must feel calm before moving on. A micro-anchor proves otherwise. You can move attention while still slightly unsettled. You can place the phone down while still wanting to check. You can return to the document while still feeling a tug towards the replay. You can walk away from a conversation and feel your steps while the mind tries to review. Calm may come later. The return comes first.

Over time, micro-anchors build trust in your own attention. You begin to know that even if a replay starts, you are not helpless. There is always a point of contact. Always a sound. Always a surface. Always a next small action. The mind may still revisit the past, but it no longer has a monopoly on where you live mentally. You have practised coming back in small, ordinary ways.

A useful phrase is: "Anchor, then act." Anchor to present contact. Act into the next small task. This phrase prevents the practice from becoming passive. It also prevents action from being frantic. The anchor steadies the transition; the action completes it. Together, they interrupt the drift into replay.

There is no need to make micro-anchors impressive. Their power is in being available when your mind is not at its best. After the awkward text. After the tense exchange. Before the meeting. After the meeting. While waiting. While walking. While tempted to reread. The ordinary world is full of handles back to the present. Use them.

The next time a replay begins, do not wait until it becomes overwhelming. Find the nearest anchor. Hear one sound. Feel one point of contact. See one object clearly. Then place attention into one small action. The past may continue to call, but each anchor teaches the mind a different response: not back there by default, but here by choice.

Chapter 10
Breaking Digital Replay Traps

Why does a message feel safer before it is sent than after it has left your hands? Before sending, the words are still private. You can adjust the tone, change the punctuation, soften the edge, remove the sentence, add warmth, wait, delete, rewrite. After sending, the same words become strangely exposed. They sit in a thread, fixed and visible, available for rereading, misreading, judging, forwarding in imagination, and measuring against every possible version you might have written instead.

The digital world gives the replay something it has always wanted: evidence that can be revisited. A spoken sentence fades into memory, but a message remains on the screen. An email can be opened again. A chat can be inspected line by line. A post can be viewed as if it were an object under examination. The mind, seeking certainty, treats this access as an opportunity. If the words are still there, surely one more look might settle the question. Did it sound cold? Was it too much? Was it too little? Did the timing seem strange? Could that phrase be taken the wrong way?

The paradox is that checking promises relief while often extending the problem. You reread to feel safer, but each reread refreshes the scene. You check for reassurance, but checking teaches the mind that reassurance must be found on the screen. You look again to reduce doubt, but the act of looking gives doubt more material. The thread becomes less like a record and more like a mirror that changes with your mood. What seemed clear when you wrote it can look blunt when you feel ashamed, needy when you feel exposed, careless when you feel guilty, and risky when you are waiting for a reply.

The central tension is that digital communication is useful because it preserves words, yet replay thrives on preserved words. Permanence can support clarity, accountability, and practical follow-up, but it can also provoke perfectionism. A sentence that would have passed naturally in speech may feel heavier when it is written, stored, and available for inspection. The mind begins to imagine the message as permanently judgeable, as though every word might be held against you indefinitely. That feeling is rarely proportionate, but it is powerful enough to keep the loop alive.

This matters because digital replays do not stay inside the mind. They shape behaviour. You may delay sending simple messages because they do not feel perfectly safe. You may over-edit ordinary replies until they lose warmth. You may check whether someone has read something, then build a story around the delay. You may scroll to avoid the discomfort of waiting, only to absorb more cues that unsettle you. You may confuse activity with action: opening, checking, rereading, comparing, refreshing, hovering. The body feels busy, but nothing is completed.

The cost is attention. Each check seems small, almost harmless, but the pattern trains the mind to keep returning. A replay fed by fresh digital stimuli becomes harder to close because the screen keeps offering new hooks: a timestamp, a read receipt, a short reply, a lack of reply, a visible online status, a post that appears to mean something, a detail that was not noticeable before. The more cues you collect, the more the mind believes there is a hidden meaning to solve. Yet most of the time, the real task is not to gather more evidence. It is to stop feeding the uncertainty.

A healthier relationship with digital communication requires friction in the right places. Not dramatic restriction. Not fear of technology. Simple, deliberate boundaries around the behaviours that keep the replay alive. Rereading and checking need limits because reassurance that depends on repeated inspection rarely lasts. Screenshot thinking needs proportion because written words are not automatically permanent verdicts on your character. Online cues need to be converted into grounded action because relief usually comes through completion, not through another round of second-guessing.

The path is practical: notice the checking cycle before it becomes automatic, return to a "good enough to send" standard before perfectionism rewrites the message endlessly, and replace hovering with one real-world action that matches your value in the moment. Sometimes that action is rest. Sometimes it is work. Sometimes it is repair. Sometimes it is connection. Sometimes it is one clarifying sentence instead of twenty minutes of rereading. The screen may hold the words, but it does not have to hold your attention hostage.

So the sharper question is not, "Can I make this message impossible to misread?" That is too much power to give any sentence. The better question is, "What am I doing with the screen right now: communicating, repairing, completing, or feeding the replay?"

Rereading and Checking Cycles

Digital replays often begin with a perfectly ordinary impulse: you want to make sure. You want to make sure the message was clear. You want to make sure the tone was not too cold. You want to make sure the email did not sound careless, needy, blunt, defensive, arrogant, vague, or excessive. The screen is right there. The words are still visible. So you look again.

The first reread may feel reasonable. You are checking for a typo, a missing detail, an accidental edge. This is practical. There is nothing wrong with reviewing a message before sending it or confirming a necessary fact afterwards. The problem begins when the purpose changes. You are no longer checking for information. You are checking for emotional safety.

That shift can be subtle. A practical check has an end. You look, confirm, correct if needed, and stop. A reassurance check does not end cleanly because it is trying to answer a question the screen cannot answer: "Am I safe in how I have been received?" The message can show you what you wrote. It cannot show you every possible interpretation. It cannot tell you the other person's mood, assumptions, attention, private reaction, or later memory. So the mind checks again, hoping the same words will finally provide what they cannot provide.

This is why rereading rarely settles the mind for long. It may lower discomfort for a moment. You look at the message and think, "It is probably fine." The body softens slightly. Then uncertainty returns. A phrase that seemed harmless now looks a little abrupt. A sentence that seemed warm now looks too eager. A full stop seems cold. An exclamation mark seems excessive. The mind is not discovering new facts; it is viewing the same evidence through a changing emotional state.

The screen becomes a mood mirror.

When you are calm, the message may look clear. When you are ashamed, it may look embarrassing. When you are anxious, it may look risky. When you are tired, it may look more serious than it is. The words have not changed. The state from which you are reading them has changed. This is one of the main traps of digital replay: because the message is fixed, the mind assumes that another look will produce a stable judgement. But the judgement keeps shifting because the reader is no longer neutral. The reader is you, activated.

Checking cycles usually follow a familiar sequence. A trigger appears: you remember what you sent, notice no reply, receive a short response, or think of a possible misunderstanding. Anxiety rises. The mind opens the thread. It inspects the wording. Relief arrives briefly or a new concern appears. Either way, the thread becomes more important. Later, anxiety rises again, and the mind returns. The cycle teaches itself: discomfort leads to checking, checking offers temporary relief, temporary relief teaches the mind to check next time.

This is how checking becomes reassurance-seeking. The behaviour is not only about the message; it is about reducing the feeling. The mind wants the screen to say, "You are fine. They are not annoyed. You did not sound foolish. Nothing bad will happen." But screens do not say that. They offer fragments: timestamps, wording, read receipts, online status, short replies, delayed replies, punctuation, silence. The replay turns those fragments into material for more interpretation.

The problem is not that digital information is useless. Sometimes rereading is appropriate. If you are checking whether you attached the right file, included the correct time, answered the actual question, or sent the message to the right person, that is practical checking. It is connected to a specific fact. Once the fact is confirmed, the check is complete. Rumination begins when checking continues after the practical question has already been answered.

A useful distinction is this: practical checking asks, "Is there an objective error to correct?" Reassurance checking asks, "Can I feel certain that this will be received well?" The first question can usually be answered. The second cannot. You can correct a typo. You cannot guarantee another person's interpretation. You can add missing information. You cannot make a message impossible to dislike. You can apologise for a clear impact. You cannot use rereading to control the emotional life of the reader.

Digital checking becomes especially sticky because it offers immediate access. In face-to-face conversation, the moment passes. You may remember it, but you cannot reopen the exact scene. With messages, the scene remains available. The mind takes this availability as permission. If the thread can be reopened, perhaps it should be reopened. If the email can be inspected, perhaps there is something to find. If the reply can be checked, perhaps meaning is hiding there. Accessibility becomes temptation.

This temptation is strongest during waiting. After you send a message, the space before the reply can feel charged. The mind wants to do something with that charge, and rereading provides an action. It feels better than doing nothing. But the action often deepens the attachment. Each reread tells the nervous system that the message is a threat worth monitoring. The more you monitor, the less ordinary the message feels. Soon a simple exchange becomes an event.

The same pattern appears with social posts. You post something, then check how it is being received. You look for reactions, silence, changes, absence, tone, signs of approval or disapproval. If engagement appears, the mind may feel brief relief. If it does not, the replay begins inventing meanings. Was it badly worded? Too personal? Too boring? Too strong? Too weak? The post becomes a public object in your imagination, even if other people are barely thinking about it.

Emails carry their own version of the trap. Because they can feel formal, permanent, and professional, the mind may treat every line as evidence of competence. After sending, you reread and notice what could have been sharper, warmer, clearer, shorter, more polished. The mind compares the real email with an imaginary perfect one. The gap becomes regret. Then checking begins again, not because the email needs correction, but because the mind wants relief from the idea that it could have been better.

The cost is more than time. Checking keeps the emotional charge fresh. Every time you reopen the thread, you re-enter the social situation. The body may tighten again. The face may heat again. The stomach may drop again. The mind may generate another interpretation. What might have faded through non-engagement is reactivated through contact. The screen becomes a replay button.

Breaking the cycle requires friction. Friction means placing a small, deliberate obstacle between the urge and the behaviour. Not because you are weak, but because design is more reliable than willpower when the mind is activated. If the phone is in your hand, the thread is one tap away. If the email remains open, the reread is effortless. If notifications remain visible, the mind receives constant invitations. Friction gives attention a chance to choose.

One form of friction is a reread limit. Before sending, choose a reasonable number of checks for the type of message. A casual message may need one read for clarity. A more important email may need a fuller review. But after the limit is reached, the message must either be sent, saved for a defined later review, or closed. The point is not to rush careless communication. The point is to stop the mind from pretending that the next reread will make the message emotionally risk-free.

After sending, use a different boundary. Do not reread unless there is a practical reason. "I need to confirm the time I suggested" is a practical reason. "I need to see if it still feels safe" is not. This boundary may feel uncomfortable at first because the mind is used to receiving reassurance through inspection. That discomfort is the training ground. You are teaching the system that uncertainty does not automatically earn another look.

Another friction tactic is the intentional pause. When the urge to check appears, pause before opening the thread. Name the urge: "This is checking for reassurance." Then wait briefly while doing something concrete: feel both feet, put the phone down, take a sip of water, stand up, open the next task. The pause does not need to be long. It only needs to interrupt the automatic sequence. Urge does not have to become action.

A checking window can also help. Instead of letting the mind check whenever anxiety rises, choose when you will look. After lunch. After finishing the document. At the end of the work block. Tomorrow morning. The timing should fit the situation, but the principle is consistent: checking becomes chosen rather than compulsive. This reduces the repeated negotiation that fuels rumination. You do not ask every few minutes whether now is the time. The decision has already been made.

For messages that involve repair or uncertainty, a waiting rule is useful. Send the clarification or apology once, then do not reread it for emotional reassurance. Let the message stand. If the other person replies with new information, respond to that. If there is no new information, do not create new action out of old anxiety. The mind may say, "Just check once." But in a checking cycle, "once" is rarely once. It is the opening of the door.

The body will often protest when checking is blocked. You may feel restless, exposed, unfinished. This does not mean the boundary is wrong. It means the mind has been using checking as a regulator. When that regulator is removed, discomfort becomes more visible. Treat this as information. "My body wants the relief of checking." Then choose another regulator: movement, breath, touch, sound, a task, a written closing line, or a deliberate shift away from the screen.

A useful replacement sentence is: "The message will not become safer by rereading it." This is not always literally true before sending, when genuine editing may improve clarity. But after the practical review is complete, it becomes psychologically true. The next reread is unlikely to create lasting safety. It is more likely to create another angle. Another doubt. Another imagined reader. Another loop.

There is also value in separating review from send. Do not compose emotionally charged messages in the same state in which you decide their final meaning. Draft if needed. Pause. Return once with a clearer eye. Then send or revise. The boundary is important: one return, not endless polishing. The replay wants total protection against being misunderstood. Good communication aims for clarity, respect, and proportion. These are achievable. Perfect immunity from interpretation is not.

The phrase "good enough to send" belongs here. It does not mean careless. It means the message is clear enough, kind enough, accurate enough, and proportionate enough for its purpose. A message to confirm a time does not need literary elegance. A brief apology does not need a moral essay. A workplace reply does not need to prevent every possible judgement. "Good enough" protects communication from perfectionism. It returns the message to its job.

Once the message has done its job, your attention has a new job. Move into action. This is crucial because stopping checking without assigning attention elsewhere can leave a vacuum. The mind may drift straight back to the thread. Choose a physical or practical next step. Close the app. Put the phone away. Stand up. Wash the cup. Return to the document. Walk outside. Begin the next task. Completion needs movement.

Digital checking cycles are not broken by insight alone. They are broken by repeated boundaries at the point of behaviour. The mind learns through what you do after discomfort appears. If discomfort leads to checking, checking becomes the pathway. If discomfort leads to labelling, pausing, anchoring, and returning to action, that pathway strengthens instead.

There will be slips. You will reread sometimes. You will check after deciding not to. You will reopen a thread and feel the old pull. The response is not self-punishment. Punishment only adds shame, and shame fuels more checking. The response is recognition: "I entered the checking cycle." Then close the thread and return to the boundary. A slip does not require a full restart of the loop.

A helpful question is, "What am I hoping this check will give me?" If the answer is factual, proceed once and stop. If the answer is reassurance, certainty, proof of being liked, proof of not being judged, or relief from shame, the check is unlikely to satisfy for long. That is the moment to use friction. The question brings honesty to the behaviour. It reveals whether the screen is being used for communication or emotional control.

Over time, the aim is not to become rigid or afraid of looking at your own messages. The aim is to stop letting the screen become the place where your worth is repeatedly evaluated. You can use digital tools without turning them into replay machines. You can send, check appropriately, repair when needed, and close. The thread can remain on the device without remaining open in your mind.

The next time you feel the pull to reread, pause at the doorway. Ask whether there is a practical question or an emotional demand. If there is a practical question, answer it once. If there is only the demand to feel safe, do not ask the screen to provide what it cannot give. Put friction between urge and action. Let the message stand. Let the uncertainty exist. Let your attention return to a life larger than the thread.

Preventing Screenshot Thinking

Screenshot thinking is the fear that every digital expression can be preserved, judged, shared, and remembered forever. It is the feeling that a message is not merely a message, but a record. A post is not merely a post, but evidence. A sentence is not merely a sentence, but something that could be held up later and used to prove that you were foolish, careless, needy, rude, uninformed, dramatic, or wrong.

This kind of thinking can make ordinary communication feel strangely high-stakes. Before sending, the mind begins to imagine the words as if they are already frozen on someone else's screen. You picture the recipient reading them in the least generous tone. You imagine the message being shown to another person. You see one phrase detached from its context and judged without your intention attached. The words no longer feel like part of a living exchange. They feel like a permanent exhibit.

This is not entirely irrational. Digital words do have a different texture from spoken ones. They can be reread. They can be searched. They can be saved. They can remain visible long after the emotional moment has passed. But screenshot thinking takes this fact and inflates it into a threat. It treats every message as if it must be polished for hostile review, every reply as if it must survive forensic analysis, every post as if it must represent your entire character without error.

The result is digital perfectionism. You do not simply try to be clear. You try to become unmisreadable. You do not simply try to be kind. You try to remove every possible edge. You do not simply try to answer. You try to sound intelligent, warm, concise, unbothered, thoughtful, confident, humble, and impossible to criticise all at once. No sentence can carry that much pressure without becoming stiff.

Screenshot thinking turns communication into self-protection. Instead of asking, "What needs to be said here?" the mind asks, "How can I make sure this cannot be used against me?" That question may feel prudent, but it often leads away from honest expression. You begin writing for an imagined critic rather than for the actual person. You over-edit warmth until it sounds calculated. You soften clarity until it becomes vague. You remove personality until the message is safe but lifeless.

The mind believes this will prevent regret. Often, it creates it.

A message shaped by fear can feel wrong after it is sent because it does not quite sound like you. A post edited to avoid every possible judgement may feel hollow. A reply that tries to be perfectly neutral may come across as colder than intended. The effort to prevent misinterpretation can produce a different kind of miscommunication: not a mistake of wording, but a loss of presence.

This is why preventing screenshot thinking is not about becoming careless online. Carelessness has consequences. Words matter. Tone matters. Context matters. Digital records can affect trust. The point is not to pretend nothing lasts. The point is to stop treating every ordinary exchange as if it must be defended against an imaginary tribunal. There is a middle ground between reckless expression and anxious self-censorship.

The middle ground is proportion.

Proportion asks what the communication is for. Is this a simple update? A practical arrangement? A warm reply? A clear boundary? A repair? A public statement? A personal reflection? A work email? Different purposes require different levels of care. A message confirming a time does not need the emotional polish of a delicate apology. A casual reply to a friend does not need to be drafted like a legal statement. A brief work update does not need to carry your entire professional identity.

Screenshot thinking ignores purpose. It treats all messages as high-risk. This is what makes it exhausting. If every sentence must be permanent-proof, then every sentence becomes an ordeal. The mind starts applying the same level of scrutiny to minor communication as it would to something genuinely sensitive. That is not responsibility. It is misallocated vigilance.

A useful question is: "What is the actual weight of this message?" Not the imagined weight. Not the weight shame gives it. The actual weight. Who is receiving it? What is the relationship? What is the context? What is the likely consequence of an imperfect phrase? Is this something that truly requires careful wording, or is the mind inflating the risk because the words are visible on a screen?

Many digital replays shrink when the message is returned to its true size. "Thanks, I will check and come back to you" is not a character statement. "Sorry, I missed this earlier" is not a moral confession. "I do not think I can make that work" is not a declaration of coldness. "Could you clarify what you mean?" is not proof of incompetence. These are ordinary sentences doing ordinary work.

Screenshot thinking also exaggerates audience. A message sent to one person may feel as if it has been sent to a panel of invisible judges. A post may feel as if every reader is studying it with unusual attention. A work email may feel as if it will be remembered indefinitely. In reality, people are usually occupied with their own tasks, worries, messages, deadlines, and interpretations. This does not mean nobody notices anything. It means the replay often grants other people a level of focus they may not actually give.

The imagined audience is rarely neutral. It is usually sharp-eyed, ungenerous, and oddly available. It has endless time to analyse your wording. It remembers everything. It assumes the worst. It strips context away. It treats one sentence as evidence of your whole self. This audience is not a reliable guide for communication. It is the inner prosecutor wearing many faces.

To prevent screenshot thinking, listen for the imagined audience before you send. Are you writing to the real recipient, or to the feared observer? Are you clarifying the message, or trying to protect yourself from a fantasy of public judgement? Are you improving the wording, or performing innocence for a critic who has not arrived? The answers matter because writing for fear often distorts the message.

Another feature of screenshot thinking is the belief that digital words must be final. Because they remain visible, the mind treats them as if they cannot be softened by future context. But many digital exchanges are not final statements. They are part of a conversation. You can clarify. You can add context. You can apologise if something lands badly. You can correct an error. You can say, "I phrased that badly; what I meant was..." Communication does not become perfect simply because it is written down, and it does not become irreparable either.

This is an important correction. The mind often says, "Get it perfect before sending, because once it is out there, it is fixed." But in many ordinary contexts, a message is not a sealed monument. It is a turn in a living exchange. That does not remove the need for care, but it reduces the pressure to make every sentence carry every nuance in advance.

A good enough to send rule helps here. The rule should be plain: the message must be clear enough, kind enough, accurate enough, and necessary enough for its purpose. Not perfect. Not immune to all possible misreading. Not polished until every trace of humanity has been removed. Good enough means the message does its job with reasonable care.

Clear enough means the recipient can understand the main point without unnecessary confusion. Kind enough means the tone is not careless, cruel, or needlessly sharp. Accurate enough means you are not knowingly misrepresenting facts or intentions. Necessary enough means the message has a real purpose, not merely the purpose of soothing anxiety. When these conditions are met, more editing may not improve the message. It may only feed the replay.

This rule is especially valuable when the mind keeps adjusting tone. One more "just". One more exclamation mark. One more softening phrase. One more explanation. One more sentence to prevent offence. Tone matters, but endless tone-polishing can become checking in disguise. At some point the question changes from "Is this considerate?" to "Can I guarantee no one will ever dislike this?" The second question cannot be answered.

Perfectionism also appears as over-context. You fear being misunderstood, so you add background. Then you add the reason for the background. Then you explain your intention. Then you soften the explanation. Soon the message becomes longer than the situation requires. The recipient now has more to process, and you have more to replay. Context should serve clarity. It should not be used as padding against imagined judgement.

The good enough rule protects against over-context. It asks, "What does the recipient need in order to understand or respond?" Not, "What do I need to include so I feel completely safe?" The first question creates useful communication. The second often creates clutter.

There are, of course, messages that deserve more care. Sensitive apologies. Boundaries. Work matters with consequences. Public statements. Conflict. Anything involving someone's trust, privacy, dignity, or wellbeing. Proportion does not mean treating all communication lightly. It means matching care to consequence. A serious message may deserve drafting, pausing, and rereading. But even then, it does not deserve infinite revision. Careful is not the same as endless.

A practical method is to decide the level of review before writing. For a low-stakes message, one read for clarity may be enough. For a medium-stakes message, one draft and one review. For a sensitive message, perhaps a pause before sending. The key is that the review has a limit. Without a limit, screenshot thinking keeps raising the standard. It will always imagine another possible reader, another possible tone, another possible objection.

After sending, the rule continues: do not treat the message as a museum object. Do not reopen it repeatedly to inspect whether it still seems safe. Do not imagine it being screenshotted unless there is a real, specific reason to believe that risk is relevant. Do not let the possibility of preservation become the basis for endless self-surveillance. If the message was good enough to send, it is good enough to leave alone.

If the mind says, "But what if they screenshot it?" ask, "What would the screenshot actually show?" This question restores proportion. Often, the answer is ordinary: a clear message, a slightly awkward phrase, a brief apology, a normal boundary, a human reply. The mind imagines the screenshot as shameful because it adds hostile interpretation. But the words themselves may not carry the drama the replay gives them.

If the answer is that the screenshot would show something genuinely careless, harsh, unfair, or unwise, that is useful information. Then the lesson is not to panic indefinitely, but to communicate differently. Repair if needed. Learn the boundary. Slow down next time. Do not send serious messages while activated. Good judgement improves through specific adjustment, not through permanent fear of being recorded.

Screenshot thinking also asks you to confuse permanence with importance. Just because something can remain does not mean it will matter. Many digital traces exist without becoming significant. Many messages are read, answered, and forgotten. Many posts pass through attention briefly. Many emails are used for their practical purpose and then disappear into the background of work. The mind may say, "It is still there, so it matters." Not necessarily. Existence is not significance.

This distinction is liberating. A message can be stored and still be ordinary. A sentence can be visible and still be forgettable. A slight imperfection can remain and still not deserve another minute of your attention. The replay treats visibility as danger. Proportion treats visibility as context.

One way to practise proportion is to ask what will matter after the exchange has served its purpose. Will the exact wording matter, or only whether the plan was clear? Will the punctuation matter, or only whether kindness and respect were present? Will the small awkwardness matter, or only whether you followed up responsibly if needed? Will the post matter as much as the mind claims, or is the replay turning a moment of expression into a permanent identity test?

The more you ask these questions, the easier it becomes to separate real accountability from digital self-surveillance. Accountability says, "Use words with care." Self-surveillance says, "Monitor every word as if it may condemn you." Accountability says, "Repair if harm appears." Self-surveillance says, "Prevent all possible negative interpretation." Accountability says, "Be clear and humane." Self-surveillance says, "Be flawless."

Flawlessness is not a communication standard. It is an anxiety demand.

A healthier digital standard is responsible imperfection. This means you accept that even careful messages may not be perfectly worded, that written tone may sometimes need clarification, that you may occasionally revise your approach, and that not every imperfection requires repair. Responsible imperfection is not an excuse for carelessness. It is an acceptance that human communication remains human even when it is typed.

This standard creates more honest messages. You can be warm without overperforming warmth. You can be direct without becoming harsh. You can apologise without turning the apology into a self-punishing essay. You can set a boundary without cushioning it until it collapses. You can send a simple reply without making it represent your whole personality.

If screenshot thinking is intense, use a pre-send pause. Not an endless pause. A brief one. Ask: "Is this clear? Is this fair? Is this necessary? Is this mine to send?" If yes, send. If no, revise the specific issue. Do not reopen the entire message unless the purpose has changed. The pause should improve judgement, not become a doorway into rumination.

For posts, add another question: "Am I willing for this to stand as a normal human expression, not a perfect self-portrait?" If the answer is no because the post is careless or too reactive, do not post yet. If the answer is no because you fear any judgement at all, the issue may be anxiety rather than content. A public expression does not need to be a flawless representation of your entire self. It needs to be aligned with what you genuinely choose to say.

After sending or posting, close the loop deliberately. "Good enough to send. No rereading." Pair the statement with action. Put the phone down. Close the laptop. Stand up. Move into the next task. This matters because screenshot thinking feeds on post-send inspection. The mind wants to examine the artefact it has just created. Do not give it unlimited access.

If a real issue arises, respond then. If someone misunderstands, clarify. If someone is hurt, repair. If you made an error, correct it. This is a more stable way to live than attempting to prevent every possible issue through anxious perfection. The mind may argue that response after the fact is too risky. But repair is part of communication. It is not evidence that you failed by not predicting everything.

The deepest shift is from defensive writing to purposeful writing. Defensive writing asks, "How do I avoid being judged?" Purposeful writing asks, "What am I here to communicate?" Defensive writing centres the imagined critic. Purposeful writing centres the actual task, relationship, or value. The same words may become simpler, clearer, and more alive when they are not forced to carry the entire burden of your self-protection.

Screenshot thinking will not disappear just because you recognise it. The mind may still imagine the capture, the judgement, the future reader. When it does, name the process: "This is screenshot thinking." Then return to proportion. What is the message for? What is the actual risk? What can I influence? What standard is enough? What action is needed, if any? Naming the pattern stops it from masquerading as wisdom.

There is no perfect digital safety. There is only careful communication, proportionate review, willingness to repair, and the discipline to stop inspecting once the message has done its job. If the words are clear enough, kind enough, accurate enough, and necessary enough, let them leave your hands.

A sentence does not have to be immortal-proof to be worth sending.

Replacing Online Cues with Action

Online cues are powerful because they seem to offer information without ever quite giving enough. A message sits unanswered. A reply looks shorter than usual. A post receives less response than expected. Someone appears active but has not replied. A thread is visible, readable, searchable, and endlessly available for inspection. The mind turns these fragments into questions, and the questions begin to multiply.

The problem is not that online cues are meaningless. Sometimes they do matter. A message may need a reply. A misunderstanding may need clarification. A practical detail may need correction. A repair may need to be made. The problem begins when cues become substitutes for facts. The mind sees delay and calls it rejection. It sees brevity and calls it irritation. It sees silence and calls it judgement. It sees a visible thread and treats it as an unfinished task.

This is how scrolling and second-guessing become part of the replay. You are not only looking at the screen; you are trying to manage uncertainty through the screen. You open the thread, check the wording, glance at the time, inspect the reply, move to another app, return again, read the message once more, then search for relief in something else online. The behaviour looks small from the outside, but internally it keeps the loop alive. Each cue becomes another spark. Each spark asks for another interpretation.

Action breaks this pattern because action changes the present. Checking only rearranges your relationship with uncertainty. Rereading only gives the mind another chance to reinterpret the same material. Scrolling only adds more stimuli to an already restless system. A real action, even a small one, moves the energy somewhere useful. It gives the mind completion rather than more material.

The action does not have to be dramatic. In fact, dramatic action is often another form of anxiety. The useful action is usually modest and matched to the value that matters in the moment. If the value is repair, the action may be one clear sentence. If the value is work, the action may be opening the document and writing the next paragraph. If the value is rest, the action may be putting the phone away and beginning the evening shutdown. If the value is connection, the action may be making a warm, direct contact rather than monitoring a thread for signs of approval.

The first step is to name what the online cue has triggered. "This is waiting anxiety." "This is rereading for reassurance." "This is story-building." "This is screenshot thinking." "This is the urge to check." The label matters because it stops the cue from pretending to be an instruction. A delayed reply is not an instruction. A short message is not an instruction. A low response to a post is not an instruction. These things may become information if enough context exists, but they are not commands.

After naming the cue, ask what value is being pulled into the replay. This is more useful than asking what the cue means, because meaning is often unavailable. Perhaps you value being understood. Perhaps you value kindness. Perhaps you value competence. Perhaps you value not seeming needy. Perhaps you value trust, clarity, respect, or steadiness. The replay is usually protecting something real, even when its method is poor. Once the value is named, you can choose an action that serves the value directly rather than feeding the loop indirectly.

Suppose you keep rereading a thread because you worry that your message sounded abrupt. The replay wants another inspection. A value-based action asks, "Is clarity genuinely needed?" If yes, the action may be to send one proportionate clarification: "I realise that may have sounded brief. I meant to be concise, not dismissive." Then stop. If no clarification is needed, the action may be to close the thread and return to the task in front of you. Both are actions. One repairs. The other refuses to feed the replay.

This is the difference between relief through reassurance and relief through completion. Reassurance is fragile. It depends on checking, rereading, receiving the right tone, or seeing the right response. Completion is sturdier. It comes from doing the next honest thing and then closing the loop. You cannot always make another person reply warmly. You can make your own next action clean.

Online cues become more dangerous when attention has no assigned destination. You put the phone down, but there is no next step, so the mind drifts back. The hand reaches again. The thread opens again. The old question returns. To replace online cues with action, you need a landing place. Not "I will stop checking," but "I will close the app and wash the cup." Not "I will stop scrolling," but "I will open the file and work on the next section." Not "I will not think about it," but "I will write the one clarification, send it, and then put the phone in another room."

The action should be concrete enough that the body can follow it. Abstract intentions are weak when the nervous system is activated. "Be less anxious" is not an action. "Stop caring so much" is not an action. "Move on" is not an action. Stand up. Put the device down. Write the sentence. Close the tab. Walk to the kitchen. Read one page. Finish one task. Send one clear repair. Begin the shutdown routine. These are actions because they change what happens next.

There is a particular trap in scrolling. It can feel like leaving the replay, but often it only changes the scenery of the loop. You stop looking at the thread and start absorbing new cues: other people's updates, tones, comments, achievements, silence, visibility, comparison. The mind remains in a state of scanning. It is no longer replaying one message directly, but it is still searching for emotional regulation through the screen. This is not rest. It is stimulation wearing the mask of rest.

If the value is rest, choose rest directly. Do not ask the screen to provide it while the screen is also feeding your agitation. Rest may mean dimming the lights, making a drink, stretching gently, reading something non-demanding, taking a shower, stepping away from notifications, or lying down without the phone in reach. The action should reduce input, not replace one stream of cues with another.

If the value is work, choose the next unit of work. A replay after a digital exchange can consume the exact attention needed for meaningful progress. The mind says, "Check first, then work." But checking rarely gives lasting permission to begin. A stronger sequence is: label the cue, close the thread, choose one work unit, and start before the mind has built another case. The first few minutes may feel uncomfortable. That is expected. The aim is not to feel perfectly settled before working. The aim is to stop making work dependent on reassurance.

If the value is repair, choose repair rather than hovering. Hovering is rereading the thread, drafting and deleting, waiting for the perfect moment, imagining how the other person will respond, and checking whether the wording still feels safe. Repair is simpler. It names the issue and offers the next clean step. For example, instead of rereading a thread for twenty minutes, draft one clarifying sentence: "I want to clarify what I meant earlier: I was referring to the timing issue, not criticising your idea." Send it if it is genuinely needed. Then stop repairing.

If the value is connection, choose contact that is real rather than surveillance. Watching whether someone has viewed, replied, posted, or appeared online is not the same as connection. It is monitoring. Connection may mean sending a warm message with no hidden demand for reassurance. It may mean calling someone you trust. It may mean speaking to the person in front of you instead of half-listening while checking a thread. It may also mean allowing the other person space without interpreting that space as rejection.

Replacing cues with action requires one important boundary: the action should not be designed to force certainty. A clarifying message is useful if it clarifies. It becomes another trap if its hidden purpose is to make the other person respond in a way that settles your anxiety. Work is useful if it returns you to what matters. It becomes avoidance if it is used to dodge a clear repair. Rest is useful if the body needs recovery. It becomes numbing if it is only a way to refuse an honest next step. The value keeps the action clean.

A simple practice is to ask, "What is the next action that matches my value?" This question is stronger than "What do I feel like doing?" because anxiety often feels like checking. It is stronger than "What will make me feel better fastest?" because the fastest relief is often the behaviour that keeps the loop alive. Values point beyond immediate discomfort. They ask who you want to be in the next small moment.

After an online cue, the answer may be: "I value clarity, so I will send one clear sentence." Or, "I value steadiness, so I will not reread." Or, "I value rest, so I will put the phone away." Or, "I value responsibility, so I will correct the mistake." Or, "I value attention, so I will return to my work." These statements are powerful because they make behaviour intentional. The cue no longer decides. The value does.

There will be resistance. The mind may say that action is premature, that more checking is needed, that one more look will help, that you cannot leave the thread alone until you feel calm. This is the old bargain: reassurance first, life second. It sounds reasonable, but it keeps attention dependent on the screen. The new bargain is different: action first, calm may follow. Not always immediately. Not perfectly. But often more reliably than another round of checking.

A useful friction tactic is to make the action easier than the cue. If the phone remains in your hand and the next task is vague, checking will win. If the phone is placed across the room and the next task is open in front of you, action has a chance. If the thread is closed and your clarifying sentence is written on paper before being typed, the message is less likely to expand into an anxious essay. If your shutdown notebook is beside the bed and the phone is not, rest becomes easier to choose.

The environment should support the decision you want your mind to make. Replay-prone minds should not have to rely on heroic restraint. They need sensible design. Close the app. Remove the notification. Put the device down. Decide the next checking time. Keep the next task visible. Write the action on a sticky note. Stand up before the urge has time to negotiate. These are small moves, but they interrupt automaticity.

Completion should be marked. After the action, say what has been completed. "Clarification sent." "No action needed." "Phone down." "Work started." "Rest chosen." "Thread closed." This may sound too simple, but the mind needs signals. Digital loops often remain open because nothing tells the system that the behaviour is finished. A brief closing statement gives the action an edge.

Then do not reopen the loop unless new information arrives. This is where the practice either holds or collapses. You send the clarification, then the mind asks whether the clarification was clear enough. You start work, then the mind asks whether there is a reply yet. You put the phone away, then the mind argues that checking once would be harmless. Answer with the boundary: "No new information, no new action." This keeps the replay from turning action into another object of analysis.

Sometimes the correct action is to wait. Waiting can be an action when it is chosen with boundaries. "I will check after dinner." "I will not assign meaning to silence." "I will return to my task until then." This is very different from passive waiting, where the body hovers, the phone stays in reach, and the mind keeps checking internally. Active waiting has a plan. It gives uncertainty a container.

The hardest part is allowing the emotional residue to remain after the action. You may send the clarification and still feel exposed. You may put the phone away and still want to check. You may return to work and still feel a pull towards the thread. That does not mean the action failed. It means your nervous system has not caught up yet. Do not use lingering discomfort as evidence that more online behaviour is needed. Let the body settle after the behaviour has changed.

Online cues are designed, by their nature, to invite attention. They are visible, immediate, and easy to revisit. But ease of access is not the same as importance. A thread can be available without deserving another look. A post can be visible without needing another check. A reply can be brief without requiring an investigation. A delay can exist without becoming a story.

The shift from cue to action is a shift from passive interpretation to chosen living. Instead of asking the screen to tell you whether you are safe, acceptable, understood, or forgiven, you ask what the present moment requires from you. Sometimes the answer is a sentence. Sometimes it is a boundary. Sometimes it is movement. Sometimes it is sleep. Sometimes it is work. Sometimes it is simply leaving the device alone.

The next time the online cue appears, pause before entering the thread. Name the cue. Name the value. Choose the action. Then let the action be the relief. Not relief through certainty. Relief through completion.

Chapter 11
The Letting-Go Routine

Why can letting go feel like something you understand, yet still fail to do when the replay begins? You may know the moment is over. You may know the lesson is small. You may know another hour of reviewing will not change what happened. Still, the mind returns. It asks for one more look, one more explanation, one more imagined repair, one more chance to feel certain before the scene is allowed to close.

The difficulty is that letting go is often treated as a mood, when it needs to be treated as a sequence. A mood depends on whether you feel ready. A sequence can be followed while you still feel unsettled. This distinction matters. If you wait until the mind naturally releases every awkward conversation, every delayed reply, every mistake, every unfinished silence, then the loop remains in charge. It decides when you are free. A routine gives freedom a shape.

Letting go is not the same as forgetting. It is not the same as pretending the moment did not matter. It is not emotional numbness, moral laziness, or refusal to learn. Real letting go happens after the useful work has been done. The replay is named. The feeling is allowed without being turned into a larger story. One lesson is extracted. One next step is chosen, if a step is genuinely needed. Then the scene is closed on purpose. The mind may still mutter at the door, but it no longer owns the room.

The central tension is that the mind wants certainty before release, while life often asks for release before certainty. You may not know exactly what someone thought. You may not feel fully calm. You may still wish you had used a different phrase. You may still feel the residue of embarrassment in the body. If certainty is the price of closure, many scenes will never close. The routine does not promise certainty. It gives you a way to act responsibly without waiting for certainty to arrive.

This matters because replays consume more than time. They train attention. Each time the mind is allowed to circle without boundary, circling becomes easier. Each time discomfort is answered with checking, checking becomes more automatic. Each time shame is treated as proof, shame gains authority. A repeatable release sequence interrupts this training. It teaches the mind that uncomfortable moments will be handled, but not endlessly hosted.

The routine must be light enough to use under stress. Complicated systems fail at the exact moment they are needed most. When the body is activated and the mind is already pulling towards the replay, you need a path that is brief, plain, and familiar. A few minutes. Clear steps. No elaborate self-analysis. No search for the perfect meaning. The purpose is not to produce a polished emotional insight. The purpose is to get the mind out of the loop and back into life.

Small moments become the training ground. A slightly awkward text, a sentence you would phrase differently, a quiet pause after you speak, a meeting comment that felt clumsy: these are not merely annoyances. They are practice opportunities. Low-stakes replays allow the routine to become familiar before a larger emotional moment demands it. The mind learns through repetition, and it learns best when the stakes are not already overwhelming.

Progress must also be understood with care. The goal is not to become a person who never replays. That standard would only create another performance to fail. Progress may look like noticing sooner, checking less, closing more quickly, choosing a smaller repair, returning to the present with less argument. A replay may return strongly on a tired day, after conflict, during stress, or when a valued relationship feels uncertain. That does not erase progress. It reveals where the routine needs to be used again, without drama and without self-punishment.

The question now is not whether you can make the mind perfectly quiet. The sharper question is whether you can give the replay a clear path to completion before it takes another evening. When the old scene returns and asks for unlimited access, will you follow it into another loop, or will you run the routine and close the door?

A Repeatable Release Sequence

Letting go becomes far more realistic when it stops being a vague emotional command and becomes a sequence you can actually run. The mind does not respond well to "just move on" because the phrase gives no route. Move on from what, exactly? With which feeling still present? After which lesson has been taken? With which action chosen? Without those steps, "move on" becomes another thing to fail at.

A repeatable release sequence gives the replay a defined pathway. It does not ask the mind to be instantly calm. It does not demand that the body stop feeling embarrassed, anxious, guilty, or exposed. It simply gives the loop a beginning, a middle, and an end. That structure matters because rumination feeds on open-endedness. If no one closes the scene, the mind keeps assuming there is more to review.

The sequence is deliberately light: label the replay, allow the feeling, extract one lesson, choose one next step, close the scene. That is the whole shape. It is not designed to be impressive. It is designed to be usable when you are tired, activated, ashamed, waiting for a reply, or tempted to reread a message for the fifth time. A routine that cannot survive stress is not a routine; it is only an idea.

Begin by labelling the replay. This first move shifts you out of the content and into the process. Instead of entering the argument again, you name what is happening: "This is a replay." "This is checking." "This is story-building." "This is the post-message loop." The label should be plain enough to believe. You are not saying the event did not matter. You are saying the mind has begun re-running it, and that re-running is now part of the problem.

The label creates a small space between you and the loop. Without it, the replay sounds like reality. With it, the replay becomes an event in the mind. That difference may feel subtle, but it is decisive. You cannot work with a loop you still believe you are inside. The label places a handle on the experience. It says, "I see the machinery."

Next, allow the feeling. This does not mean indulging the feeling or turning it into a dramatic story. It means locating the emotional charge in the body before the mind uses it as evidence. Shame may sit as heat in the face. Anxiety may tighten the chest. Regret may feel like heaviness in the stomach. Embarrassment may create the urge to disappear, explain, or repair too quickly. For a moment, let the feeling be sensation rather than conclusion.

This part of the sequence prevents a common mistake: using the replay to justify the emotion. The mind says, "I feel bad, so something must be wrong." The release sequence says, "I feel bad, and I can notice that before deciding what it means." That pause protects you from converting every bodily alarm into a full investigation. A feeling can be real without being accurate in the story it creates.

Stay with the feeling briefly. Not for an hour. Not as a deep emotional excavation. Just long enough to stop fighting it. "This is shame in my chest." "This is anxiety in my stomach." "This is regret in my throat." These sentences are simple, but they lower the need for mental drama. The feeling has been acknowledged. It does not need to recruit the whole past to prove its right to exist.

Then extract one lesson. One. This limit is essential. Rumination wants many lessons because many lessons justify more thinking. It wants to redesign your personality, rewrite your social style, repair every possible interpretation, and protect you from future embarrassment forever. Learning is humbler. It asks for one useful adjustment that can be carried into the next real moment.

A lesson should be specific, behavioural, and small enough to practise. "Pause before replying when I feel defensive." "Add warmth before critique." "Do not send important messages when tired." "Ask for clarification instead of guessing." "Apologise briefly when I interrupt." "Stop rereading once the message has been checked." These are usable. They give the future self a clear instruction.

A statement such as "I need to be less awkward" is not a lesson. It is a vague punishment. "I must never upset anyone" is not a lesson.

It is impossible control. "I should be better at everything" is not a lesson. It is self-attack disguised as growth. The release sequence requires the lesson to remain close to the ground. What can you actually do differently next time?

After the lesson, choose one next step. Sometimes the next step is external: send the clarification, apologise, correct the mistake, ask the question, prepare differently, return to the task. Sometimes the next step is internal: stop checking, let the silence remain unfilled, accept that no action is needed, allow the feeling to fade without another message. The step should match reality, not anxiety.

This is where the sequence protects you from both avoidance and over-action. If repair is genuinely needed, the next step gives it a form. If repair is not needed, the next step prevents you from manufacturing one to soothe discomfort. The question is not "What would make me feel safe fastest?" The question is "What does this situation reasonably require from me now?"

The next step should be small enough to do. "Fix my communication style forever" is not a next step. "Send one clear sentence" is. "Stop caring what people think" is not a next step. "Put the phone down until after dinner" is. "Become more confident" is not a next step. "Prepare the first line before tomorrow's meeting" is. Small steps return authority to the present. Rumination keeps trying to solve the whole self. Action handles the next piece of life.

Then close the scene. Closure must be explicit because the mind often does not infer it. Say the line. "Lesson taken, scene closed." "My part is handled." "No further review needed." "Repair chosen, now I move on." "No new evidence, no new action." The wording should be firm and believable. It should not pretend that all feeling has vanished. It simply states that the useful process is complete.

Pair the closing line with a small physical action. Stand up. Close the notebook. Put the phone down. Wash the mug. Open the next document. Walk to another room. Send the email and close the app. This matters because the body needs evidence of transition. Rumination has physical habits: staring, hunching, rereading, lying still, hovering over the phone. A small action tells the system that the scene is over and attention is moving.

The whole sequence may sound almost too plain. That is its strength. Under stress, the mind does not need a complex philosophy. It needs a route it can remember. Label. Feel. Learn. Step. Close. The order keeps you from falling into the usual traps: believing the replay, fighting the feeling, extracting ten lessons, taking anxious action, or leaving the scene open.

The routine can be run in a few minutes. A message replay might look like this: "This is post-message checking. I feel tightness in my chest and embarrassment in my face. The lesson is to add one sentence of warmth when I am being brief. No further action is needed because the message was clear enough. Lesson taken, scene closed." Then the phone goes down and attention moves to the next task.

A work replay might look like this: "This is the meeting replay. I feel exposed and tense. The lesson is to pause before challenging an idea and acknowledge the person's point first. The next step is to make a note for tomorrow's meeting; no apology is needed right now. Review complete." Then the note is written, the notebook is closed, and the body moves.

A relational replay might look like this: "This is rupture scanning. I feel anxiety in my stomach. The lesson is that I need to ask directly instead of guessing when something feels off. The next step is one calm check-in tomorrow if the concern still feels real. Not tonight. Scene parked." This gives the mind a boundary without pretending the concern is meaningless.

There will be times when the replay returns after the sequence. That does not mean the sequence failed. A well-practised loop may knock again. The key is not to restart the entire review every time. If no new information has appeared, repeat the closing line and return to the chosen action. "Already reviewed. Lesson taken." The mind may want another hearing. You do not have to grant it one.

If new information does appear, the sequence can be run again. Perhaps someone replies with a concern. Perhaps you realise a repair is genuinely needed. Perhaps a practical consequence emerges. In that case, the routine remains useful because it stops the new information from becoming a flood. Label the replay, allow the feeling, extract the lesson, choose the step, close again. The structure holds even when the content changes.

The sequence should not become another perfection project. Do not ask whether you performed it beautifully. Do not turn it into a test of mental control. Some days you will label late. Some days the feeling will still be strong. Some days the lesson will be rough. Some days closure will need repeating. That is normal. The purpose is not to execute the routine flawlessly. The purpose is to shorten the distance between being caught and coming back.

It helps to write the sequence somewhere visible until it becomes familiar. Not as a decorative affirmation, but as a working tool. Keep the words plain: "Label. Feel. Lesson. Step. Close." Use them after small replays, not only painful ones. A slight awkwardness, a delayed reply, a message you are tempted to reread, a small mistake at work: these are practice ground. The lower the stakes, the easier it is to learn the route.

Repetition matters because the mind under stress does not rise to theory; it falls to training. If the only practised response to discomfort is replay, replay will come quickly. If the release sequence has been practised many times, even briefly, it becomes available sooner. You begin to catch the loop before it has taken the whole evening. You begin to feel the first pull and know what comes next.

The deepest benefit of the routine is that it teaches the mind to trust completion. It learns that uncomfortable moments will not be ignored, but they will not be endlessly hosted. Feelings will be allowed, lessons will be taken, action will be chosen, and scenes will be closed. This is a very different relationship with the past. The past becomes a teacher, not a landlord.

A replay will always argue for exception. It will say, "This one matters more." "This one needs more thought." "This one is not like the others." Sometimes it will be right; some moments do need serious attention. But serious attention still benefits from structure. The more important the moment, the more dangerous it is to let rumination run without boundaries. The sequence does not trivialise the issue. It protects your ability to handle it well.

Letting go, then, is not a single emotional leap. It is a series of small, deliberate completions. Name what is happening. Let the feeling exist. Take the one lesson available. Choose the next honest step. Close the scene. Move the body. Return to life.

The mind may still glance back. That is all right. It does not get to move back in.

Practising After Small Moments

Letting go is easiest to learn when the stakes are low. This is not because small moments are unimportant, but because the mind has more room to practise before shame, fear, or urgency takes over. A slight awkwardness, a message you are tempted to reread, a pause after you speak, a tiny mistake in wording, a passing concern that you sounded blunt: these are not interruptions to your progress. They are the training ground.

Many people wait until a replay is painful before they try to use the tools. By then, the loop has gathered force. The scene feels vivid, the body is activated, the imagined consequences are already expanding, and the mind is arguing for one more review as if your safety depends on it. Trying to learn a release routine in that state is possible, but harder. It is like trying to build a bridge while standing in the river.

Small moments let you build the bridge before the water rises.

A low-stakes replay might begin after something ordinary. You send a brief message and wonder whether it sounded too cold. You leave a conversation and remember that you interrupted once. You make a small joke and do not get much response. You ask a question in a meeting and later think it might have sounded obvious. None of these moments is catastrophic. Precisely for that reason, they are useful. The mind may still try to start its familiar machinery, but the emotional charge is not yet overwhelming.

This is the moment to practise. Label the replay while it is still small. "This is post-message checking." "This is the meeting replay starting." "This is shame trying to make a small thing global." Then allow the feeling briefly. Perhaps there is a little heat in the face, a small tightness in the chest, a flicker of embarrassment. Let it be there without turning it into a case. Extract one lesson if one exists. Choose whether any action is genuinely needed. Close the scene.

The whole sequence may take less time than rereading the message would have taken.

This is why small loops should not be dismissed as trivial. A minor replay is a rehearsal for a larger one. Each time you run the routine on something small, the mind learns the route. It learns that discomfort does not automatically require checking. It learns that uncertainty does not automatically require another message. It learns that a feeling can be allowed without becoming a story. It learns that a lesson can be taken without putting the self on trial.

The aim is not to become hyper-aware of every thought. That would only create another form of monitoring. The aim is to recognise the familiar first movement of a replay and respond while the mind is still flexible. Early practice is lighter. Later intervention often requires more force because the replay has already built its world. Small moments give you the chance to interrupt before the scene becomes theatrical.

Think of a simple social example. You say goodbye to someone and afterwards wonder whether you sounded distracted. The replay begins to offer interpretations: perhaps they noticed, perhaps you seemed rude, perhaps you should send a message. This is a perfect practice moment. The stakes are low, the evidence is thin, and the urge to repair may be more about discomfort than reality. You might say, "This is a small replay. I feel a little uneasy. The lesson, if any, is to slow down when leaving conversations. No action needed. Scene closed." Then you move into the next task.

That small act matters. You have just refused to train the loop.

Every time you follow the replay into unnecessary analysis, the mind learns that this route is worth taking. Every time you close a small loop cleanly, the mind learns another route. This is how a steadier baseline is built. Not by one dramatic breakthrough, but by many ordinary completions. The mind starts to trust that uncomfortable moments will be handled without being endlessly reopened.

Small moments also help you learn proportion. When a replay is intense, the mind tends to argue that this particular case is exceptional. It says, "This one really matters." "This one needs more thought." "This one could change everything." Sometimes a situation does deserve careful attention. But if you have practised on small loops, you become better at recognising the difference between real significance and emotional magnification. You know what a replay sounds like before it becomes convincing.

Practising after small moments also reveals your common trigger categories. You may notice that you often replay after sending messages, after speaking in groups, after moments of possible misunderstanding, or after receiving brief replies. This is useful information. It allows you to prepare gentle interventions at the places where your mind is most likely to drift backwards. The more predictable the doorway, the easier it is to place a micro-anchor there.

For example, if you often replay after sending messages, practise a post-send ritual every time the stakes are low. Send the message. Say, "Sent is sent." Put the phone down. Feel both feet. Move to the next task. Do this after ordinary messages, not only emotionally charged ones. The mind learns that sending is followed by closure, not by inspection.

If you often replay after meetings, practise a closing ritual after uneventful meetings. Write one factual note: what matters next. Then close the notebook. Stand up. Move your body. Do not wait for the difficult meeting to begin training. Use the ordinary ones. The routine becomes familiar before pressure tests it.

If you often replay after social moments, practise after brief, low-risk interactions. A chat with a neighbour, a short exchange in a shop, a quick conversation with a colleague. Notice the mind's urge to audit your tone. Then close the scene without analysis. Not every human exchange needs a review. Many simply need to end.

This practice is especially helpful because replay-prone people often treat recovery as something that should happen naturally. When it does not, they criticise themselves. But recovery is a skill. Skills improve through repetition under manageable conditions. You would not expect to become fluent in any skill by practising only during crisis. The same applies here. Low-stakes repetition builds availability.

There is another benefit: small practice reduces fear of the feeling itself. If you repeatedly experience mild embarrassment and discover that you can allow it without replaying, embarrassment becomes less alarming. If you repeatedly feel uncertainty after a message and do not check, uncertainty becomes more tolerable. If you repeatedly close a small scene while a little discomfort remains, the mind learns that discomfort is survivable. It does not need to be solved every time.

This is one of the deepest shifts in the work. You stop treating emotional residue as a command. A feeling may remain after a scene is closed. That does not mean closure was false. It means the body is still catching up. Small moments give you repeated evidence that feelings can fade after attention moves on. The mind does not have to supervise the fading.

Practising on small loops also prevents the routine from becoming associated only with distress. If you use the release sequence only when you are overwhelmed, the mind may begin to treat it as an emergency tool. But if you use it lightly after ordinary discomfort, it becomes part of how you move through life. It becomes familiar, almost boring. That is good. Boring tools are often the ones that work under pressure.

The practice should remain gentle. Do not turn every minor awkwardness into a formal exercise. That would become another audit. Use enough small moments to build the habit, then let many moments pass without attention. The goal is not to become an expert at analysing tiny loops. The goal is to become skilled at closing them quickly.

A useful phrase is: "This is a training rep." Not because the moment is meaningless, but because it is usable. A training rep does not require drama. It requires repetition. Notice the loop. Run the sequence. Move on. The mind may complain that the process is too simple. Let it be simple. Complexity is often how rumination sneaks back in.

Some small replays will still hook you. You may intend to practise and find yourself twenty minutes into rereading, imagining, defending, or criticising. That is not a reason to abandon the work. It is another practice moment. The instant you notice, begin there. "I am already in the loop." Allow the feeling of frustration. Extract one lesson from the slip: perhaps the phone needs to be placed farther away, or the post-meeting note needs to happen sooner. Choose the next step. Close again.

Progress is not measured by never entering the loop. It is measured by how soon you recognise it, how gently you interrupt it, and how reliably you return to the present. Small moments teach this without requiring a heroic emotional effort.

Over time, these repetitions change the texture of your day. A small awkwardness no longer automatically becomes an evening soundtrack. A brief delay no longer becomes a full investigation. A message no longer becomes an object to inspect until it feels safe. The mind still notices discomfort, but it does not always build a house around it. Recovery becomes quicker because the route has been practised.

There is real confidence in that. Not the brittle confidence of believing you will never be triggered, but the sturdier confidence of knowing what to do when you are. You have run the routine on small things. You have felt the pull and returned. You have closed scenes while still slightly uneasy. You have practised not checking.

You have survived uncertainty without making it someone else's responsibility. Those repetitions accumulate.

The next time a small replay appears, do not sigh at it as another annoyance. Use it. Let it become a quiet rehearsal for freedom. Label it, feel what is present, take one lesson if there is one, choose the next step, close the scene, and return to life. The moment may be small, but the habit you are building is not.

Tracking Progress Without Obsession

Progress with mental replays can be surprisingly easy to turn into another replay. You begin with a healthy wish to change, then the mind starts measuring itself with the same harshness it once used on conversations and mistakes. "Did I handle that well enough?" "Why did I still replay?" "How long did it last?" "Am I improving fast enough?" The project of freedom quietly becomes another performance.

This is why progress must be tracked gently. The aim is not to become a person who never replays, never checks, never feels embarrassed, never wakes at night with an old scene returning. That standard is not liberation. It is perfectionism in calmer clothing. A replay-prone mind can take any goal, even a healing goal, and make it into a scoreboard. If you are not careful, you stop replaying conversations and start replaying your attempts to stop replaying.

Real progress is less dramatic than that. It often looks like noticing sooner. The replay begins, and instead of losing the whole evening, you catch it after a few minutes. It looks like checking once instead of repeatedly. It looks like writing one clear apology instead of drafting a long emotional defence. It looks like closing a message thread even while part of you still wants to inspect it. It looks like feeling shame in the body without allowing shame to write the whole story.

These changes can feel small because they are not glamorous. They do not announce themselves as transformation. Yet they matter because they alter the pattern. A replay that once lasted all afternoon now loses strength after a short routine. A night-time thought that once became a full investigation is now parked for morning. A delayed reply still bothers you, but it no longer controls your behaviour. This is progress: not perfect calm, but quicker recovery and more present action.

The difficulty is that the mind may dismiss anything less than total freedom. It may say, "I still replayed, so nothing has changed." That is poor measurement. If a habit has been practised for years, the first sign of change is rarely disappearance. More often, the first sign is interruption. You notice the loop. You name it. You return. You relapse into it. You return again. The old route still exists, but it is no longer the only route.

Tracking progress without obsession means looking for direction rather than perfection. Are you catching loops earlier? Are you taking lessons more cleanly? Are you apologising more simply? Are you checking less often? Are you allowing more uncertainty before acting? Are you returning to tasks, relationships, rest, and ordinary life more quickly? These are the markers that matter. They show that attention is becoming more available, even if the mind still visits old scenes.

The tracking itself should be light. A brief note is enough. Not a full diary of every replay, not a detailed emotional audit, not a chart that turns your inner life into a project of constant assessment. A simple line can do the work: "Caught the replay after sending the message; checked once; closed the thread." Or, "Night replay returned; parked it instead of debating." Or, "Awkward meeting comment; took one lesson and moved on." The note should show recovery, not reopen the scene.

There is a danger in tracking too much detail. The mind may begin collecting evidence about itself: how long the replay lasted, how intense the feeling was, whether the technique worked, whether the closing statement felt convincing enough, whether the routine was performed correctly. This can become rumination about rumination. The point is not to monitor yourself with a clipboard. The point is to notice that change is happening and to strengthen the behaviours that help.

A useful rule is to track only what you want to reinforce. If you track every failure, you may train the mind to look for failure. If you track every emotional fluctuation, you may become more watchful of your feelings. Instead, record the moment of interruption, the skill used, or the return to life. "Named the loop." "Stopped rereading." "Sent the repair." "Chose no action." "Returned to work." These are the behaviours that build freedom.

Progress also includes how you respond when the replay returns strongly. There will be days when the loop comes back with force. Stress, tiredness, conflict, uncertainty, hormonal shifts, pressure, loneliness, and old sensitivities can all lower your threshold. A replay that seemed manageable last week may feel sticky again. The mind may seize this as proof that you have gone backwards. Be careful. A difficult day is not a failed identity. It is a difficult day.

A strong replay is a signal, not a sentence. It may signal that your body is depleted, that the issue genuinely matters, that you need rest, that a repair is still incomplete, that a boundary is needed, or that an old trigger has been touched. It does not automatically mean the work has failed. The question is not, "Why am I back here?" spoken with contempt. The better question is, "What support does this moment need?" Perhaps the answer is the release sequence. Perhaps it is sleep. Perhaps it is one clear action. Perhaps it is no action and a return to the present.

Self-judgement after a setback is especially damaging because it creates a second loop. First, you replay the original moment. Then you replay your failure to handle the replay. Now the mind has twice as much material. "I should know better by now." "I thought I had moved past this." "Why am I still like this?" These sentences are not progress tools. They are old harsh scripts wearing the language of self-improvement.

A more useful response is procedural. "The replay is strong today. I will run the routine again." That is enough. No drama. No verdict. No emotional trial about why it returned. The routine exists for exactly these moments. You do not need to feel inspired to use it. You do not need to believe perfectly in it. You only need to begin:

label the replay, allow the feeling, take one lesson, choose one step, close the scene.

Tracking progress should also include signs of increased living. This is easy to miss because the mind tends to focus on symptoms. But the real goal is not simply fewer replays. The real goal is more life available after replays. Are you more present with people? Do you return to work sooner? Do you sleep with fewer mental hearings? Do you send messages with less editing? Do you leave conversations without auditing every sentence? Do you recover enough attention to enjoy what comes next? These are the gains that matter most.

There is a quiet moment when progress becomes visible: you realise that a scene which once would have taken the evening has taken only a small part of it. You still felt the pull. You still cared. You still had to choose. But you did not surrender the whole night. That is not minor. That is a change in ownership. The replay appeared, but it did not get unlimited access.

Another sign of progress is a reduction in reassurance-seeking. You may still want to ask whether everything is fine, but you pause long enough to decide whether the question is genuinely needed. You may still want to reread the message, but you notice that the urge is for relief rather than information. You may still want to apologise again, but you recognise that the repair has already been made. This pause is powerful. It is where freedom begins to show itself in behaviour.

Progress may also appear as more accurate language. Instead of "I ruined that," you say, "That felt awkward." Instead of "They hate me," you say, "I do not know what they thought." Instead of "I always do this," you say, "This is a familiar trigger." These changes in wording are not cosmetic. They alter the nervous system's sense of threat. They keep the event at the right size. They allow the mind to learn without attacking the self.

Do not underestimate quicker closure. The ability to say, "Lesson taken, scene closed," and mean it even partially is a sign of growth. At first, the statement may feel mechanical. Later, it begins to carry authority because you have used it and survived. The mind learns that scenes can end without perfect certainty. It learns that emotional residue can remain without demanding more review. That learning is central.

The best tracking practice may be a brief weekly reflection rather than constant measurement. Ask what helped, where the loop was strongest, and what one adjustment would make the next week easier. Keep the answers practical. "Phone away after sending messages." "Parking note before bed." "One apology, no over-explaining." "Micro-anchor after meetings." This kind of reflection turns progress into support rather than surveillance.

Avoid ranking your days as success or failure. Human minds are not machines, and emotional patterns do not improve in a straight line. A day with a replay can still be a day of progress if you noticed it sooner, used a tool, avoided one unnecessary check, or returned to the present after being pulled away. A day without a replay is pleasant, but it is not proof that you are now permanently cured. Stay steady. Take the evidence lightly.

There is also no need to compare your progress with anyone else's. Some people release quickly from certain triggers and struggle with others. Some are most vulnerable at night. Some replay social moments. Some replay work mistakes. Some check messages. Some rehearse conversations. Your pattern is yours. The only useful comparison is between old automaticity and new choice.

The language of progress should be kind, but not vague. "I am improving" may be true, but the mind often benefits from clearer evidence: "I checked less." "I recovered faster." "I chose one action." "I did not reopen the thread." "I slept after parking the thought." These observations are specific enough to build confidence without becoming obsessive. Confidence grows when the mind sees proof that a different response is possible.

When the replay returns strongly, do not erase your progress by treating the return as a collapse. Think of it as a flare. A flare can be uncomfortable without being permanent. It asks for the same skills, perhaps with more patience and support. You may need to run the routine twice. You may need to rest before reviewing. You may need to write the data down because the mind is too charged to hold it clearly. You may need to choose no action and tolerate the discomfort. None of this means you are back at the beginning.

The mature measure of progress is not whether you never fall into the loop. It is whether you have a way out and use it with less self-punishment each time. That is a profound shift. A person who can recover is less afraid of being triggered. Less fear means fewer secondary loops. Fewer secondary loops means more trust. More trust means the mind does not need to monitor itself as aggressively.

Tracking progress without obsession is ultimately about protecting the work from the old pattern. The old pattern wants to turn everything into evidence against you. Do not let it turn healing into another trial. Notice the gains. Learn from the difficult days. Adjust the routine lightly. Keep living.

The question is not, "Am I finished with replays forever?" The better question is, "Am I returning to myself more quickly than I used to?" If the answer is yes, even sometimes, progress is already happening.

Chapter 12
Maintaining Change When Stressed

Stress has a way of making old loops sound convincing again. You may have built a steadier relationship with replays, learned to close scenes more quickly, stopped checking as often, and become better at taking one lesson rather than reopening the whole past. Then pressure rises. Sleep shortens. Conflict appears. A message lands badly. A conversation feels unfinished. Suddenly the mind reaches for its familiar route: replay, analyse, scan, correct, imagine, worry.

This return can feel discouraging if you mistake it for failure. The mind says, "I thought I was past this." That sentence is dangerous because it turns a stressful moment into evidence against your progress. Change is not proven by never being triggered again. It is proven by what happens when the old pattern returns. Stress does not erase what you have learned; it tests whether the tools are still available when conditions are less favourable.

A replay-resistant life is not a perfectly calm life. It is a life designed with fewer open loops, clearer endings, and gentler recovery points. The goal is not to eliminate every awkward moment, avoid every conflict, or make communication so polished that nothing ever requires repair. That would be another form of control. The goal is to build habits that reduce unnecessary rewinding and support quicker return when rewinding begins.

The central tension is that stress narrows attention at the exact time when you need perspective. When you are tired, hungry, pressured, lonely, overstimulated, or emotionally bruised, the mind is more likely to treat uncertainty as danger and discomfort as proof. A delayed reply feels heavier. A small mistake feels more revealing. A tense exchange feels more final. The old loop does not come back because you are weak. It comes back because your system is under strain and has reached for a familiar protection strategy.

This matters because the way you respond to setbacks determines whether one replay becomes a passing flare or a full return to old habits. If you meet the flare with self-criticism, the loop gains fuel.

If you treat it as useful information, it becomes a signal. Perhaps you need rest. Perhaps a boundary has been crossed. Perhaps a repair is genuinely needed. Perhaps the day has too many unfinished edges. Perhaps your mind is simply overworked and looking for something to solve. A setback is not a verdict. It is data.

Maintaining change means learning how to reset without drama. A difficult day does not need to become a difficult week. One night of replaying does not mean the routine is broken. One anxious check does not undo the practice of checking less. The mind loves all-or-nothing conclusions, especially under stress. Maintenance asks for something less theatrical and more powerful: return to the tool, return to the body, return to the next honest step.

A replay-resistant life is built through ordinary design. How you leave meetings matters. How you send messages matters. How you close the workday matters. How you move into the evening matters. If every transition is left open, the mind has more loose material to collect later. If each transition includes a brief closing point, the mind receives a different instruction: this is complete enough for now. A note, a closing statement, a planned next step, a phone boundary, a small physical shift: these are modest habits, but they protect attention.

The work ahead is to treat setbacks skilfully and design daily rhythms that give the mind fewer reasons to rewind. Stress will still happen. Tiredness will still lower perspective. Conflict will still leave residue. But you can build a reset day instead of sliding into a reset week. You can end conversations and tasks with clearer closure. You can change a post-conversation habit from replaying to noting one lesson and one next step. Maintenance is not a grand transformation. It is the quiet repetition of choices that keep the past from taking over the present.

The question now is not, "How do I make sure I never replay again?" That question belongs to perfectionism. The better question is, "When life becomes strained, what structure will help me return before the old loop takes the day?"

Handling Setbacks Skilfully

A setback can feel like betrayal. You thought you were getting better. You had begun to notice replays sooner, close scenes more cleanly, leave messages alone, sleep with fewer late-night investigations, and speak to yourself with less cruelty. Then one stressful week arrives, one tense exchange happens, one delayed reply touches the wrong nerve, and suddenly the old machinery is loud again.

The mind replays. The body tightens. The sentence returns. The imagined reactions gather. The phone becomes tempting. The inner voice says, "I thought I had moved past this." That line hurts because it turns a human return into a personal verdict. It suggests that progress only counts if it is permanent, smooth, and unbroken. But that is not how change works. A replay returning under stress does not mean you are back at the beginning. It means your system is under pressure and has reached for a familiar strategy.

Stress narrows the mind. It reduces patience for ambiguity. It makes ordinary uncertainty feel more threatening. A comment that might not bother you on a rested day can feel sharp when you are tired. A short reply may feel colder when your body is already strained. A small mistake can seem more revealing when you have been carrying too much. The replay is not necessarily stronger because the event is more serious. It may be stronger because your capacity is lower.

This is the first skill in handling setbacks: read the replay as a signal, not a sentence. A sentence says, "You have failed." A signal says, "Something needs attention." Perhaps you need sleep. Perhaps you need food, space, movement, or a simpler evening. Perhaps a repair is genuinely unfinished. Perhaps a boundary has been crossed. Perhaps you have been absorbing too much stimulation, conflict, or pressure without a closure point. The replay may be pointing to a need, but it is not automatically telling the truth about the event it has chosen.

When a setback happens, the most damaging response is usually self-criticism. "Why am I still like this?" "I should know better." "I have ruined my progress." "All that work was pointless." These thoughts do not restore steadiness. They add shame to an already activated system. Now you are not only replaying the original moment; you are replaying your failure to handle the replay. The loop doubles.

A skilful response begins with dropping the drama. Not the care. Not the responsibility. The drama. "The loop is back today" is a far better sentence than "I am back where I started." It names what is happening without turning it into identity. It gives you somewhere to work from. The old pattern has appeared. That is all. It does not get to write the story of your progress.

A setback should be met procedurally. That means returning to the tools rather than reopening the entire emotional argument. Label the replay. Allow the feeling in the body. Extract one lesson if there is one. Choose the next honest step. Close the scene. If the loop is strong, run the routine more than once. If the body is exhausted, reduce the demand. If the mind is too activated to think clearly, anchor first and decide later. Skill is not always elegance. Sometimes skill is simply returning to the plain steps when you least feel like doing them.

It helps to ask, "What made me more replay-prone today?" This question is not an accusation. It is a diagnostic. Look for the conditions around the setback. Were you tired? Hungry? overstimulated? under pressure? waiting for an important response? dealing with tension? trying to perform well in front of people whose opinion matters? moving through too many unfinished tasks? A replay rarely exists in isolation. It grows in a climate. Understand the climate, and you can respond more intelligently.

Sometimes the setback reveals that your day lacked closure. You moved from one conversation to another, one message to another, one demand to another, without giving the mind a place to put anything down. By evening, the mind starts collecting loose material. It chooses one moment and begins to circle. In that case, the solution is not deeper analysis of the chosen moment. The solution may be a reset: write down what remains unfinished, close what is complete, decide one next step, and stop allowing the mind to sort the whole day in fragments.

A reset day is a useful concept. It is not a day of punishment, withdrawal, or dramatic self-repair. It is a day where you deliberately lower friction and rebuild steadiness. You do the basics. Sleep as well as circumstances allow. Eat properly. Reduce checking. Make one clean repair if one is genuinely needed. Clear one small task that has been hanging over you. Use simple anchors. Avoid turning the setback into a full review of your character. The aim is not to become perfect by tomorrow. The aim is to stop one difficult loop becoming a difficult week.

A reset day also protects against the all-or-nothing trap. Replay-prone minds often believe that once a loop has taken hold, the day is ruined. That belief is dangerous because it removes incentive to return. If the day is already ruined, why not keep checking? Why not keep replaying? Why not give up on the routine? A skilful reset rejects this. A day can contain a replay and still contain recovery. A morning can be messy and the afternoon steadier. A night can be difficult and the next day handled well. Progress is often recovered in the middle, not preserved perfectly from the start.

Setbacks also expose whether the tools have become too complicated. Under stress, the mind does not want an elaborate framework. It needs the nearest usable handle. "This is a replay." "Feeling is not evidence." "One lesson." "One step." "Scene closed." These simple phrases may seem basic, but basic is what works when capacity is low. Complexity often belongs to rumination. Simplicity belongs to recovery.

There will be setbacks where action is needed. Perhaps you did speak sharply. Perhaps the message was unclear. Perhaps you avoided a conversation for too long. Skilfulness does not mean dismissing every replay as stress. It means separating the useful signal from the exaggeration around it. Ask what is known, what is guessed, what is yours to do, and what is outside your control. Then choose a proportionate action. A short apology. A clarification. A practical correction. A boundary. A decision to wait. Once that action is chosen or taken, do not let the mind continue punishing you as if punishment improves the repair.

There will also be setbacks where no action is needed. This can be harder. Stress makes inaction feel unsafe. The mind wants to do something: check, explain, reread, apologise, ask, reopen. But if the facts do not support action, then the skilful response is restraint. Not passive restraint, but deliberate restraint. "No new evidence, no new action." "This is discomfort, not a task." "If real information appears, I can respond then." These lines hold the boundary while the body settles.

When the replay returns strongly, watch for old behaviours trying to re-enter through reasonable doors. Rereading may call itself reviewing. Over-explaining may call itself clarity. Reassurance-seeking may call itself checking in. Self-punishment may call itself accountability. Avoidance may call itself giving space. The language can be persuasive. Look at the function. Is this behaviour helping the situation, or is it trying to reduce anxiety for a few seconds? Function reveals what the label hides.

A setback is also a chance to refine your prevention points. If you replayed after a meeting, perhaps you need a two-minute debrief immediately afterwards: one fact, one lesson, one next step. If you replayed after sending messages, perhaps the phone needs to be placed away after pressing send. If night-time loops returned, perhaps the shutdown routine needs to happen before you are exhausted. If conflict triggered a spiral, perhaps you need a clearer repair rule. The point is not to blame yourself for being triggered. The point is to adjust the environment so the old route is less available next time.

Be careful not to use setbacks as proof that you are fragile. A sensitive system is not a broken system. It is a system that notices threat quickly, sometimes too quickly. The work is not to become blunt or indifferent. The work is to become more accurate. You can notice discomfort without treating it as a command. You can care about impact without giving uncertainty unlimited access. You can feel shame without letting shame decide the meaning of the event.

The language you use after a setback matters deeply. Replace "I have failed" with "The loop is active." Replace "I am back to square one" with "This is a flare." Replace "I should be over this" with "My system is strained, and I need the routine." Replace "Nothing works" with "What is the next smallest stabilising step?" These sentences are not cosmetic. They change whether the nervous system hears threat or direction.

Setbacks also become easier when you remember the evidence of past recovery. The mind in a loop forgets that loops have ended before. It treats the current replay as permanent because it feels intense. You may need to remind yourself plainly: "This has happened before, and it passed." Not as forced reassurance. As historical accuracy. The feeling is real. The permanence is not.

If you have tracked progress gently, use that evidence. Maybe you now catch replays earlier than you used to. Maybe you check less often. Maybe you apologise more simply. Maybe you return to work sooner. Maybe you sleep after parking a thought that once would have kept you awake. A strong replay does not erase those changes. It only shows that under strain, the old pathway still exists. That is not surprising. Old pathways often remain available. The question is whether they still dominate every time.

Skilful setback handling is therefore a practice of returning without humiliation. You return to the body. Return to the facts. Return to the controllable part. Return to one lesson. Return to one next step. Return to closure. Return to the day. Not because the replay has politely left, but because you are no longer willing to make its presence the centre of the whole room.

There is a quiet power in saying, "This is a hard day, not a failed life." That sentence restores scale. The loop may be loud. The body may be tired. The old urge may be strong. Still, the day can be handled. The scene can be processed. The next step can be small. The setback can remain a setback, not a collapse.

The next time the old replay returns after a period of improvement, do not treat its arrival as evidence against you. Treat it as a knock on the door from an old pattern that still knows the address. You do not need to invite it in for the evening. Label it, steady the body, take the useful information, make the needed adjustment, and close the scene again.

That is maintenance. Not never being pulled back. Coming back with less fear each time.

Designing a Replay-Resistant Life

A replay-resistant life is not a life without mistakes, awkwardness, conflict, uncertainty, or regret. It is not a life so carefully managed that nothing uncomfortable ever has the chance to happen. That would be a smaller life, not a freer one. The aim is not to remove every trigger. The aim is to design your days so that fewer moments are left emotionally open, fewer transitions become replay zones, and fewer small uncertainties are allowed to grow into full mental investigations.

The mind rewinds most easily when moments have no ending. A meeting finishes, but no lesson is captured. A message is sent, but no boundary is placed around checking. A conversation feels slightly tense, but nothing is named, repaired, or released. The workday ends, but unfinished tasks and unresolved impressions follow you into the evening. These open edges become invitations. The mind returns to them later, not always because they are important, but because they have not been clearly put down.

A replay-resistant life is built around closure points. These are small, deliberate signals that tell the mind, "This part is complete enough for now." They are not dramatic rituals. They are brief acts of mental housekeeping. After a meeting, you write one useful note and one next step. After sending a message, you place the phone down and move into a chosen task. After a difficult conversation, you ask whether repair is needed, choose the next action if there is one, and stop holding the scene open. After work, you capture tomorrow's tasks before they become night-time intruders.

This kind of design matters because attention follows habit. If the habit after speaking is auditing, the mind will audit. If the habit after sending is checking, the mind will check. If the habit after tension is scanning for damage, the mind will scan. These habits may feel automatic, but they are not fixed laws of personality. They are repeated pathways. A replay-resistant life creates different pathways: close, capture, act, return, rest.

Start with how you end meetings. Meetings are common replay triggers because they combine visibility, performance, judgement, group dynamics, and incomplete interpretation. You may leave wondering whether you said too much, too little, too sharply, too hesitantly, too confidently, or not confidently enough. Without a closure point, the mind may review the meeting later as if the review itself is responsible behaviour.

A better ending is simple. Before moving on, write one factual outcome and one next step. Not a self-evaluation. Not an emotional audit. Just outcome and action. "Decision: send revised timeline. Next step: draft update by tomorrow." If there was a moment you want to learn from, add one clean lesson: "Next time, pause before challenging the plan." Then close the notebook or document. The physical closure matters. It tells the body that the meeting is no longer an open mental file.

Do not use the post-meeting note to prosecute yourself. That defeats the purpose. The note is there to reduce replay, not formalise it. Avoid sentences such as "I sounded awful" or "Everyone probably thought I was difficult." Those are interpretations, not closure. Keep the note grounded in what happened, what matters, and what will be done. A replay wants to keep asking, "How did I come across?" A closure point asks, "What is useful now?"

Messages need their own design because digital communication keeps the scene available. If the phone remains in your hand after pressing send, the checking cycle has an easy entrance. The mind can reread, inspect, compare, and wait with a level of intensity the situation may not deserve. A replay-resistant life treats sending as a transition, not an invitation to monitor.

Create a post-send rule. Send the message, then place the device down. Feel one physical anchor: feet, hands, chair, breath, sound. Then move into a specific next task. The rule can be as plain as: "Send, down, next." This may seem small, but it retrains the sequence. Instead of send, check, reread, worry, you teach the mind: send, close, act.

The message itself should have a standard of completion before it leaves you. Clear enough. Kind enough. Accurate enough. Necessary enough. Once it meets those conditions, it does not need to be made immune to every possible interpretation. A replay-resistant life does not depend on perfect wording. It depends on reasonable wording and a willingness to repair if real information later shows repair is needed. That is a stronger standard than endless editing because it is liveable.

Conversations also benefit from gentle endings. Many replays begin because an exchange ends with emotional residue: an odd pause, a quick goodbye, a moment of tension, a feeling that something was not quite settled. You cannot end every conversation with a full debrief, and you should not try. That would make ordinary social life heavy. But you can give yourself a brief internal close.

After a conversation, ask one question: "Is there anything real to do here?" If yes, choose the smallest honest action. Clarify, apologise, follow up, or make a note to address it later. If no, close it: "Nothing needed. Let it pass." This is not denial. It is proportion. Not every odd moment is a rupture. Not every silence is a signal. Not every feeling deserves a social intervention.

For conversations that genuinely matter, design a repair habit that is brief and proportionate. If you spoke sharply, say so plainly. If you misunderstood, clarify. If you interrupted, apologise without making it a grand confession. Repair becomes easier when it is normalised. It should not feel like a dramatic rescue operation. It is simply part of human contact: something lands imperfectly, you adjust, and the relationship continues.

Evenings are especially important because the mind often uses quiet to collect unfinished material. A replay-resistant evening does not require a long routine. It requires a boundary between the active day and the sleeping mind. Capture what must be remembered. Close what has already been reviewed. Park what belongs to tomorrow.

Then stop giving the day new opportunities to reopen itself through screens, threads, and late-night analysis.

A simple evening capture might include unfinished tasks, one concern for tomorrow, and one line of closure for any replay-prone moment. "Clarify budget question tomorrow." "Meeting comment: lesson taken, no action needed." "Message sent; no more checking tonight." These short notes are powerful because they prevent the mind from trying to remember, solve, and monitor everything in bed. The mind relaxes more easily when it trusts that important material has been stored.

Transitions are the hidden architecture of a replay-resistant life. Moving from work to home, from conversation to silence, from phone to task, from day to night, from conflict to repair: these are the places where the mind either closes or rewinds. If no transition is designed, the mind fills the space with whatever is most emotionally charged. A transition ritual gives that space a better job.

The ritual can be very small. Close the laptop and write tomorrow's first task. Leave the meeting and take one breath before opening messages. Finish a difficult call and stand up before analysing it. Put the phone down after sending and touch the desk. Walk into the evening and say, "Work is parked." These are not decorative habits. They are protective boundaries around attention.

A replay-resistant life also requires fewer unnecessary inputs. This does not mean withdrawing from digital life or becoming rigid. It means noticing which cues repeatedly feed your loops. Read receipts. Visible online status. Late-night message checking. Reopening sent emails. Scanning social posts for reaction. If a cue reliably increases replay, place friction around it. Reduce visibility. Set checking windows. Keep the phone out of reach during vulnerable times. Choose when to engage rather than allowing the cue to summon you.

Friction is not weakness. It is intelligent design. A person who wants to stop eating biscuits at midnight does not keep the open packet on the pillow and rely on moral strength. A person who wants to stop rereading messages does not keep the thread open and rely on willpower while anxious. Design the environment for the behaviour you want from your most tired self, not from your most ideal self.

Relationships need design too. Replay-prone people often suffer from unspoken expectations: expecting others to reply quickly, read tone perfectly, understand intention without clarification, or offer reassurance when ambiguity rises. A replay-resistant life includes clearer communication before the loop begins. Ask directly when something matters. State needs plainly. Use proportionate repair. Let people have their own timing without immediately turning it into a story.

This does not make you emotionally detached. It makes you less dependent on guessing. Guessing is fuel for rumination. Directness, used with warmth, reduces the number of invisible meanings the mind has to invent. "Can I clarify what you meant?" is often cleaner than an hour of interpretation. "I need a little time to think before I answer" is cleaner than silence followed by replay. "I meant the timeline, not your idea" is cleaner than hoping the other person understood.

A replay-resistant life also respects the body. Replays worsen when the body is depleted. Tiredness, hunger, overstimulation, and stress make the mind more vulnerable to threat interpretations. This does not mean every replay can be solved by a meal or sleep, but it does mean maintenance must include physical care. A mind running on exhaustion will not handle ambiguity generously. A body under strain will make small uncertainties feel louder.

When you notice replays increasing, check the body before attacking the mind. Have you slept poorly? Are you hungry? Have you been still for too long? Have you had too much stimulation and too little quiet? Have you been carrying tension without movement? The replay may be attached to a conversation, but the intensity may be coming partly from depletion. A replay-resistant life does not treat the mind as separate from the body that carries it.

Build reset points into stressful periods. When life is busy, closure habits are often the first things abandoned, yet they are needed most then. A reset point can be a brief midday note, a phone-free walk, a proper meal, a five-minute desk clear, a single sentence debrief after a difficult task, or a shutdown routine before bed. These small resets stop loose material from accumulating until the mind has to process it all at night.

One of the most useful habits is replacing post-event replay with post-event learning. After a conversation, meeting, message, or task, ask for one lesson and one next step. Then stop. This habit turns reflection into a contained practice. It tells the mind, "You will get the lesson, but you will not get the whole evening." Over time, this reduces the mind's fear that letting go means losing information. The information is captured. The loop is not needed.

The language you use throughout the day also shapes resistance. Replace dramatic internal phrases with operational ones. Not "I was terrible," but "That was uneven; one adjustment." Not "They are annoyed," but "No evidence yet." Not "I need to fix this feeling," but "Feeling present; no action needed." Not "I cannot stop thinking about it," but "The loop is active; run the routine." Operational language lowers emotional heat. It gives the mind instructions rather than accusations.

Do not try to make the whole life replay-proof in one ambitious redesign. That becomes another pressure. Choose the biggest leak. Where do replays most often enter? After messages? Meetings? Night-time quiet? Ambiguous replies? Social mistakes? Begin there. Add one closure point. Practise it until it becomes ordinary. Then add another. Sustainable change is usually built through small systems, not sweeping declarations.

For example, if messages are the main trigger, design around messages. Use a good-enough-to-send rule. Read once for clarity. Send. Put the phone down. Check at chosen times. No rereading for emotional reassurance. If meetings are the main trigger, design around meetings. Prepare one point. After the meeting, write one outcome, one next step, and one lesson if needed. Then close the notebook. If nights are the main trigger, design around evenings. Capture, close, cue sleep.

This targeted approach is more effective than trying to be generally less anxious. General goals are hard to act on. Specific replay zones can be redesigned. The question is not, "How do I stop being someone who replays?" The question is, "Where does the replay usually begin, and what closure point can I place there?"

A replay-resistant life still leaves room for real reflection. Some moments deserve time. Some conflicts deserve conversation. Some mistakes deserve repair. Some patterns deserve deeper work. The point is not to rush everything closed. The point is to stop giving ordinary discomfort the same amount of attention as genuine harm. Proportion remains the central discipline.

There is also a profound emotional shift in accepting that some uncertainty must remain. No life design can remove every unknown. People may still misunderstand you. Replies may still be delayed. Your tone may still land differently than intended. You may still feel awkward after a conversation that was objectively fine. The design is not meant to abolish uncertainty. It is meant to stop uncertainty from automatically becoming rumination.

The strongest design principle is this: finish what can be finished. Capture what must be remembered. Repair what genuinely needs repair. Release what cannot be controlled. Return attention to what is next. This principle can be applied everywhere: work, relationships, digital communication, evenings, conflict, sleep, and private self-talk. It is simple, but it becomes powerful through repetition.

A replay-resistant life is ultimately a life with clearer endings. Not harsh endings. Not avoidant endings. Clean endings. The meeting has a next step. The message has been sent and closed. The apology has been made. The uncertainty has been named. The lesson has been taken. The evening has a shutdown. The body has rest. The mind has fewer reasons to keep knocking on yesterday's doors.

You will still replay sometimes. That is not a defect in the design. It is part of being human. The difference is that the replay no longer finds a house full of open doors. It meets boundaries, routines, anchors, notes, closure statements, and actions that return you to the present. The past may visit. It does not get to stay without permission.

Design your days so the mind has fewer unfinished loops to collect. End things on purpose. Move between moments with intention. Give the body rest before it starts searching for danger. Let lessons be small and clear. Let repairs be proportionate. Let ordinary moments remain ordinary. That is how a life becomes less available to rewinding and more available to being lived.

About the Author

Aria Kostova writes about the small, repeatable skills that help people meet their own minds with steadiness. Her work focuses on the gap between insight and change: why we can understand a pattern perfectly and still get pulled into it on a tired Tuesday evening. She is drawn to the everyday places where rumination blooms - the walk home after a tense meeting, the silence after you press send, the bedtime moment when the day demands a verdict.

Kostova approaches self-development with a practical, humane sensibility. She favours tools you can use in real time, language that reduces shame rather than dressing it up, and routines that support attention instead of fighting emotion. Her guiding belief is that learning from experience should make life larger, not smaller - and that the point of reflection is to return you to action, relationship, and rest.

A subtle thread running through her perspective is a respect for older forms of closure: letters that were finished and folded, conversations that ended at the doorway, evenings marked by a simple ritual before sleep. In a culture of endless drafts and constant availability, she is interested in what it takes to create clean endings again, so the mind does not have to keep replaying in search of one.

www.ingramcontent.com/pod-product-compliance
Lightning Source LLC
LaVergne TN
LVHW100727061126
851857LV00011B/422
9788169888417